WRITING IN THE MARGIN

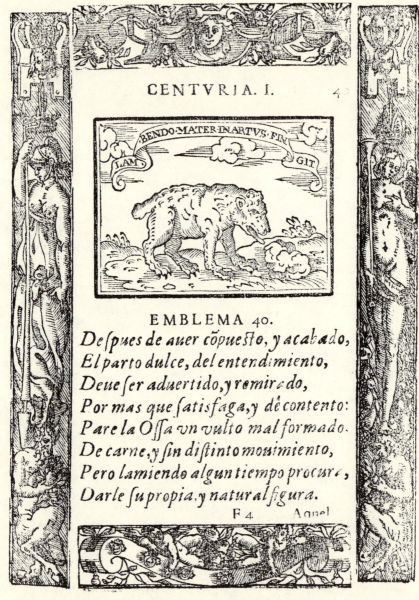

EMBLEMA 40.

Despues de auer cōpuesto, y acabado,
El parto dulce, del entendimiento,
Deue ser aduertido, y remirado,
Por mas que satisfaga, y dé contento:
Pare la Ossa vn vulto mal formado.
De carne, y sin distinto monimiento,
Pero lamiendo algun tiempo procure,
Darle su propia, y natural figura.

F 4   Aquel

The she-bear licks its cub into shape: an emblem of the artistic process (see p. 18). From Sebastián de Covarrubias Orozco, *Emblemas morales* (Madrid, 1610). By permission of the Syndics of Cambridge University Library.

Writing in the Margin

SPANISH LITERATURE OF THE GOLDEN AGE

PAUL JULIAN SMITH

CLARENDON PRESS · OXFORD
1988

Oxford University Press, Walton Street, Oxford OX2 6DP

Oxford New York Toronto
Delhi Bombay Calcutta Madras Karachi
Petaling Jaya Singapore Hong Kong Tokyo
Nairobi Dar es Salaam Cape Town
Melbourne Auckland

and associated companies in
Beirut Berlin Ibadan Nicosia

Oxford is a trade mark of Oxford University Press

Published in the United States
by Oxford University Press, New York

British Library Cataloguing in Publication Data

Smith, Paul Julian
Writing in the margin: Spanish literature
of the Golden Age.
1. Spanish literature—Classical
period, 1500–1700—History and
criticism
I. Title
860.9'003   PQ6064
ISBN 0-19-815847-5

Library of Congress Cataloging in Publication Data

Smith, Paul Julian
Writing in the margin.
Bibliography: p.
Includes index.
1. Spanish literature—Classical period, 1500–1700—
History and criticism. I. Title.
PQ6064.S65   1988   860'.9'003   87-21948
ISBN 0-19-815847-5

Filmset by Eta Services (Typesetters) Ltd, Beccles, Suffolk
Printed in Great Britain by
Biddles Ltd, Guildford and King's Lynn

PREFACE

This study was initially prompted by a reading of Terence Cave's *The Cornucopian Text: Problems of Writing in the French Renaissance* (Oxford, 1979). In its completed form my work differs from Dr Cave's in at least three main ways. First (with the exception of the chapter on Cervantes) I have treated not single authors but genres, in the attempt to cover as much as possible of the literary field in my chosen period. Second, I have dealt at length with modern criticism on these genres, in the belief that this critical tradition is not easily separable from the creative works on which it feeds. Third, I have made explicit my appeal to modern theorists of writing and subjectivity, in the hope that readers unfamiliar with literary theory will be able to follow up the references themselves. Although this book is general in scope it is not a history of Golden Age writing in any traditional sense. Conventional surveys of this kind already exist. Rather it is an attempt to reread well-known texts in the light of a number of relatively unfamiliar critical discourses. Thus I offer no potted biographies and few plot summaries. In order to preserve a readable text in one language and to keep the book to a reasonable length I rarely quote from either Spanish literary texts or French theoretical ones. Because of the complexity of both kinds of writing, it is difficult to paraphrase either of them. But to offer translations of selected passages would also have been to impose a meaning on them. Although translations of variable quality now exist for many of the French texts, I have chosen to refer to the originals, and sometimes offer commentaries on terms not easily put into English ('suppléer', 'écriture'). My subtitle refers to 'literature'. However, I am well aware that the limits of the literary are somewhat arbitrary. I myself have reproduced some of these limits: although I invoke 'Golden Age Spain', I treat only male authors writing in Castilian. The question of female writing (and of sexual difference in general) is barely referred to here, and I hope to return to it in a later book. Regrettably, I am not competent to treat writing in Peninsular languages other than Castilian. The decision to exclude works in Latin (with the principal exception of Scaliger's *Poetices libri septem* in Chapter 2) comes more from a lack of space. The vernacular texts already constitute a vast corpus of writing.

My thanks are due to Professor O. N. V. Glendinning, Professor Arthur Terry, and Dr B. W. Ife, who read the whole of the book in manuscript and made many helpful suggestions. Dr Melveena McKendrick kindly corrected errors in Chapter 4. The dual focus of the book (French and Spanish) derives ultimately from the structure of the Cambridge Tripos, which enabled me to devote myself almost exclusively to modern French and Renaissance Spanish. My thanks are thus also due to my undergraduate supervisors from 1976–80: Dr Michael Tilby, Dr Leslie Hill, and Dr Robert Lethbridge for French; Dr A. J. Close and Mrs L. J. Close for Spanish. Mrs Close also supervised my doctoral thesis from 1980–4. I would like to thank all those who attended French and Spanish Research Seminars in Cambridge during the same period, and the staff and students of Queen Mary College, London, who enabled this book to be written. My knowledge of rhetoric was much enhanced by discussions with Mrs Yvonne Austin, a research student in QMC.

A revised form of the introduction was read as a public lecture at Fordham University, New York City, and Boston University, in spring 1987. The first half of Chapter 1 was read as a paper at the Fifth Biennial Conference of the International Society for the History of Rhetoric (Oxford, 1985). Chapters 2 and 3 are revised and much expanded versions of articles which first appeared in *MLN* 100 (1985), 223–46, and *MLR* 82 (1987), 88–108. I am grateful for the permission of the editors of these journals to reproduce this material here.

P. J. S.

London, 1987

CONTENTS

ABBREVIATIONS

The following abbreviations have been used both in the footnotes and in the Bibliography:

ASSQJ	*Anglo-Spanish Society Quarterly Journal*
BCom.	*Bulletin of the Comediantes*
BHisp.	*Bulletin hispanique*
BHS	*Bulletin of Hispanic Studies*
FMLS	*Forum for Modern Language Studies*
HR	*Hispanic Review*
JHP	*Journal of Hispanic Philology*
JWCI	*Journal of the Warburg and Courtauld Institutes*
MLR	*Modern Language Review*
NRFH	*Nueva revista de filología hispánica*
PMLA	*Publications of the Modern Language Association of America*
REH	*Revista de estudios hispánicos*
RF	*Romanische Forschungen*
RJ	*Romanistisches Jahrbuch*
RQ	*Romance Quarterly*
RR	*Romanic Review*
RS	*Romance Studies*

For E.

Omnis enim oratio figurata est.

J. C. Scaliger

El arte, cuyo effecto es suplir la falta de naturaleza.

Sánchez de Lima

Ce dangereux supplément.

Derrida, *citing* Rousseau

INTRODUCTION
REREADING THE GOLDEN AGE

THIS is the first study of writing in the Spanish Renaissance or
Golden Age to draw extensively on what has become known as
'post-structuralism'. As I write these words in the mid 1980s,
there is a feeling, particularly in the United States, that deconstruction has 'peaked' and is being superseded by a new pragmatism or historicism. Yet it remains the case that the newer
critical approaches have had very little influence on Golden
Age studies. It is my aim, therefore, to suggest ways in which
writing by Derrida and others may point the way to new and
more subtle readings of Golden Age texts; but also to supplement the more hermetic versions of deconstruction with a
broadly historical awareness of the relationships between different authors, of the development of literary genres, and of conflicts within the practice of Renaissance rhetorics. To say that
'there is nothing outside the text' need not mean that the literary work is a discrete, aesthetic object, but rather that the
world of discourse 'beyond' it is structured in similar ways to
the text itself and cannot be separated from it. As Terry Eagleton has suggested, evidence for just such an 'open' model of
deconstruction is offered by Derrida himself.[1]

In this study I focus on the problems of 'excess' and marginality because they tend to call into question the boundaries
between such supposed opposites as inside and outside, art and
life. The first chapter examines Golden Age theory for its treatment of linguistic excess and its relation to the perception of a
Spanish temperament. In the next three chapters I appeal to
three Derridean terms (supplement, parergon, and trace) to
explore the three most important genres of the period (lyric,
picaresque narrative, and drama). My purpose is both to displace traditional, positivist criticism and to disclose the contradictions in the texts produced by more experimental readings.
In the final chapter the popularity of *Don Quijote* is related to its
(apparent) repression of those excessive linguistic traits charac-

---

[1] *Literary Theory: An Introduction* (Oxford, 1983), 148.

teristic of other Spanish texts of the period. In the conclusion I
suggest that Spain itself is the place of 'marginality', the supplement to Europe (both excessive and essential) which at once
conceals and reveals the criteria on which its exclusion is
founded.

Hispanism, both in Spain and elsewhere, has often been considered a poor relation to French or German studies. The latter
are generally held to be both more demanding for the student
and more central to the understanding of a received 'European'
culture. Two Anglo-Saxon Hispanists have traced the history
of this devaluation or marginalization of Hispanic studies. For
John Beverley, Hispanism derives in part from the somewhat
patronizing pleasure which the nineteenth-century northerner
took in a southern land, as picturesque as it was reactionary.[2]
Barry Jordan suggests that in British Hispanism the deference
to a restricted canon of 'great literature' and a faith in its
authors' masterful ability to transcend the time in which they
lived have divorced the study of 'Spanish' from the social and
historical circumstances of Hispanic cultures themselves.[3] He
argues, as I shall myself, for a strategic attention to the difference or specificity of Spanish texts, a difference which cannot
be confined within a totalizing 'human nature'. It should be
remembered, however, that the British bias towards a loose
empiricism and an unexamined 'common sense' is often
matched by the anti-intellectualism of Spanish critics themselves. It is perhaps significant that, unlike Germany or Italy
and in spite of a prolonged and bitter experience of Fascism,
Spain produced no theorist of Marxian resistance equal to
Benjamin or Gramsci.

The 'humanist' poetics still dominant in Hispanism may
seem flexible enough, with its stress on the individuality of the
author, the relativism of points of view, and the ambiguity typical of the great literary text. However, British Hispanism especially has tended towards a formalism and moralism which
can seem oppressive. Traditional criticism is based on certain
unexamined distinctions, such as those between imaginative

---

[2] 'Hispanism Today: A View from the Left', paper read at the Midwest MLA Conference (Iowa, 1982).

[3] 'Between Discipline and Transgression: Re-tracing the Boundaries of British
Hispanism', *RS* 5 (Winter 1984–5), 55–74 (pp. 59, 66).

and critical writing, or between literary and non-literary texts. Often, in New Critical style, the virtues of literary texts are taken to be, on the one hand, unity and coherence, and on the other, tension and ambiguity. The first pair confirms the text's status as a perfect aesthetic artefact; the second invokes a plurality of meaning, which is, however, rigorously delimited by authorial intention and critical relevance. The main presupposition of such criticism, then, is that the author is the origin of the text and that he (or, rarely, she) has determined its value for all time.

Renaissance rhetorics, on the other hand, appear inflexible at first sight, but reveal themselves in practice to be both fluid and contradictory. Thus one basic distinction is that made between tropes (which involve the transference of meaning) and figures (which involve the arrangement of words). Yet the class of figures is itself divided into 'figures of speech' and 'figures of thought'. The former are dependent on the order of the words, while the latter are not; they are subject to the artful *voluntas* or will of the orator. Thus, figures of thought have much in common with tropes; indeed synecdoche, for example, may occur under both headings. The formalist binaries tend to break down when used. Ultimately, as we shall see, the use of such terms tends to call into question the most basic distinction of all: that between 'plain' language and figurative, essence and excess. The virtues of the rhetorical discourse are equally problematic. In this study I pay particular attention to two of them: clarity and decorum. Clarity has two simultaneous and mutually exclusive definitions, namely graphic brilliance and formal simplicity. Decorum is literally undefinable: it is that infinite adaptability of diction to speaker, audience, and subject matter that is constant only in its mutability. Rhetoric also tends to decentre or unsettle any simple sense of causality or determinism. For if the orator has a 'will', then his language is elicited by an audience whose response is by no means predictable. The rhetorical discipline is at once a theory and a practice of discourse, arising from within an oral society, but adapted for different purposes by literates. As in Scaliger's definition of the related art of poetics, the limits of rhetoric are impossible to fix and its parameters are constantly shifting. In particular, it fails to draw a consistent distinction between literary and non-literary discourse. Quintilian quotes indifferently from Virgil's epic poem and Cicero's forensic oratory.

The most recent theories of discourse seek to abandon binaries of all kinds. Where structuralism sought the articulation of meaning in the play of difference between two terms, post-structuralism tends to hollow out that meaning by appeal to third terms which permit neither antithesis nor the synthesis of opposites. Thus Derrida's 'supplement' is both an addition to and a substitute for another term, and its contradictory status serves to undermine our persistent faith in the 'presence' of meaning in language and of the author in the text. Other Derridean terms have a similar disturbing quality, being at once present and absent, essential and excessive. They thus participate in Derrida's continuing attack on what he sees as the 'metaphysics', or unthinking idealism, of the Western conception of being and knowledge. But these terms are not tools or instruments to be wielded by a masterful critic, somehow external to the text in question. They are generally to be found within the text itself, whether it is by Rousseau, Kant, or Freud. Derrida's practice is one of minutely, even excessively, 'close reading'. As Barbara Johnson, one of the most fluent of the commentators, reminds us, deconstruction is not so far from 'analysis' (literally, undoing) in its etymology.[4] Two qualities often attributed to the post-structuralist text are reflexivity and undecidability. Reflexivity is the capacity of the text to reflect back on its own nature as discursive construct. However, this need not imply the dogmatic formalism of the traditionalists' 'unity', since (as I suggested earlier) the text remains open in a continuing process of 'intertextuality' to the discursive acts or messages which precede or follow it. Likewise, undecidability is not (or should not be reduced to) the 'ambiguity' of the New Critic. For while Empsonian interpretation takes a multiple yet fixed number of meanings to be typical of the great literary text, the post-structuralist reading takes plurality of meaning to be the general condition of discourse as a whole. Just as there is no original or final basis for authority, so there is no simple or univocal language from which the complexities of the literary may diverge.

---

[4] See the intro. to her trans. of Derrida's *Dissemination* (London, 1981), p. xiv.

Modern theory, then, is radically sceptical towards many distinctions and values still favoured by more traditional critics. It also seeks to displace any simple teleology or causality: the writer is no longer the unique and active origin of the text, nor the reader its passive destination. If we, as critics, choose to adopt such a viewpoint, then we will be constantly aware of subjectivity (the sense of self) as a shifting process, not a fixed product, and of language as a concrete medium, not an ideal essence. Hence, what seems to unite Renaissance and post-structuralist theorists (and what separates them from positivist or humanist scholars) is that the former acknowledge from the very beginning that any immediate communication is impossible or illusory: there can be no direct presence of the author in the language that issues from him, no representation in language uncompromised by the discursive frame in which it is formed, and no natural human experience prior and immune to cultural inscription. What is more, the fluid movement of modern intertextuality recurs quite openly in the scholarly, citational culture of the Renaissance, with its proliferating glosses and commentaries, barely determined (if at all) by an increasingly obscured original or 'host' text. This tends to confirm the most pervasive current in post-structuralism, namely the awareness that there is no metalanguage, no vocabulary 'outside' the literary object (or the psychological subject) which can serve to 'explain' it. Traditional criticism has always fudged this issue, claiming at once that the literary text is superior to the critical, and that the latter has unique access to a truth inherent, yet invisible, in the former. Writers such as Derrida and Barthes, on the other hand, have blurred the distinction between the creative and the critical in both their theory and their practice. Hence, if in this study I pay inordinate attention to secondary readings of primary texts, it is because there can be no direct engagement with Golden Age writing: access can only be made through an extensive growth of commentary, which must also be the object of analysis. Once more, Renaissance practice may be closer to the post-structuralist here. Writers such as Herrera and Tasso are both poets and literary theorists, and the relative status of rhetoric within the trivium and poetics within the human sciences is constantly shifting, always unstable.

Given this knowledge, my own approach (like that of Renaissance commentators) is unashamedly eclectic or intertextual. Although the main substance of my argument comes from Derrida, I am aware of the trace of earlier thinkers from whom I have borrowed in often unusual ways. Thus from Marx I take a view of history as theoretical structure, not surface phenomenon, and of value as produced or relative, not innate and ideal. From Saussure I take the related theory that linguistic value is arbitrary or conventional (subject to cultural practice), but not random in character, and that language is a system of differences without positive or 'full' terms. From Freud I take a mistrust of the conscious mind and of the dominion of the intellect, and a concern for language as psychic process much developed in Lacan. From Lacan himself I derive the concept of the 'imaginary' (that is, the realm of delusory representation necessary for the construction of identity), and of subjectivity itself as a linguistic practice, not an ideal essence. Yet, if there is in Lacan and Derrida no ultimate basis for either psychic identity or textual value, this does not mean that the experience of madness or of subjection is any less 'real'. Rather it draws our attention more closely to the problems of power, punishment, and surveillance closely associated with Foucault.

I do not claim to be alone in appealing to such writers. If there is a 'New Hispanism' in Golden Age studies it began in France with the structuralist poetics of Maurice Molho and the sociocriticism of Edmond Cros. While the work of both has been new and challenging it has tended to confirm Anglo-Saxon prejudices against technical vocabularies, with its often hermetic lexicon and frequent claims to 'scientific' mastery or detachment. This last claim is, of course, openly refuted by Lacan, Derrida, and the later Barthes. If there is to be a renaissance in Golden Age studies it may well come from scholars in North America. Thus among a number of scholars (some of whose work is yet to be published), John Beverley and James Iffland have offered structural Marxist readings of Góngora and Cervantes. Henry W. Sullivan has pursued a Lacanian approach to the comedia. Javier Herrero, Harry Sieber, and Ruth El Saffar have studied Golden Age prose in the light of semiotics, narratology, and feminism. One elder statesman of North American Hispanism, Elias L. Rivers, has made a general treatment of Hispanic literature, which draws like my own on a variety of new approaches.[5] While British scholars have made little overt contribution in this area at least two of their number (Anthony Close and M. J. Woods) are preparing responses to the challenges posed by the newer theories.

In one area at least I myself have been conservative, and that is in the preservation of a 'canon' of great authors and texts. Why limit my principal chapters to lyric, picaresque, and serious drama? There are obvious gaps in this study. Among the 'literary' texts excluded are *cancionero* and epic poetry; chivalric and pastoral narrative; and comic and religious drama. Another important absence is the allegorical narrative, such as the *Sueños* or *Criticón*, works which would tend to confirm my thesis of the Spanish 'difference' as one of verbal and conceptual overloading. But if I appear to reiterate and thus reconfirm a canon of great authors (and a particularly limited one at that) it is not because I consider them to embody the essence of writing in the period or because I lack the space or energy to deal with lesser-known authors, or with 'non-literary' texts, such as religious manuals or chronicles of historical events. Indeed, I take it for granted that the canon is specific to a particular time and place, and is thus a variable product, not a timeless essence. The changing fortunes of Góngora in this century are a case in point. Yet, as I have already suggested, the fact that value is conventional does not make it any less 'real' in its effects. The canon has been created in part by the sheer force of critical attention; but that critical attention is itself an object of my study. Thus, although my ultimate aim might well be the dissolution of the canon and the emergence of a less rigid domain of 'cultural studies', a necessary prerequisite of such a change is the displacement of those values (humanism, essentialism, ahistoricism) which critics claim to see exemplified in 'great authors'. If Garcilaso and Lope are not the pure presences they have been thought, then the prescriptive rigour of traditional criticism is seriously undermined. And if the supposed artificiality of Góngora and Calderón is common to all literary discourse, then the conventional distinction between art and nature must also be called into question.

---

[5] *Quixotic Scriptures: Essays on the Textuality of Hispanic Literature* (Bloomington, 1983).

I may also be criticized for a lack of concern for history, in a traditional sense of the word. Again, as I have suggested, I take it for granted that there is a specific, if variable, relationship between art and life, or (in Foucault's terms) between discursive and non-discursive practices. Yet it is clear that historical incident or epiphenomenon does not determine a literary text in any direct way, although we may choose to call the mediation between the two by any number of names including 'convention' or 'ideology'. And if empirical history does not explain the text, then the text often determines, to some extent at least, the way in which history itself is experienced. For example, it seems likely that the picaresque novel presented contemporary readers with a 'picture' of society which both was and was not their experience, close enough to be recognizable, yet distant enough to be flattering or consoling. If literature feeds the 'imaginary' in this way, then any access to a 'real' beyond it is problematic indeed. To take another specific example, was the sense of a Spanish 'difference' (the starting-point of my study) a literary delusion or a historical reality? The answer is at once both and neither. Spanish culture is indeed typified by 'excess', but that excess is, as I shall argue, highly volatile in character, and typical of literary discourse as a whole. The rigid distinction between the concrete and the discursive (history and literature) is scarcely tenable.

Finally, a note of caution. In the next few years, Hispanism may find itself (as English or French studies do now) in a highly uncomfortable position. On the one hand, there will be the newer, 'strong' critics, whose work will be unpopular and often inaccessible to their colleagues; and on the other, the older, traditional critics, perhaps dissatisfied with earlier methods, yet unwilling to surrender to current fashion. This study is an attempt to fill that gap, or absence, as it is in the process of arising. To that end it blends, somewhat uncomfortably perhaps, Renaissance and modern theories of writing. It will no doubt seem too historical to some readers, and too theoretical to others. However, as the book proceeds, the emphasis shifts from the former to the latter, in an attempt to introduce the reader to the less familiar ideas without the threat of intellectual violence. This is not an attempt to synthesize opposites by means of a transcendental third term. For there was no simple opposition in the first place. Neither ancient nor modern criticism is a monolithic structure; each is a mixture of disparate ideas and traditions. Indeed, the modern debate is rather similar to the Góngora controversy in the early seventeenth century. For the simple dichotomy of 'culteranismo' and 'conceptismo' scarcely existed in reality, and the perverse novelty of Góngora was already implicit in the often artificial mannerisms of Herrera and even Garcilaso. Terry Eagleton's *Literary Theory: An Introduction* ends with a praise of rhetoric as critical activity 'inseparable from . . . writers and readers, orators and audiences' (p. 206). Rhetoric, in its broadest sense, is indeed the closest link between all theories of literary discourse. Even those approaches which claim to be innocent of any theoretical basis may succumb to its ardent interrogation. And perhaps the 'jargons' of twentieth-century French thinkers are not so far removed from the 'jerigonzas' of the seventeenth-century Spaniards. It is surely no accident that Lacan cites Gracián and Barthes praises Góngora.[6] In both French and Spanish writers the density and materiality of the language denies the reader the illusion of stylistic transparency and the comfort of intimate communion with the author. It is a lesson which should not be forgotten, and one which the peculiarly complex and intricate writing of the Golden Age is uniquely qualified to demonstrate.

It has become a commonplace of recent criticism that any theory of writing or reading carries within it a corresponding critical practice. Hence in my own case the arguments above are not simply theoretical or abstract. They are the substance of the thesis to be developed throughout this book. However, the question 'How do changes in theoretical bias affect our reading of a specific text?' is a legitimate one, which can be illustrated, if not answered, at this preliminary point of the study. I will thus offer three different readings of a well-known sonnet by a poet whom I do not consider in the chapter on lyric, Francisco de Quevedo. The readings are traditional, Renaissance rhetorical, and modern theoretical. As I stated earlier, the distinctions between critical schools are never hard

---

[6] See Malcolm Bowie, 'Lacan and Literature', *RS* 5 (1984–5), 1–26 (pp. 9, 15); and my own 'Barthes, Góngora, and Non-sense', *PMLA* 101 (1986), 82–94. For a rhetorical study of a single Golden Age author see my *Quevedo on Parnassus* (London, 1987).

and fast, and the readings should be seen as exemplary, even parodic. And of course there can be no innocent example. The poem attempts to represent in language a portrait of the poet's lady contained in a ring. It thus offers particular scope for the appeal to those notions of reflexivity and undecidability typical of modern theory. However, the New Critic also favours the sonnet as preferred object of close reading; and the Renaissance rhetorician is attracted to the conventionality of topic and complexity of language we find in Quevedo's poem.

> En breve cárcel traigo aprisionado,
> con toda su familia de oro ardiente,
> el cerco de la luz resplandeciente,
> y grande imperio de Amor cerrado.

> Traigo el campo que pacen estrellado
> las fieras altas de la piel luciente;
> y a escondidas del cielo y del Oriente,
> día de luz y parto mejorado.

> Traigo todas las Indias en mi mano,
> perlas que, en un diamante, por rubíes,
> pronuncian con desdén sonoro yelo,

> y razonan tal vez fuego tirano
> relámpagos de risa carmesíes,
> auroras, gala y presunción del cielo.[7]

In a brief prison I hold captive, with all its family of burning gold, the resplendent circle of light, and the great empire of love enclosed. I hold the starry field on which the lofty beasts of shining skin graze; and, hidden from heaven and from the East, a day of light and better birth. I hold all the Indies in my hand, pearls which, in a diamond, through rubies speak sonorous ice with scorn, and sometimes give forth a tyrannical fire, scarlet lightning flashes of laughter, dawns, pomp and presumption of heaven.

For the New Critic, much of the poem's value lies in its aesthetic unity.[8] The 'brief prison' of the ring is also that of the sonnet itself, which constrains disparate elements within a coherent formal structure: the poet refers periphrastically to the

---

[7] Text from *Poesía original*, ed. José Manuel Blecua (Barcelona, 1974), no. 465.
[8] For a survey of modern criticism on this poem, see ch. III of my *Quevedo on Parnassus*. For two recent readings of it see Julián Olivares, *The Love-poetry of Francisco de Quevedo* (Cambridge, 1983), 68–74; and D. Gareth Walters, *Francisco de Quevedo, Love Poet* (Cardiff, 1985), 79–80.

golden rays of the sun in the first stanza, the stars in the heavens in the second, and the jewels of the Indies in the third. Each of these terms represents parts of the lady's beauty: her hair, eyes, and mouth, respectively. The order of the cosmos is thus reflected in a discrete, yet parallel, order, that of the woman's features. Hence on both the figurative and literal levels (heavenly body and feminine beauty) the sonnet embodies a natural unity of image and referent, a unity which both reflects the poet's skill and reproduces his (authentic and authenticating) emotion. This combination of artistic control and affective charge is by no means contradictory. Rather it guarantees that the poem's imagery is not decorative or superfluous, but organic and essential. It also infuses the sonnet with a sustained tension, at once formal and existential. The theme of enclosure is contrasted with that of expansion: the infinite wealth of the cosmos strains against the tiny limits of the poet's ring and hand. Likewise the poet claims he can comprehend his lady's beauty, but he cannot withstand her cruelty. In the first tercet she speaks scornfully to him; in the second, she speaks with 'tyrannical fire' and laughs with 'scarlet lightning'. The startling synaesthesia of this last image reveals both the originality of Quevedo the poet (he breathes new life into the commonplaces of Petrarchan lyric) and the paradoxical feelings of Quevedo the man (he adores his lady's beauty but fears her wrath). The poem takes on a newly ambiguous light: natural forces are both beautiful and cruel, just as love can bring both life and death. What is more, the lover who seeks to confine his beloved finds himself, in turn, taken captive by her beauty. These ambiguous tensions (pleasure and pain; freedom and servitude) are couched by the author in language that is at once naturally organic and artfully wrought. And the poem's final significance is at once peculiar to Quevedo the suffering individual and general to an unchanging human predicament. Quevedo's prison-house of love is not his alone. It is also ours.

The first priority of the Renaissance rhetorician is to explore the figures, tropes, and erudite references of the sonnet and thus facilitate its reception by the reader. Thus a seventeenth-century editor of the poem tells us that the 'golden family' is the sun's rays and the 'starry field' the heavenly firmament, which must remain hidden ('a escondidas') after dawn breaks

('Oriente').[9] Such images may seem obscure to the modern reader if they require explanation of this kind. But if they lack immediacy they lend the poem a graphic brilliance which is highly prized. In his simplicity of syntax and complexity of metaphor Quevedo thus exhibits that curious combination of qualities that the Renaissance called 'clarity'. This density of figuration also raises the question of decorum. Renaissance readers would probably see the poem as an example of 'allegoria' or 'icon', extended metaphor in which the literal term is omitted. The elevated diction seems appropriate to the omnipotence of the lady, (absent) object of praise. On the other hand, the status of the love sonnet in general is uncertain in the period. Such high-flown language would be more fitting for the noble themes of epic than for the mean or middle style of lyric. It is unlikely that the poem would be taken as testimony to personal experience: poetry dealt with universals not particulars. But even if it was, it would not receive that transcendental value attributed to it for that reason by some modern critics.

Renaissance critics are also less confident in distinguishing between organic and artificial imagery, between decorative and functional language. It is perhaps significant that the seventeenth-century editor does not comment on those images thought by the modern critic to be the most complex and ambiguous (the sonorous ice and scarlet lightning), but dwells on the poet's use of the deadest of metaphors (the ruby lips). He also cites the belief that diamond and ice are composed of the same substance, subject to varying degrees of freezing. Such information hardly seems relevant when the terms are used figuratively to stand for the mouth of the lady and her scorn for the poet, respectively. It suggests, however, that the same criteria apply to figurative and non-figurative language: even metaphorical stars cannot shine after dawn has broken; and metaphorical minerals cannot contradict the physical properties of actual creation. The space of poetry thus opens out on that of other disciplines, such as the natural sciences. The sonnet is not the closed, aesthetic and experiential artefact of the New Critic; it is at once effect and instrument of a potentially boundless culture of erudition.

[9] The editor is José Antonio González de Salas. His comments are reproduced by Blecua under the poem.

Hence Renaissance scholars do not think to praise the poet for his originality. There is as little concern for thematic novelty as there is for organic form or authentic language. If the editor's commentary had been fuller, he might have noted similarities between Quevedo and other poets who treat the topic of the ring, such as Marino and Góngora. He might have noted that Horace's lady, like Quevedo's, both laughs and speaks in a well-known ode. The image of 'flashing scarlet' would be praised not for its novelty, but for its subtle recasting of a commonplace which can be traced from Dante and Petrarch to Tasso and Marino. The image itself would be seen not as synaesthesia (sensuous expressivity), but transferred epithet (rhetorical ingenuity). This infinite regress from one poet to another, this indefinite expansion from one area of knowledge to another, suggests that Renaissance erudition resists any attempt at closure: the problem of intertextuality has no simple solution. Hence the question of the subject (of the poet's integrity of language or sincerity of emotion) does not arise. In spite of the stress on the first-person singular in the poem ('traigo'), the extreme rhetoricity of Quevedo's language tends to decentre or displace any notion of the poet as unique, self-possessed, individual.[10]

A modern theoretical reading might take off from these unvoiced assumptions of Renaissance rhetoric. As I have said, post-structuralism is generally hostile to overly schematic binary oppositions. It is also suspicious of transcendent origins or definitive ends. If we read the sonnet with this kind of linguistic scepticism in mind then the fundamental preconceptions of other critics may be erased or dissolved by the action of the poem itself. These preconceptions involve the supposed distinctions between figure and ground, form and content, and subject and object. I have suggested that, rhetorically, the relationship between figurative and non-figurative language is highly problematic. The figure stands in for the proper or native term, but also goes beyond it in verbal potency. It both substitutes for and adds to plain language. In Derrida's word, the action of the figure is 'supplementary' (from the French 'suppléer', meaning both to displace a term which is present

[10] For an attack on the supposed 'individuality' of Quevedo's poetry see my 'Affect and Effect in the Lyric of Quevedo', *FMLS* 22 (1986), 62–76.

and to substitute for one which is absent). I explore the supplementarity of Golden Age lyric at length in Chapter 2. However, Quevedo's sonnet is an extreme example of the way in which the figurative term, supposedly secondary and derivative, displaces and exceeds the primary referent. In spite of the efforts of the commentators, it is by no means clear what some of the images claim to represent; if the pearls are teeth and the rubies lips, how can the sum of these two parts (the mouth) be a diamond? This is not an artfully directed conceit, nor an arbitrary piece of hyperbole. It is a symptom of the disseminating play of figuration which always surpasses the 'proper' term for which it is intended to substitute. Quevedo's ornamental language at once amplifies the lady's beauty and attracts the reader's attention to her exclusion from the sonnet. When metaphor is so dominant it merely points up the absence of both plain language and original referent. It could be argued that this tendency towards verbal exorbitance is determined by Quevedo's historically marginal position, almost last in a tradition of great lyric poets. But (as I argue in Chapter 2) this assumes the possibility of a natural or neutral language untainted by the ravages of figuration, a language which is not to be found even in the earliest and simplest of Golden Age poets. And (as I argue in Chapter 4) the alienating 'trace' of cultural inscription precedes the most 'natural' of Spanish geniuses. The dispersal of the woman's presence and the lack of unmediated feeling in Quevedo's sonnet need not be assigned to a climate of baroque deviance. They point rather to the roles of difference and alienation in writing and reading at all times.

The distinction between figure and ground (primary and secondary terms) is further subverted by Quevedo's tendency to remetaphoricize metaphorical terms. Thus the 'lofty beasts of shining skin' represent the constellation of Taurus, which represents in turn the flashing eyes of the lady; or the East stands for the dawn, and the dawn for the reappearance of the lady. Of course this second-stage metaphor is common in the period, particularly in Góngora. It is familiar enough to rhetoricians to be given the name of metalepsis (from the Greek verb meaning both to partake in something and to interchange one thing with another). But its implications for poetic language are wide-ranging: metalepsis suggests the possibility of an interminable chain of substitution in which antecedent and consequent (literal and figurative) endlessly displace one another. The lady is in the cosmos and the cosmos is in the lady. Indeed, as we shall see, the peculiar potency of the poem derives from unexplained swerves or slippages of perspective of this kind. The form of the sonnet (and of the ring) can be read as a parergon, a margin or frame at once necessary and contingent which calls into question the distinction between centre and periphery, inside and outside. In Chapter 3 I explore the relationship between the parergon and the supposed 'picture' offered by the frame-tale of the picaresque. But by making the overt object of his poem the portrait of a woman, and by stressing both the rigid constraints of that portrait and its curiously fluid transformations, the poem also calls the reader's attention to the problem of representation itself.

I call the portrait the 'overt' object of the poem, because when we reach the tercets the image held in the lover's hand speaks and laughs. Here the rhetorical structure of the poem seems to shift from ecphrasis (the reproduction in words of a pre-existing image) to pintura (the 'painting' in verse of an original model). We may speculate that the poet is hallucinating; or that the miniature depicts the woman in the act of laughing and speaking. But it could hardly depict both: the painter, unlike the poet, cannot represent consecutive action. There is thus a slippage from imitation to original as motive of the poem, one which has not been noted by modern critics, enthralled by the seductive 'presence' of the lady. The poem is reflexive, because, on closer reading, it points up the margins of representation itself. But it is undecidable, because it deprives the reader of any stable referent 'outside' itself. We may succumb to the hallucinations of the lover, but only by reproducing uncritically the shifts and turns of his desire.

One modern critic suggests: 'At the conclusion we may ask: "who indeed is the prisoner?" ' (Olivares, p. 74) But this uncertainty need not serve to reinforce orthodox belief in the supposed psychological torment of the individual and the universal truth it holds for the reader. Rather and more radically, it suggests the inadequacy of all theories that presuppose an essential and substantial identity outside language. In particular it corresponds to Jacques Lacan's theory that the process through

which the subject comes into being is one of specularity or reflection. For Lacan, as for Quevedo, the eye is an organ of desire, as well as of perception.[11] Lacan cites the well-known
story of the painters Zeuxis and Parrhasios. The former's picture of a bunch of grapes was so perfect that birds were
deceived by it. But the latter's picture of a curtain made his
rival ask what was behind the picture so real did it appear. For
Lacan, what is at issue is not the illusionistic quality of the
images. On the contrary, the objects need not have been represented with any precision. Even the most schematic of images
would have deceived birds (unfamiliar with pictorial conventions) and a human witness (unused to the depiction of house-
hold objects). The eye is thus imprisoned not by the essential
qualities of the object, but by its own willingness to be 'taken
in'. The picture serves merely as a lure or decoy, relaying a
message to the subject already carried by the look itself. Thus
the lady's portrait is like that of the grapes in that its lack of
photographic realism does not prevent it from serving as a perfect object of desire; and it is like that of the curtain in that its
opacity provokes the (male) witness to seek satisfaction behind
it. The poet's gaze slips beyond the picture to the absent model,
cause of his grief; the critic's gaze slips beyond the poem to the
absent author, cause of his seduction.

   The object is thus deprived of integrity, because it is always
already implicated in the look. But the subject himself is also
decentred. Where does he speak from? As master of the woman,
he is outside the frame; as her prisoner, he is caught inside it.
And this discontinuity confirms what is for Lacan the necessary
asymmetry of the look of love, the fact that 'You never look at
me from the place from which I see you.' (p. 103.) The subject's
position is displaced in relation to that of the beloved, but the
two can never coincide. Thus, at a surface level, there can be no
communication between the two: the lady remains absent and
unknowable. Just as the figure displaces the proper term it
claims merely to represent, and the picture supersedes the

[11] See Lacan's essay 'Of the Gaze as Objet Petit a', in *The Four Fundamental Concepts of
Psychoanalysis*, trans. Alan Sheridan (Harmondsworth, 1977), 67–119. The references to
Zeuxis and Parrhasios are on pp. 103 and 111–12. For a lucid commentary on this pas-
sage see Elizabeth Wright, *Psychoanalytic Criticism: Theory in Practice* (London and New
York, 1984), 119.

model on which it claims to be based, so desire endlessly surpasses the object it claims for its origin. The poem ends with a
promise of new dawns for the lady-sun, and a richness to rival
the heavens: 'auroras, gala y presunción del cielo'. The movement of the celestial bodies, stressed throughout the poem, is
similar to that of desire itself: it offers circularity without
reciprocity.

In spite of the implicitly totalizing claims of Lacanian
theory, this condition may not be universal. In particular, it is
tempting to see Quevedo's brief prison, both brilliant and oppressive, as a speculum: the curved, distorting mirror which
seeks to shed light on woman's darkness and integrate her supposed formlessness. This image (derived from modern theory) [12]
has a curious precedent in one Golden Age text, Caramuel's
encyclopaedic *Mathesis*. [11] Commenting on the verse 'Now we
see through a glass darkly', Caramuel claims that no mirror
can represent an object perfectly. Convex mirrors offer images
smaller than life, flat mirrors exchange the right side for the left,
and concave mirrors exchange the top for the bottom. Our perception of God in the world is thus limited by the necessary
deficiencies of all mechanical reflection. The divine image we
see in our mind's eye is much smaller than the original. The
world is thus heavy with the sure sign of the convex mirror:
'mundus enim convexi speculi praerogativă pollet.' (Thesis
xlviii, p. 168.)

The context of this passage is of course theological. But when
dealing with a culture of polymaths it is not perhaps improper
for the modern critic to move, as his predecessors did, from one
art to another. The significance for literature would seem to be
the writer's sensitivity to the formal and material limits of
representation and perception. And the combination of literate
self-consciousness and intense concentration we find in
Caramuel's image is typical not just of Quevedo's sonnet, but of
much Golden Age writing in general. The sign of the convex
mirror is a fitting device for literature in the period. What

---

[12] For a critique of the tyrannical male gaze and an implicit refutation of Lacan's
model of specularity see Luce Irigaray, *Speculum, de l'autre femme* (Paris, 1974). For an
analysis of this motif in Irigaray see Toril Moi, *Sexual/Textual Politics: Feminist Literary
Theory* (London and New York, 1985), 129–31.

[13] I have referred to the edition published in Louvain, 1644.

Caramuel fails to examine, of course, is the primacy of vision itself as the privileged mode of perception, and in the following chapter I suggest that half-erased metaphors of light and seeing form the 'blind spot' of contemporary poetics. However, the frontispiece to Caramuel's work offers a second device for our study: it shows a she-bear licking its new-born cub into shape, with the motto 'Informia formo'. The image is a familiar one from bestiaries and emblem books throughout Europe. And when Covarrubias glosses it he refers to another legendary Greek painter, Apelles.[14] This artist could never finish a painting until his friends hid his paints and brushes: the painting could always be altered and improved. Thus he signed his works 'Apelles pingebat' (rather than 'pinxit'), the imperfect tense suggesting continuous, uncompleted action. Covarrubias advises the prospective artist or writer to polish a work ('limar') and to lick it ('lamer'), just as the mother-bear licks its formless young into shape. Like the convex mirror, the image of the bear suggests a process of condensation or concentration. Unlike it, it suggests that the artistic process is interminable, always uncompleted. And what is more, natural process is itself artful: the poet imitates not innocent or brute objects but a coherent world which is already overburdened with motivation and significance. There can be no space 'outside' these densely worked systems of meaning. And as we shall see, the metatextual aspirations of Spanish theorists are inevitably doomed to failure.

[14] *Emblemas morales* (Madrid, 1610), i. 40.

THE RHETORIC OF EXCESS IN
GOLDEN AGE THEORY

I. THE SPANISH DIFFERENCE

'SPAIN is different.' So ran the advertising slogan of the sixties. Designed by the Franco government to attract foreign tourists, it was sometimes echoed with ironical intent by the regime's political opponents. For the student of Renaissance rhetoric or poetics also, Spain is different; and it is with the nature and status of this difference that this chapter is concerned. As in the case of the slogan, 'difference' may be subject to more than one interpretation.

Literary theory in Spanish begins later than elsewhere and is, initially at least, overwhelmingly dependent on Latin and Italian antecedents. The first rhetoric to be published in the Spanish vernacular is Miguel de Salinas's wholly traditional preaching manual of 1541, and the second (excluding summaries of the first) is Juan de Guzmán's of 1589. Rhetoricians such as these borrow wholesale from Cicero, Quintilian, and the *Ad Herennium*, and add little, if anything, of their own. This historical belatedness and cultural dependency are perceived as such by Spanish theorists themselves in the sixteenth and seventeenth centuries and, as we shall see, play a large part in the development of an indigenous theory of writing in Spain.[1]

As in Italy, the rhetorical tradition precedes and informs literary criticism in general,[2] the latter denoted in Spanish by the generic term 'preceptiva' or 'prescription'. Indeed, while the rhetorics proper have little intrinsic interest, more marginal texts, less easy to classify, have an importance which transcends their historical and geographical limitations. The three texts or

---

[1] For Spanish 'belatedness' see Ernst Robert Curtius, *European Literature and the Latin Middle Ages*, trans. Willard R. Trask (London, 1953), 541–3.

[2] See Craig Kallendorf, 'The Rhetorical Criticism of Literature in Early Italian Humanism from Boccaccio to Landino', *Rhetorica*, 1.2 (1983), 33–59.

collections with which I am concerned here span the second half of what is known as the Golden Age. They are Fernando de Herrera's *Anotaciones* to the poems of Garcilaso de la Vega (published 1580); documents relating to the dispute over the poems of Góngora, the major literary controversy of the period (1610s and 1620s); and, finally, Baltasar Gracián's manual of wit or erudition, the *Agudeza o arte de ingenio* (revised edition 1648). I will pay particular attention to prologues in these works, liminary passages in already marginal texts.

The belatedness of the primary texts has until recently been reflected in the secondary literature. Studies of rhetoric or poetics have received less attention from Hispanists than from scholars in other language areas. There has been no work in Spanish as detailed and wide-ranging as that of Weinberg in Italian or Fumaroli in French. Two general treatments of rhetoric in the Golden Age have been published, by Antonio Martí and José Rico Verdú, respectively.[3] Both suffer, however, from brevity of exposition and uncertainty of definition. For example, Rico Verdú devotes barely one page to Gracián, undeniably the greatest and most original *preceptista* of the age, while Martí offers just six pages, no doubt judging him to be insufficiently rhetorical. Yet, as I will suggest later, Gracián is profoundly compromised by the rhetorical tradition from which he seeks to distance his theoretical practice.

The sense of a Spanish 'difference' may be related to the common perception of an excess or superfluity both intrinsic and extrinsic to Spanish culture as a whole. It seems fair to say that Spain itself, geographically separate from the rest of Europe, has often been considered as marginal, even redundant, certainly less 'central' than France or Italy to a received 'European' culture. The prose, poetry, and drama of the Golden Age have had relatively little resonance abroad, condemned as they are from the seventeenth century onwards as excessively extravagant and immoderate. Until recently the commonplace of 'baroque excess' was echoed to a large extent by Spanish critics themselves. For the great nineteenth-century scholar Menéndez y Pelayo, the first to pay close attention to Spanish *preceptiva*, the transition from the sixteenth to the

---

[3] José Rico Verdú, *La retórica española de los siglos xvi y xvii* (Madrid, 1973); Antonio Martí, *La preceptiva retórica española en el siglo de oro* (Madrid, 1972).

seventeenth century, or from the poetry of Garcilaso to that of Góngora, reveals a marked decline from noble plainness to redundant ornamentalism. And this decline is also reflected in the growing, inordinate complexity of theoretical writing in the same period, and the increasing historical decadence of Spain as imperial power.[4]

According to Menéndez Pelayo and most subsequent critics, seventeenth-century poetry and theory are split into two camps: the 'culteranismo' of Góngora and his supporters, characterized by a redundant verbal excess, and the 'conceptismo' of Quevedo and Gracián, noted for its knotty conceptual difficulty. The distinction between the two is the rhetorical one of *res* and *verba*. However, recent research has shown that this opposition is untenable, for the terms were unknown to the writers to whom they are often still applied and would, indeed, have been unintelligible to them.[5] It is clear that a more sophisticated approach is required. My own thesis is twofold: that the apparent contradiction between the poetic plainness and theoretical dependency of the sixteenth century and the poetic excess and theoretical autonomy of the seventeenth is in fact a gradual progression in which the final extravagance is already implicit in the initial sobriety[6] and that the exclusion or marginalization of Spain in relation to Europe is relative rather than absolute, and the two terms are mutually defining, not rigorously divorced. My evidence for these very broad generalizations is drawn from statements in preceptiva of the period which we may now examine in some detail.

In the introduction to his *Arte poética en romance castellano* (1580) Sánchez de Lima rehearses the Horatian argument that in the case of the poet or rhetor art must supply the deficiencies of nature. Yet this artistic supplement ('suplemento') is particularly necessary in Spain, where native wits ('ingenios') remain dangerously unrestrained by precept.[7] More complex, but rather similar, is Herrera's argument in the same year, de-

---

[4] See *Historia de las ideas estéticas en España* (Santander, 1947), esp. ii. 329.

[5] See Andrée Collard, *Nueva poesía: Conceptismo, culteranismo en la crítica española* (Madrid, 1967).

[6] See Arthur Terry, 'The Continuity of Renaissance Criticism', *BHS* 31 (1954), 27–36.

[7] Ed. Rafael de Balbín Lucas (Madrid, 1944), 12.

veloped at some length in the opening pages of his *Anotaciones.*[8]
On the one hand, Herrera intends to 'illustrate' and 'enrich'
the Spanish culture of his day by supplying it with those alien
poetical and rhetorical concepts of which it has hitherto re-
mained ignorant. This ignorance is the result of Spain's martial
history, which has produced its people's characteristic bias towards arms rather than letters. On the other hand, Herrera
praises the Spanish language for its supreme copiousness and
abundance, greater than all other tongues, which makes it a
worthy instrument of the mighty empire throughout which it is
spoken. He vigorously rejects accusations made by Italian
theorists such as Tomitano that the Spanish are ignorant and
unlettered.

Herrera, then, both acknowledges and refutes Spain's dependency on Europe, looks back to the rhetorical nakedness of
the emergent, warring kingdoms and forward to the poetic
plenitude of an established imperial dominion. However, both
of these states appear to coexist at the time he is writing. The
contrast between past ignorance and future knowledge is
repeatedly expressed in such pairs as nakedness and clothing,
poverty and richness, deficiency and excess. Yet the Spanish
language in its current state seems to comprehend both terms
in each of these oppositions, according to a twin perspective
of praise and vituperation which Herrera develops
simultaneously.

A contradiction of the same order is seen in Herrera's treatment of 'clarity', which he takes as the principal elocutionary
virtue. 'Claridad' is the supreme goal to which a poet can
aspire, and it seems at first to correspond to an ornamental brilliance or decorative luminosity. However, the excesses of verbal
elaboration are to be avoided: language should not deviate
from its natural plainness, and obscurity is tolerated only in the
matter of the discourse, not in its expression.[9] Clarity thus has
two values (luminosity and simplicity), which are produced respectively by the exploitation or the repression of the resources
of figurative language. Linguistic complexity is both positive,
in that it is proof of erudition, and negative, in that it is a symp-

[8] *Garcilaso de la Vega y sus comentaristas*, ed. Antonio Gallego Morell (Madrid, 1972),
305.
[9] *Garcilaso de la Vega*, p. 342.

tom of immoderation. It may be that this ambiguity is also found in the authorities normally cited by Spaniards in this context, Cicero and Quintilian. But it should be noted that the problems of clarity and of excess seem to be linked to the peculiar sensitivity of Spanish rhetoricians to the marginal status of their culture.

The same arguments (and authorities) recur in the thirty or forty years which separate the *Anotaciones* from the Góngora controversy, although the emphasis seems to change very gradually. The Aristotelian López Pinciano in 1596 still laments the poverty of Spanish theory, which has confined itself to prosody. He also gives a prudent warning on the dangers of the excessive vice of hyperbole.[10] The Platonist Luis de Carballo (1602) claims that more rhetorical works are urgently needed, not in order to confine the subtle wits ('ingenios') of Spanish poets, but rather in order to enlighten the ignorant populace who still consider poetry to be extravagant and disorderly.[11] The academic rhetorician Jiménez Patón (1604) suggests an increasing confidence in the value of Spanish copiousness. In the prologue to his *Elocuencia española* he states his intention as being to preserve the Spanish language in its current exalted state by drawing attention to the lofty ornament characteristic of contemporary writing. He thus illustrates the figures of his rhetoric with vernacular rather than classical examples.[12] An uncompromising tone is set by Luis Carrillo's *Libro de la erudición poética* (published posthumously in 1611). Carrillo claims that since the time of Garcilaso the practice of poetry in Spain has come to rival that of Italy. And it is perhaps significant that he describes this increasing poetic abundance and richness as 'excesso' ('excess'), evidently attaching no negative connotations to the word. His aim in writing his treatise is to attack those who oppose the linguistic elaboration of the new poetry and would strip the Spanish muses of the elocutionary garments which they have only recently acquired.[13] Carrillo appeals, like Herrera before him, to the traditional metaphor of style as garment. And as in the

[10] *Philosophía antigua poética*, ed. Alfredo Carballo Picazo (Madrid, 1953), i. 9; iii. 56.
[11] *Cisne de Apolo*, ed. Alberto Porqueras Mayo (Madrid, 1958), 23.
[12] Cited by Rico Verdú, p. 49.
[13] Ed. Manuel Cardenal Iracheta (Madrid, 1946), 8–9.

case of Herrera, he is acutely conscious of foreign claims that Spain is rhetorically naked. The question of stylistic excess is thus linked once more to that of national anxiety; but unlike in earlier preceptiva, here verbal difficulty or obscurity is an unqualified good, proper linguistic apparel for the aristocratic and manly Spaniard who (like Carrillo) dedicates himself to both arms and letters.

Such praise of obscurity paves the way for the commonplaces of the Góngora controversy in the 1610s and 1620s. Here, again, theoretical debate attempts to set the necessary limits of the essential and the excessive, and to situate a relatively novel poetic practice within the traditional confines of a rhetoricized poetics. In his *Antídoto* against the first *Soledad* (written around 1614) Juan de Jáuregui attacks Góngora's monstrous 'swelling' of words, his great 'heaps' of figures and metaphors, both cause and effect of a discursive superfluity ('hinchazón', 'montones', 'superflua loquacidad'). And in his defence of Góngora some ten years later Pedro Díaz de Rivas lists eleven objections to the 'new poetry', supposed transgressions of the rhetorical norm. These are the excessive use of neologism, trope, and hyperbaton and the obscurity which consequently results; the extravagance of metaphor, dissonance of style, and improper mixture of low and high diction; unnecessary repetition, hyperbole, and extension of the length of sentences. The final objection comprehends all the rest: 'redundancy or excessive copia in diction'.[14]

Yet the defenders of Spanish novelty are forced to take up their theoretical position firmly within the confines of traditional (that is, foreign) authority. Rivas tends to refer to Aristotle and Hermogenes, Cicero and Quintilian, Scaliger and Minturno, but rarely cites the native Spanish theorists, such as Herrera, who had by now produced a substantial body of work.[15] Spanish deviance is thus supported by European orthodoxy and an autonomous poetic practice emerges from a dependent rhetorical theory.

Inversely, the opponents of Góngora (supporters of tradition and reaction) are led by their nationalism to reject the canonic

[14] Cited by Eunice Joiner Gates in the intro. to her edn. of these texts, *Documentos gongorinos* (Mexico City, 1960), 20–1.

[15] See C. C. Smith, 'On the Use of Spanish Theoretical Works in the Debate on Góngora', *BHS* 39 (1962), 165–76.

authorities and assert Spanish deviance at the same time as they proclaim its orthodoxy. Góngora's greatest critic is Quevedo, fellow poet and scholar, and the latter's most sustained theoretical exercise is the introduction to his edition of the poetry of Luis de León (1629).[16] Fray Luis's work is presented by Quevedo as the paradigm of a plain and 'moderate' sixteenth-century lyric, explicitly opposed to Góngora's seventeenth-century excess. Yet the authorities Quevedo cites are idiosyncratic and his argument is frequently obscure. He cites Statius on clarity and Petronius on avoidance of the vulgar, apparently indifferent to the widespread reputation of the first for obscurity and the second for obscenity. He appeals to the fifteenth-century Spanish prosodist Enrique de Villena, to markedly little effect. And he closes his discourse with an exegesis of 'clarity' based mainly on Demetrius Phalereus, which quite openly proposes verbal redundancy as the key to graphic brilliance. For Quevedo the techniques which produce 'claridad' include anaphora (the repetition of a single word at the beginning of consecutive lines); cacophony (emphatically discordant play on the phonetic value of single words); and what he calls 'menudencia' or 'smallness' (the appeal to improperly 'low' or physical detail for the purpose of heightened pictorial expressiveness). These 'brilliant' figures of speech come dangerously close to the excessive vices of gongorism to which Quevedo claims to be opposed. Indeed, Quevedo's list bears some resemblance to that of Díaz de Rivas some fifteen years before. By the late 1620s the 'clarity' originally thought to be absent in Góngora is thus produced (paradoxically) by those verbal strategies characteristic of him. In practice, the differences between the poetry of Quevedo and Góngora cannot be reduced to the *res/verba* dichotomy. And in theory, their respective traditionalism and innovation are profoundly implicated in one another. For each is sustained by its ambiguous and rather different relationship with a European tradition which it can neither accept nor ignore.

The ambiguous status of 'clarity' in this debate is perhaps reinforced by apparent contradictions inherent in the use of related terms by Cicero and Quintilian. In the former's treat-

---

[16] Reprinted in *Obras completas: Prosa*, ed. Luis Astrana Marín (Madrid, 1932). I refer to pp. 1482–8.

ment of the elocutionary virtues it is first denoted by the adverb 'plane' and the adjective 'dilucidus' (*De oratore*, iii. 37–8), implying a value close to 'simplicity' or 'plainness'. Yet elsewhere Cicero seems to use 'illustration' and 'decoration' as synonyms (iii. 152), and the figures themselves are often called 'lumina' (*Orator*, xxxix. 134). In Quintilian too 'perspicuitas' also seems to mean 'facility' at one point, given again by the adjective 'planus' (VIII. ii. 22). Yet previously the figures of 'emphasis' (similar to the techniques recommended by Quevedo above) are assigned, after some hesitation, not to 'perspicuitas' but to 'ornatus' (VIII. ii. 11). Clarity is thus associated at different points with two of its sister elocutionary virtues, purity and ornament, and this lack of resolution may be echoed in Spanish vernacular debate.

An increasingly important term and one equally dependent on foreign precedent is 'concepto'. For if 'claridad' seems to swing between purity and ornament, then 'concepto' oscillates between idea and sensation. Until recently 'concepto' has been read as a synonym of the English 'conceit'. Yet recent research has shown that on the one hand it has the value of 'concept' in the common sense of the word, and on the other it can denote an example of figurative language more decorative than conceptual. This later development seems to rely on Italian theory of the late Cinquecento and in particular Camillo Pellegrino's *Del concetto poetico* (written around 1598).[17] As in the case of clarity, the lexical ambiguity of the term in Spain is preceded by the uncertainty of its exposition elsewhere, and the terms claimed by Spanish critics as their own are already saturated with meaning from humanist debate abroad.

This assertion of freedom within authority is reinforced by increasing reference in the early seventeenth century to Spanish-born Latin authors. Thus Quevedo praises Martial, Lucan, and Seneca as stylistic models and theoretical commentators to the relative neglect of Virgil and Cicero. The rise of Silver Age Latin in Spain has a particular resonance as it is thought to exhibit the unchanging rhetoric of a 'Hispanic' temperament. The potential excesses of its style (verbal and conceptual) are resolutely defended by those, such as Quevedo,

---

[17] See Collard (p. 26) for the role of Pellegrino's text in the semantic development of 'concetto'.

committed in theory to a prudent moderation of language. Yet, once more, much of this sense of self has its roots outside Spain, and Quevedo's praise of the hyperbolic Lucan is to some extent a reactive gesture to the vituperations made against the Latin poet by the hated Julius Caesar Scaliger.

The awareness of a Spanish difference, and of the refusal of foreigners to appreciate its quality, is fundamental to the most important and complex of Spanish theoretical treatises, Gracián's *Agudeza y arte de ingenio* (1648), which remains unjustly ignored outside Hispanism. I shall return to the two major terms in the title, but for the moment I render 'agudeza' as 'wit' and 'ingenio' as 'intellect'. In its final version the *Agudeza* is a vast work in two parts and sixty-three 'discursos', which is nothing less than a general theory of literary discourse. Although it appears initially to be random in construction, it moves with a certain coherence from a polemical introduction, to an extensive formal classification of simple wit (or single 'conceptos'), to a shorter treatment of compound wit (multiple 'conceptos'), and concludes with a brief definition of terms. The *Agudeza* is both highly technical in vocabulary and (at times) affectingly idiosyncratic in tone, its prescriptive rigour interrupted by the occasional personal reference and a constant stream of examples from poetry, prose, and sermons. There is much repetition and redundancy in the *Agudeza*, but this reveals (in spite of the author) the impossibility of reducing literature to a single 'scientific' method.

The foreword cites with approval the Silver Latin models already favoured by Quevedo some twenty years before: Martial, Seneca, Tacitus, and Pliny.[18] And it claims that while the French are noted for erudition, the Italians for eloquence, and the Greeks for invention, the Spaniards are known for their wit. The first discourse places this sense of uniqueness in a historical context: the ancients, although skilled in logic and rhetoric, had no sensitivity to wit. They admired it in epigrams but did not observe or examine it, still less define its characteristics. It is hard, Gracián complains, to begin anew ('inventar'), easy to continue those traditions already laid down by precedent. Yet this attempt at invention *ex nihilo*, the only strategy

---

[18] Ed. Evaristo Correa Calderón (Madrid, 1969), i. 45–7.

(Gracián suggests) that can do justice to the uniquely disinherited status of the Spanish genius, is compromised from the outset by its necessary engagement with the classical rhetoric which has excluded or marginalized Spanish wit. In the foreword, again, Gracián uses the metaphor of the family to describe the relationship between the traditional arts and his own innovatory theory. 'Conceptos' have often occurred in the past, but like orphaned children they have been entrusted to an improper mother, the rhetorical eloquence which could not have given birth to them.

The image of the family tends to suggest, against the avowed intentions of the author, the 'relative' status of the terms involved. As Gracián states a little later, wit is a second-stage system, taking the figures of rhetoric as the primary matter from which it creates its own distinctive structures. Innovation is thus grounded in the tradition it seeks to reject. The main division of the *Agudeza* (that between simple and complex wit) reduplicates the conventional rhetorical distinction between figures *in verbis singulis* and *in verbis conjunctis*. Indeed, much of Gracián's lexicon is drawn from logic and rhetoric. He uses such traditional names as amphibologia, equivocatio, and paranomasia, as well as his own classifications, and even such apparently neutral terms as 'sujeto' and 'término' seem to be used in the logical sense of 'subject' and 'predicate'. Even Gracián's well-known definition of the 'concepto' as an 'act of the intellect expressing the relation between objects' is prefigured by Matteo Peregrini's *Acutezze* of 1639.[19] Gracián's ideal of the penetrating Spanish intellect is not dissimilar to that of Peregrini or the later Italian theorist Tesauro. It seems unlikely that the *Agudeza* plagiarizes the *Acutezze* to any significant extent. It is more important to acknowledge that, in the very attempt to establish an autonomous and peculiarly Spanish theory of discourse, Gracián coincided inadvertently with contemporary developments outside Spain.

What is more, as in the cases of 'claridad' and 'concepto', the terms privileged in Spanish theory, 'agudeza' and 'ingenio', are preceded (like their Italian equivalents) by an indeterminate Latin origin. In Quintilian's treatment of the oration the

---

[19] For Góngora's dependence on scholastic logic and Italian concettisti see M. J. Woods, 'Gracián, Peregrini, and the Theory of Topics', *MLR* 63 (1968), 854–63.

'acutum' is an ingeniously witty quality produced, none the less, by proper use of ornament (VIII. iii. 49). And in his study of the orator, the copia of 'ingenium' is both subservient to the other virtues of judgement and prudence ('iudicium', 'consilium') and superior to the practical exercises and imitation of models by which those lacking in 'ingenium' seek to supply their deficiency (X. i. 29; X. ii. 12). 'Ingenium' is thus both excessive, dangerously unstable and volatile; and essential, a natural gift which human effort cannot reproduce. Gracián stresses the divine perfection of wit in his opening panegyric: it is the nourishment of the soul. And his proposal of a genetic Spanish gift perhaps echoes and intensifies the Roman conception of 'ingenium' as a natural or innate quality. Yet it is typical of Spain that what Gracián praises above all is the variety of 'agudeza', its multiple diversity. The subtleties of the fecund intelligence are more numerous than the stars in heaven or flowers in the field (p. 56).

But what is copia to the Spaniards is excess to others. In a well-known letter of 1662 Jean Chapelain attacks the Spanish for their lack of 'sens' and love of 'agudezas'. An overactive imagination stifles the powers of judgement. He thus reiterates Quintilian's triad with a prescriptive bias: 'ingenium' must be subordinate to 'iudicium' and 'consilium'. Adrien Baillet in 1685 derives Spanish extravagance from the Jewish and Moorish temperament inherited by Christian contemporaries, an argument which was, understandably in the light of Spanish racism, more popular abroad than in Spain itself.[20] Yet this supposed excess of wit need not be attributed to spurious 'oriental' influences. For, as we have seen, for over a century the growth of a rhetoricized poetics in Spain had been profoundly compromised by an awareness of that 'European' tradition from which it felt itself to be excluded. Marc Fumaroli has recently suggested a hidden history of vernacular apologetics in France, in which he contrasts the 'naturalness' of the mother tongue as praised by Vaugelas and others with the lofty imperialism of the *patrius sermo* promoted by Port Royal.[21] Such a division does not seem to hold for Spain in a slightly earlier

---

[20] Both Chapelain and Baillet are cited by Collard (pp. 91–3).
[21] See 'L'Apologétique de la langue française classique', *Rhetorica*, 2. 2 (1984), 139–61.

period. For while there is pervasive concern for the deficiencies of Spanish culture, there is also an uncompromising assertion that the richness of the Castilian language makes it equally fitting for both the natural simplicity of private speech and the heroic gravity of public proclamation. Hence the persistence of the return (from Herrera to Gracián) to the problem of copia, multiplicity or excess. For a rich rhetorical diversity was born from an anxious awareness of difference.

The great eighteenth-century dictionary of the *Autoridades* defines 'excesso' as 'the portion or part which is left over . . . and goes beyond the regulation and natural order of anything'. The rhetoric of excess in the Golden Age reveals the extent to which Spain goes beyond (while remaining within) the European culture from which it still perhaps feels itself to be at once subjected and disinherited. But it also reminds us that the 'natural' is a strategic not an essential term in rhetorical or prescriptive discourse, that it varies according to both time and place. Indeed, the nature invoked by theorists in order to support their discourse often exposes the cultural assumptions of that discourse to the critical gaze of the reader.

2. LANGUAGE AND VISION

El diálogo de la lengua

I return to the question of 'natural' language at the end of the chapter, in my discussion of another, much earlier work: Juan de Valdés's *Diálogo de la lengua*. From the preceding discussion, however, three main problems arise which deserve closer examination; these are imitation, interpretation, and language.[22] I will take each of these in turn. The problem of imitation centres on the status of the poetic object. As is well known, the term 'imitation' is used to denote both the depiction of nature and the reworking of previous texts.[23] The first case is generally taken to be a simple or primary process. But as we have seen with the emblem of the she-bear and its cub, nature is not always perceived as aesthetically neutral. Rather it per-

---

[22] In the opening chapters of *The Cornucopian Text* Terence Cave treats these points with reference to Erasmus and the French humanists.

[23] See Bernard Weinberg, *A History of Literary Criticism in the Italian Renaissance* (Chicago, 1961), 60, 483.

forms within itself a kind of exemplary, self-sufficient crafts-manship. But if nature sometimes serves as the model of a pre-existing quasi-artistic order, at other times it is taken as an authoritative example of rampant disorder. Thus Pedro Mejía, author of the popular miscellany *Silva de varia lección* (1540), jus-tifies the random structure of his collection by appeal to the pleasant irregularity of plants and trees to be found in the forest ('selva').[24] The frequent claims by theorists that art serves to supply deficiencies in nature also tend to problematize 'primary' imitation. When Sánchez de Lima seeks to define art (the faculty which determines the quality of imitation) he can-not do so without incorporating the word 'art' itself into his definition (p. 12). This is not simply an example of careless reasoning by a minor scholar. Rather it betrays a certain in-security as to the relative positions of poetic skill and natural faculty in the artistic process.

The imitation of authors is even more problematic. Here, by means of the process known as homology, the term that was once secondary (the first poet's copy of nature) now becomes primary (the model from which the second poet works). Homo-logy is rather similar to the figure of metalepsis we met in the Introduction. Both present the opportunity for an indefinite substitution of terms, each superseding the next. Critical theory itself provides a clear example of the action of homology. Thus traditional rhetoric and poetics take speech or text as their object; but the new manuals of wit in the seventeenth century seize on the traditional arts as 'matter' for their dominant 'form'. This process is repeated in the twentieth century, when the would-be metalanguages of semiotics or mythology are rapidly superseded by newer theories which question their authority.[25] Hence critical theory (like imitation) has no simple origin and no definitive end.

Perhaps the subtlest treatment of imitation comes from López Pinciano, who struggles to accommodate Aristotelian precept to a pragmatic awareness of the diversity of literary

---

[24] Cited by R. O. Jones in *A Literary History of Spain: The Golden Age: Prose and Poetry* (London and New York, 1971), 15.

[25] For the relationship between homology, mythology, and semiotics see the final essay in Barthes's *Mythologies* (Paris, 1957), 'Le Mythe, aujourd'hui', 191–247 (pp. 195–202).

forms. For El Pinciano, imitation is primarily an innate human faculty: even babies learn by mimicking their elders. Likewise, tailors and cobblers make garments which imitate or reproduce the parts of the body they are intended to cover (i. 196). El Pinciano distinguishes between primary and secondary imitation. The poet who carries out the first is a portraitist ('retratador'); he who carries out the second is just a painter ('simple pintor', i. 197). One modern critic suggests that the first process is natural, and the second is not.[26] But if, as El Pinciano has already said, all human action is a kind of imitation, then any representation of it must be secondary and deficient to some extent. What is more, the frequency of El Pinciano's appeal in his own work to textual rather than natural authority tends to work against the assumption that the first must be inferior to the second. The distinction itself and the value we should attribute to it are by no means clear.

When El Pinciano treats the dramatic poem, the status of the object seems to change once more. He asks whether the action we see performed actually took place in the way we see it. The answer, of course, is no. In this case, El Pinciano reserves the name of imitation for the depiction of an action ('obra') which did not take place, but could have done so (ii. 308). The dramatist has no pre-existing object in the world; it is enough that his imitation satisfy the conditions of verisimilitude. Here, then, the very condition of the object is that it does not exist in nature: the actual object of poetry in general is displaced by the virtual object of drama. Yet, in his discussion of drama, El Pinciano frequently invokes nature not as a principle of possibility (that which could take place), but as one of propriety (that which does and ought to take place). For example, he says that actors' gestures should be noble and in accordance with nature (iii. 286–8). There seems to be a conflict here between the twin demands of variety and fidelity. By supplying the necessary copia of invention the poet inevitably distances himself from literalist notions of imitation. The objection may seem small to modern readers. But El Pinciano is highly sensitive to the charge that drama is false, even pernicious, because it has no simple origin in the world. He is not helped by his

---

[26] See Sanford Shepard, *El Pinciano y las teorías literarias del siglo de oro* (Madrid, 1962), 49.

global definition of 'poesía' or imaginative writing: he claims that it is subject to no single discipline and that it encompasses everything that is in the world (i. 234). This limitless expansion increases the scope of poetics, but undermines its stability. How can the theorist approach an infinite object?

El Pinciano's concept of interpretation is also problematic. In rhetoric there are four different ways of reading a text, traditionally given as historical, allegorical, topological, and anagogical (see Jiménez Patón, pp. 352–3). The reader is thus offered a certain freedom of action within well-defined limits. El Pinciano is concerned by the potential breakdown of this transmission or production of meaning. Thus he distinguishes between three kinds of obscurity. The first derives from the poet's discretion, when he withholds information which should not become public knowledge, such as the identity of the lady to whom he writes. The second derives from the poet's use of allegory, when he disguises an idea with 'dark' language so that it may shine more brightly when uncovered by the reader. The third is when the poet mixes up ('confunde') his words in such a way that it precludes understanding by the reader (ii. 162). The first two forms of obscurity are praiseworthy; the third is to be avoided. The problem of this division is that it fails in its attempt to reconcile the antagonistic roles of writer and reader. The ultimate goal of El Pinciano's rhetoricized poetics must be the proper communication of the poet's message to the audience. But this depends on the definition of 'audience'. Discretion and allegory improve the reception of the message by a learned audience through their very withholding of information. On the other hand, the subtle pleasures of the hidden meaning will be lost on the vulgar audience generally envisaged by the Aristotelians. In spite of the confidence of El Pinciano's assertion, there can be no verifiable point at which 'good' obscurity becomes 'bad'. When allegory is put to the service of heightened imitation the act of interpretation is held in a kind of perpetual suspension between the poet and the reader. Each is necessary to the process, but the duties of neither can be rigorously defined.

Elsewhere, El Pinciano shows his fear that inflated or affected language may obstruct the process of communication. In the section on tropes he quotes three examples to be avoided. One speaker, wishing to praise a mason, claimed that he could roof the highest towers while standing on the ground. For El Pinciano, such hyperbole serves merely to diminish the object it seeks to amplify. His second example is that of a preacher who, wishing to decry adultery, said that he would rather sin with two virgins than with one married woman. The third example is that of a prudish nun who, instead of saying 'testicles', used a circumlocution so laboured that El Pinciano dare not repeat it (iii. 56–7). The examples show that, when used improperly, the 'dark' tropes or schemes of hyperbole or periphrasis confound the speaker's intention instead of enforcing it. This is not the well-defined plurality of interpretation favoured by traditional hermeneutic, but an uncontrollable surplus of meaning, which gives rise to wholly unintended and often comic effects. But, as in the case of good and bad obscurity, the supposed distinction between proper and improper language can have no fixed or definitive status: El Pinciano appeals rather to an unvoiced consensus between speaker and audience always already in place. It is perhaps significant that two of the examples refer to the taboo subject of sexuality. Both literary and social behaviour are subject to the conventional or arbitrary control known as 'decorum'.

Herrera's references to obscurity (which El Pinciano would have known) also raise questions concerning the process of interpretation and the relation of meaning to language. Thus, commenting on a sonnet by Garcilaso which he considers particularly 'brilliant', he declares, in the space of a few lines, first that meaning is enclosed ('encerrado') within words; secondly that words are the pictures ('imágenes') of thoughts; and thirdly that clarity is born ('nace') from words (H-78, p. 342[27]). The relationship of language to meaning is successively instrumental (the word merely encloses the concept within), proportionate (the word directly reflects the concept), and genetic (words produce a textual effect). Of course these terms are figurative: Herrera does not literally believe that words are boxes which contain a physical meaning, pictures which reproduce visual thoughts, or mothers who give birth to poetic offspring. But it is not enough to say that these hermeneutic models are 'simply' metaphorical; or that the metaphors are 'in' Herrera's text. Because to do so is to reproduce, without

---

[27] 'H' stands for Herrera.

examination, those conventional distinctions between plain and figurative language, and between external form and internal substance, which are themselves problematized by the intermittence and plurality of Herrera's own writing. As in all learned discourse of the period, the burden of Herrera's argument is carried by the figures, which cannot be subtracted from it in an attempt to lay bare the presumed substance of the text. And once more we are confronted with the problem of reflexivity. In writing on the figurative process Herrera (unknowingly) incorporates into his argument those same motifs of light and vision, inside and outside, that he perceives in the poetry he takes as his model.

A similar kind of rhetoricity is evident in the opening lines of the *Anotaciones*, where Herrera defends the richness of Spain's language and laments the poverty of its culture. Here the nakedness of the linguistic body is covered by 'ornaments and jewels' (p. 307). Such images can only be read within a kind of rhetorical repertoire in which the garment of style serves the purposes of both modesty and luxury; hence it is impossible to say at what point figurative decoration becomes superfluous. And when Carrillo cites the same motif, the word used to denote the richness of apparel is 'arreo', which means at once (decorative) trappings and (functional) harness (p. 18). Figurative language is a kind of cover; but without it, the poem-steed lacks direction and guidance.

The other image repertoire developed by Herrera is so pervasive as to be almost imperceptible: it is that of sight and vision. In the introduction he claims modestly that he can 'see' little in the 'fog' of Spanish ignorance; and that he will not shed more 'light' on his chosen topic than is appropriate for his 'weak-eyed and short-sighted' readers. Otherwise, they risk being 'blinded' by his erudition. Just as the stylistic garment both conceals and displays, so the light of erudition both blinds and illuminates. But once more, it is insufficient to say that the metaphor is 'in' the text: any paraphrase of Herrera's argument is likely to fall back itself on such half-erased metaphors as 'perspicacity'. Figuration is at once superfluous and unavoidable. But if it cannot be separated from argument, it reveals, none the less, the unspoken assumptions of that argument. The first assumption is that vision is associated with order. Carballo states explicitly that the 'blindness' of the Spaniards is their ob-

stinate belief that poetry is vain and frivolous. When it is over-
come, they will realize that poetry is as ordered and coherent as
any other discipline (pp. 23–4). The power of this kind of
unacknowledged metaphor is that it passes off an aesthetic
preference (the love of order) for the simple act of perception
(the ability to see). Sight thus implies the notion of mastery, for
it asserts the 'natural' precedence of the subject who claims to
possess it: only Carballo (or Herrera, or López Pinciano) can
'see' the truth. The position of Gracián is rather similar, if more
emphatic. In the opening lines of his address to the reader he
describes his own theory as 'flamante' (both 'bright, flaming'
and 'brand new'). And he goes on to claim that although some
of the subtleties of agudeza 'shine through' in rhetoric they are
but glimpses or flashes ('vislumbres') of the real thing (i. 45).

The privilege of light, then, is that, like language itself, its
omnipresence renders it invisible. The potency of light, again
like language, is that it enables communication but takes no
active part in it. Hence poetic 'brilliance', much discussed in
the period, is at once a property inherent in the poem and a
faculty brought to it by the attentive reader. This is particularly
the case with seventeenth-century theorists such as Gracián or
the Italian Emanuele Tesauro, who present their theories of
discourse as means of exploring the world. Gracián seeks to discover the relationship between objects; Tesauro to acquire
knowledge of distant objects. Yet, disconcertingly, they seem to
use 'clarity' and 'perspicacity' as synonyms. In both, the line
between perception and interpretation (between the acknowledgement and the imposition of value) is tenuous indeed.

Derrida has a famous essay on metaphor in the text of philosophy.[28] In it he argues that figures based on the sun, dawn, or
light (which he punningly baptizes 'heliotropes') ensure the
persistence of supposedly neutral or objective discourses such as
philosophy. This is also the case with the texts of Golden Age
theorists, who would not perhaps have been unwilling to
acknowledge the figurative status of their own writing. The
force of Derrida's argument, however, is that *all* writing is constitutively figurative. Hence, although rhetorical contradiction

---

[28] 'La Mythologie blanche', in *Marges, de la philosophie* (Paris, 1972), 247–324. For a
commentary on this essay see Christopher Norris, *Deconstruction: Theory and Practice*
(London and New York: 1982), 82.

is perhaps more evident in the later theorists, whose writing is notoriously complex and intricate, it seems possible that similar contradictions are also implicit in much earlier Spanish treatises. We can therefore test Derrida's hypothesis of universal figuration by examining a chronologically early work, and one often claimed as the most natural and spontaneous of its kind in the Golden Age: Juan de Valdés's *Diálogo de la lengua*, which was written around 1535.

As an Erasmist who lived much of his life in Italy, Valdés is something of a marginal figure. Yet this very marginality seems to ensure the subtlety of his account of the Spanish 'difference' and of its peculiar relationship to Europe. Of course, Valdés is by no means disengaged from Spanish culture: his treatise is in part a sustained refutation of his main predecessor and fellow humanist Nebrija. And by both lamenting the poverty of Castilian and advocating its use as the language of empire, Valdés not only anticipates writers such as Herrera; he also echoes Nebrija himself. Thus Valdés is neither the origin of Golden Age linguistic thought, nor an objective commentator on it. Yet the *Diálogo* has often been read for its supposed originality and objectivity. Modern critics have praised the plainness of style both advocated and exemplified by Valdés, his overt concern for the primacy of spoken language, and his preference for the natural wealth of vernacular proverbs, as against the academic authority of classical precepts.[29] Hence, whatever its status in the lifetime of its author, the *Diálogo* is thought to exemplify, perhaps for the first time, many of those linguistic qualities thought to be peculiarly Spanish. These 'natural' virtues of simplicity and objectivity have been called into question by the latest scholars, more rhetorically aware than their predecessors.[30] But the purpose of my own reading is not to suggest that the *Diálogo* does not possess the qualities often attributed to it, but to propose that those qualities are deconstructed at the very moment of their exposition by a submerged and antithetical rhetoric of linguistic surplus or gratuity.

As the *Diálogo* begins, a simple opposition is set up between plain language and rhetoric, the latter understood as super-

[29] See e.g. Jones, *A Literary History*, pp. 24–6.
[30] See Cristina Barbolani's intro. to her edn. of the *Diálogo* (Madrid, 1982), 49–55. References to Valdés's text are to this edn.

fluous ornament. When the learned Italian Marcio asks the
Valdés character if he is willing to answer questions on the Castilian language, he replies somewhat curtly that he cannot
understand the question, so overburdened is it by rhetorical
decoration (p. 118). Marcio is forced to repeat his request. A
second distinction is also implied here, between the improper
excesses of Italian and the noble precision of Spanish. A little
later, Marcio makes a third distinction, between native and
acquired languages. The mother tongue is sucked from the
breast; subsequent languages are learned from books, and are
merely 'pegadizas' (both 'sticky' and 'parasitic') (p. 122). The
natural organicism of the first language is thus contrasted with
the unnatural artifice of the second. The first is essential to
human development, the second prevents or inhibits it. It is not
surprising, therefore, that Valdés consistently privileges speech
over writing. The only rule in spelling is to write as one speaks;
the usage of pronunciation is the greatest of authorities; style is
'natural' when it takes its origin in speech (pp. 171, 184, 233).
Hence, Valdés appeals to proverbs as the unique source of a
natural, oral wisdom.

The wealth of Spanish proverbs perhaps reflects Valdés's
sense of the heterogeneity of the Spanish language, which (even
more than other vernaculars) cannot be reduced to simple precept (p. 153), and the copiousness of its lexicon, which can be
learned only by prolonged intercourse with native speakers,
even uneducated peasants (p. 209). Yet this alleged cornucopia
or vibrant, natural effusion tends to work against Valdés's
opening distinctions. For example, Valdés claims several times
that Spanish is 'purer' than Italian. Yet, according to Valdés
himself, its development is halting and compromised at every
stage: the source of the Iberian language was Greek, but this
noble tongue was lost in the Peninsula after the Roman in-
vasion. The romance bequeathed by the Romans was irreme-
diably 'corrupted' by the Goths and, above all, the Arabs
(pp. 132–8). Thus, although Valdés argues vehemently that
Castilian is closer to Latin than Tuscan, and is thus more perfect (see e.g. p. 257), a partially repressed sense of the tainted
genealogy of the Spanish language keeps returning in images
which speak of the decline from or corruption of an original
linguistic plenitude. Of course, such ideas are commonplace in

the period. But they produce important contradictions in Valdés's practical recommendations. Thus he insists on re-inserting letters absent in Spanish words where the Latin original has them (e.g. 'cobdicia', not 'codicia', from 'cupidi-tas') (p. 168). By these additions he claims to render words 'full and whole', but succeeds rather in calling our attention to the irregularities and deficiencies in the supposedly primary term 'usage'. The heterogeneity of Spanish and its resistance to regu-lation come to seem a very mixed blessing. Thus art or erudi-tion tend to displace usage at critical points in the argument. If style is natural, based on speech, one must vary the level of one's style ('hazer diferencia') according to the topic on which and the person to whom one writes (p. 223). And if Spanish style is prized for its brevity, that brevity does not preclude the repetition of words when the nobility of the subject or the ele-gance of the diction are in danger (p. 237). Critics who cite the first half of these propositions generally omit the second half, in which Valdés radically qualifies his argument by a wholly tra-ditional appeal to decorum.

In both these cases the founding model of language slips or shifts imperceptibly from speech to writing. And elsewhere Valdés's overt preference for oral authority is in direct contra-diction with his equally overt preference for usage as final arbiter. Thus, in a number of examples, the proverbs cited by Valdés contain archaisms (such as 'cubil' or 'fallar') that he is obliged by his own criteria to reject (pp. 197, 199). The *refranero*, repository of the Spanish people's authentic voice, is as corrupt and alienating as the rest of language. The general status of Valdés's examples is thus called into question. They frequently fail to 'illustrate' the point he wishes to make. For example, he quotes lavishly from traditional lyric for the bene-fit of his Italian audience (and they sometimes reciprocate with Spanish verses he claims not to know himself). Yet Valdés acknowledges the idiosyncrasy of poetic diction: poetry is not to be used to teach foreigners Spanish (p. 244).

Hence, throughout the *Diálogo*, there is a kind of under-current that hints at a hidden or repressed knowledge: the inevitability of linguistic surplus. At one point Valdés admits to a fondness for the archaisms he excludes elsewhere: the an-tiquity of 'ca' ('because') gives him a certain pleasure (p. 197).

He pays great attention to puns ('vocablos equívocos'), which he claims are inappropriate in other languages, but proper ornament in Castilian (p. 211). It may not be accidental that the neologisms he would introduce to Spanish relate to multiple registers of diction (*paradoxa, decoro, estilo*) and copiousness of invention (*ingeniar*) (pp. 219–22). When asked by Marcio if these loan words are required for decoration ('ornamento') or necessity ('necesidad'), Valdés replies that it is for both reasons (p. 23). He thus gestures unknowingly at the twin status of the 'illustrated' language he desires, which is at once a substitute for and an addition to the supposedly authentic origin of a proper or native speech. Cristina Barbolani claims that Valdés takes up a position of harmonious synthesis ('medietas') between Spain and Italy, art and usage (pp. 58, 88–9). The action of the supplement we have traced, however, is more devious and less gratifying than any simple reconciliation of opposites.

The status of writing is thus of the essence. Writing initiates a play of difference of which speech is incapable. Thus, even in the spoken genre of the dialogue, Valdés often returns to written forms as the basis for linguistic purity. For example, the proverb 'Quien no aventura (no ha ventura) no gana' has two contradictory meanings according to the presence or absence of a silent 'h'. The first version reads properly, 'He who does not venture does not gain'; the second reads erroneously, 'He who has no luck does not gain' (p. 156). Elsewhere Valdés advises us to omit the letter 'h' from writing because it is not pronounced (p. 175). Here, on the contrary, it must be inserted because it is not pronounced. Only writing can offer the unvoiced difference exemplified by the silent, yet persistent, letter 'h'. Similarly, Valdés suggests that where there is a confusion in spelling between 's' and 'x', words deriving from Latin take 's', and words deriving from Arabic 'x'. The correct forms are thus 'sastre' not 'saxtre', but 'caxcavel' not 'cascavel'. The modern edition suggests that this is a phonetic rather than a purely etymological distinction (p. 183 n. 144). But it remains the case that the written distinction between the two sibilants had no stable equivalent in spoken Spanish. If there had been one, then the confusion could not have arisen. Once more, writing takes precedence over speech, and the abstract authority of philology over the dynamic example of usage. A final problem is that of written accents. At times they simply reproduce a difference in stress already present in spoken language ('hablo'; 'habló'). But Valdés also recommends a redundant tilde on *cõmo* and *mũy* for the purpose of decoration (p. 188). Or again, towards the end of the dialogue Valdés advises against inverting word order: the statement 'verdad es' might be confused with the plural noun 'verdades' (p. 235). Yet there can be no confusion in writing. Once more the distinction can be reproduced in speech only with difficulty. Like the Spanish double negative which obstinately retains a negative value in spite of Latin precedent (p. 236), writing both structures and reduplicates the forms on which language depends. Writing is the repressed term from the beginning of the dialogue with its reference to the natural plenitude of the mother tongue; but it is persistent in its return as a necessary point of reference. The property of the written letter is its insistence or adherence. Like the acquired language, it is 'sticky' or 'parasitical'.

The most enigmatic of Valdés's 'illustrations' (and the one which most clearly outstrips its supposed function) is the celebrated riddle given about half-way through the work. It is offered merely as an example of the shift from 'r' to 'l' when an infinitive is followed by an enclitic pronoun (that is, 'conocella' instead of 'conocerla'). The riddle has yet to be solved by critics, though many solutions have been offered. It begins: 'What is the thing which we can see most clearly if we don't have it and cannot recognize if we do have it?' (p. 178.) I would suggest that one answer to the riddle is writing. Those who are skilled in writing (like Valdés) look 'beyond' its lure to a Utopia of voice or nature uncorrupted by art; only those who have no writing (the illiterate) are confronted by the full force of its materiality and its ability to enforce difference. But if writing is one 'blind spot' of Valdés's linguistic theory, then vision itself is another. The absent object of the riddle (whatever it may be) is defined only by its relation to sight: it is alternately visible and invisible. And Valdés, like the later theorists we met in the first half of the chapter, couches stylistic virtues in visual terms, such as 'color'. When Valdés translated the Psalms the words he was obliged to add to the text to carry the sense of the original (but which had no direct origin in it) were written in

ink of a different colour. They served to add 'lustre' or brilliance (Barbolani, 47–8). Valdés's glowing red ink is a fitting
image of the linguistic surplus inherent in even the most rever-
ent approach to the Word. And it suggests, like the images of
clothing and adornment which occur throughout Golden Age
theory, a heightened concept of imitation, which incites the
reader's eye to penetrate its brilliant surface. In Barthes's well-
known phrase, the site of erotic desire is 'where the garment
gapes'.[31] And it is no accident that the intermittent play of
presence and absence (vision and invisibility) so common in the
theorists also leaves its trace in the love poetry of the Golden
Age.

---

[31] *Le Plaisir du texte* (Paris, 1973), 19.

2

THE RHETORIC OF PRESENCE
IN LYRIC POETRY

I. PRESENCE AND COMMUNICATION

THE three main genres of Golden Age writing are often taken
to be lyric poetry, picaresque narrative, and verse drama. Of
these, it is the poetry that has had least fortune abroad, no
doubt because of the lack of adequate translations. Yet there is
a widespread feeling that it is inappropriate, even improper, to
translate lyric verse. This is because it remains the case for
many modern readers that the poet 'speaks' more or less
directly of his most private feelings, and thus offers us the
chance of intimate communion with his inner being. Although
this criterion of authentic utterance has been questioned by
critics, it is rarely abandoned entirely. Moreover, the formal
excellence typical of the sonnet, preferred form of the lyric,
tends to promote a kind of linguistic fetishism in the reader.
The poem is often seen in traditional criticism as a verbal icon,
at once untainted by historical process, and suffused by personal ethos. Yet, as we saw in the previous chapter, the post-
Romantic bias towards both individual personality and linguistic transparency is not shared by Golden Age scholar-poets,
who are more sensitive to the necessary margins and uncontrollable excesses of literary discourse. Hence, when scholars
trained in linguistics began to undertake analyses of lyric
poetry, their practice not only constituted an implicit challenge
to the received idea that meaning was somehow 'present' in the
poem, as the author was in his language; it also suggested an
understanding of lyric as code or convention similar to that of
Renaissance poetics.

One particular term derived from linguistics is relevant to
my argument in this chapter: the shifter, or deictic. Shifters are
words such as personal pronouns and adverbs of time and place
whose referents always vary according to the context in which

they are used. They produce a sense of immediacy in the reader, of experiential intimacy. Jonathan Culler has drawn attention to the use of deictics in lyric and its association with the recreation of a speaking voice: 'A whole poetic tradition uses spatial, temporal, and personal deictics in order to force the reader to construct a meditative persona. The poem is presented as the discourse of a speaker who, at the moment of speaking, stands before a particular scene ...'[1] Shifters produce the effect of reality, of presence. And, as we shall see, they are anticipated by rhetorical terms which serve the same function: the loci or places associated with the figure known as *evidentia* or *enargeia*. Thus the lyric poet's 'I' and 'you', his 'here' and 'now', are at once constants of the genre (immutable and eternal) and variables (infinitely mobile and contingent).

As we saw in the Introduction, the model of discourse both implied and enacted by classical rhetoric is founded on the necessity of communication: the rhetor takes the object of imitation and attempts to transmit it through the medium of language to the listener or (later) to the reader.[2] The excellence of the oration is in proportion to the efficiency of this transmission. The source of the oration (the speaker), its target (the audience), and the message which passes between them (figurative language) all participate in a single process, while retaining, nevertheless, their separate identities. The three traditional ends of rhetoric (the production of pleasure, profit, and emotion) are subsumed under this general purpose or *officium* of persuasion. It is to the achievement of an ever more efficient instrument of persuasion that the rhetors subordinate the serried ranks of trope and figure in the class of *ornatus*. The rhetorical mission, then, is essentially and necessarily pragmatic and self-conscious with regard to the relative status of word and thing. Intermittently linked, the two remain essentially dis-

---

[1] 'Poetics of the Lyric', in *Structuralist Poetics* (London, 1983), 161–88 (p. 167).

[2] For the definition and aims of rhetoric see Heinrich Lausberg, *Manual de retórica literaria* (Madrid, 1966–8), paras. 32–3, 256–7. This chapter was prompted by Terence Cave's '*Enargeia*: Erasmus and the Rhetoric of Presence in the Sixteenth Century', *L'Esprit créateur*, 16.4 (Winter 1976), 5–19. For pictorialist representation in Golden Age lyric see Gareth Alban Davies, '*Pintura*: Background and Sketch of a Spanish Seventeenth-century Court Genre', *JWCI* 38 (1975), 288–313. For a treatment of three poets which is rather different from my own, see Arthur Terry, 'Thought and Feeling in Three Golden Age Sonnets', *BHS* 59 (1982), 237–46.

crete, as in the pervasive distinction between figures of speech (verbal patterning) and figures of thought (conceptual coercion). I suggested in the previous chapter that such relationships cannot be seen in terms of simple opposition. It remains the case, however, that the difference between *res* and *verba*, however shifting and asymmetrical it may prove to be, can be seen as the fundamental structuring principle of the art of rhetoric as a whole.

The figure known variously as *enargeia*, *evidentia* and *illustratio* appears at first to form a gap or fold in the sophisticated theoretical fabric within which it occurs. It aims to create a credible image which will take the audience into the presence of the object itself. The form of the thing is to be so expressed in the word that it is seen, rather than heard, and the orator's linguistic gesture will provoke emotions appropriate to this graphic persuasiveness. In its attempt to 'place things before the eyes' (the invariable definition of the figure from Cicero to Herrera and beyond) *enargeia* attempts the impossible: the fusion of word and thing, of orator and public in the single moment of representation. It is a potent and seductive ambition. However, the rhetoricians are well aware that language is inevitably mediate in character, and there are intricate instructions for the use of the figure. There are three modes or loci of attention, corresponding to the classes of deictics (persona, place, and time); and there are a variety of means by which they may be communicated (the choice of significant detail, the use of the present tense of the verb, and of apostrophe). *Enargeia* is associated with the demonstrative genre, that is formal oration used for praise or blame, and with a traditional subject matter: nature, war, catastrophe (see Lausberg, paras. 810–19). Moreover, it is always excessive. Quintilian classes his *evidentia* under *ornatus*: like all figurative language it goes beyond the clarity and verisimilitude of plain speech (VIII. iii. 61). Thus *enargeia* both makes up a lack in the unadorned (and hence impoverished) oration and forms a verbal excess, improperly outstripping the less ambitious elocutionary virtues. As we shall see, this logic of 'supplementarity' recurs, often unrecognized, in both modern and Renaissance treatments of the relation between art and nature, between poem and world. The marginality and deviance of the single figure are thus symptomatic of more general contradictions implicit in lyric poetry and literary criticism.

In spite of theoretical attempts to limit its scope and define its application, *enargeia* seems to correspond, in its initial movement at least, to an ingenuous and impassioned desire for the union of language and concept which will transcend both terms and embody a primal, linguistic plenitude. In other words, a rhetoric not of communication (relative and determinate), but of presence (absolute and integral). This nostalgia for the direct experience of nature and author is still potent today. As we saw in the Introduction in the case of Quevedo, modern readings of Golden Age lyric have suffered from just such an unwitting critical bias. The seductiveness of the 'vision' offered by *enargeia* (and as we have seen, its action is always expressed in visual terms) is also demonstrated by the attention it receives from Renaissance scholars such as Scaliger and Herrera who seem momentarily to succumb to the delights of the immediate in theoretical works whose habitual rigour and sophistication bear ample witness elsewhere to the artifice and deviance of poetic language as a whole. With the rise of *enargeia*, then, the aim of persuasion fuses with the ideal of heightened imitation in a way which will be characteristic of the rhetoricization of poetics in the second half of the sixteenth century.[3] My purpose in this chapter is to suggest that *enargeia* is of particular significance for our understanding of time, place, and personal identity in Golden Age lyric; that changes in the relative prestige and definition of the figure suggested by theorists coincide with developments in poetic practice in the sixteenth and seventeenth centuries; and finally, that modern critics have failed to recognize this rhetoric of presence and thus consistently misread the poems in which it is embodied. The shifts and turns of the supplement point to a more subtle model of lyric than that offered by the 'unity' or 'tension' of traditional critics.

The most intricate study of *enargeia* is to be found not in the Spanish treatises I examined in the last chapter, but in a Latin work: Julius Caesar Scaliger's *Poetices libri septem* (Lyons, 1561). This is not only one of the most authoritative manuals of its period, of pervasive influence in Spain, as elsewhere in Europe;

[3] See Bernard Weinberg, *A History of Literary Criticism in the Italian Renaissance*, esp. pp. 804-6.

it also contains an extensive and developed discussion of those delicate relations between nature, imitation, and audience so violently transgressed by the graphic ambitions of *evidentia*. Scaliger's treatment of the figure reveals the contradictions inherent in its action. By attending to these contradictions we can make out in emergent form traces of attitude and turns of argument which will recur with varying degrees of emphasis throughout the next century. Traditionally, the four elocutionary virtues are purity, clarity, ornament, and decorum. Scaliger's virtues (attributed as much to the poet himself as to his poem) are rather different: prudence, efficacy, variety, and sweetness. It is with the second that we are concerned. 'Efficacia' (offered explicitly as the Latin equivalent of the Greek 'enargeia') is defined as the power of the oration to represent the object in an excellent way. This power derives initially not from the words, but from the thing signified: 'although it seems to be in the words it is however first of all in the things themselves.' (p. 116.) Scaliger's first example is Virgil's depiction of the mother of Euryalus on hearing the news of the death of her warrior-son. Her expression is described by the poet as being at once terrified, dumbfounded, and furious. It seems to be the graphic combination of these varied emotions that satisfies the criteria of efficacy. But sometimes poets miss the mark, and fall into one of the two vices associated with efficacy: the excess called affectation, and the deficiency known as languor. For Scaliger, the unique excellence of Virgil lies in his moderation. He has sifted all the gold-dust from the sand of his predecessors: anything added would be superfluous and without value; anything subtracted would necessarily be precious metal. Scaliger hints here at the instability of his criteria; for if efficacy is produced by a certain appeal to verbal and conceptual excess (the multiple emotions in the grieving mother's face) then it will always be liable to topple over into affectation. It can be defined only in relative, not absolute, terms. Only the critic can draw the line between proper and improper superfluity. Improper poetry seems to involve the exploitation of the writer's power over the reader: the poet of excess (Lucan) bullies and cajoles his unwilling audience, and like a tyrant would rather be feared than loved. For Scaliger, efficacy must be tempered by prudence.

In spite of this appeal to reason and moderation, Scaliger's reaction to the Virgilian places he transcribes on the following page is immediate and unashamedly personal. When Aeneas leads his little son through the carnage of Troy, Scaliger feels that the strong man is his own father and that he himself is being led: his whole body shudders. The sufferings of Dido leave him rapt and tortured with grief; the valour of Nisus (another youthful warrior, beloved of Euryalus) transports him to the battlefield: who, he asks, could refuse to be in the presence of such a man? When, as here, the efficacy lies in the object alone, then communication is immediate and the critic has nothing to do: 'I am not the interpreter; let it be enough to have pointed out the places.' (p. 117.) This gestural presence is, however, somewhat compromised by the rest of the chapter in which efficacy is quite explicitly dependent on verbal means: the use of the epithet, of tropes such as metaphor and hyperbole, of the figures listed by rhetoricians in this connection (apostrophe, interrogation, and the rest). The opening stress on the power of the object *per se* works against such artifice, presupposing as it does the extra-linguistic priority of the thing and our unmediated experience of it. But it also relies on a shared conception of that nature whose privileged moments are taken as uniquely efficacious. We have noted that classical rhetoricians offer war as an appropriate subject for *enargeia*. Scaliger's examples are predominantly bellicose in character. His men are invariably heroic, his women implacably distraught. In spite of Scaliger's denials, the reader can have no access to Euryalus's mother except through the linguistic medium of Virgil's epithets. It is the knowledge of this necessary mediation or artifice which *enargeia* represses in the name of a 'natural' order of apparently immutable human phenomena which is in fact determined by patriarchy. Like the 'brief prison' of Quevedo's portrait of his lady, *enargeia* is not a flat mirror reflecting the real in all its vividness and particularity, but a curving lens or speculum which reproduces only through distortion.

By his use of the term 'representation' Scaliger seems to acknowledge the possibility that presence in language is always second-hand. But on closer reading, Scaliger seems to anticipate such later Spanish critics as Sánchez de Lima by suggesting

that nature itself is also deficient. This is implicit in the closeness of Scaliger's attention to 'efficacia in verbis'. It is explicit in
an earlier chapter on the four poetic virtues. Here the poet is
likened to a painter selecting elements from nature, such as
form, light, and shadow. Yet he does not so much learn from
the natural world, as compete with it. Although all perfection
lies within nature, the contingencies of its expression in the
world impede human perception of it. Scaliger's example of
this natural deficiency is (not surprisingly) woman: was there
ever a case of female beauty which did not leave something to
be desired by the discriminating (male) judge? (p. 113.) Hence
nature (like her eternal figure, woman) is both integral and
lacking, and art (like the male gaze) is both extrinsic and
intrinsic. Scaliger's 'efficacia', no less than the rhetors' *evidentia*,
is supplementary in character. Yet if Scaliger has some scorn
for nature, the ultimate ambition of his poetics is to absorb it
entirely. His 'search for poetic principle among ideas that exist
outside the poem itself' must lead ultimately to a subject matter
that is universal and to a poet who is also historian, natural
scientist, and geographer (see Weinberg, pp. 750–1). I will suggest that an increasing awareness both of the incursion of
poetics into nature and of the supplementary relationship
between the two is characteristic of the development of lyric in
the Golden Age. Yet, as we shall see, this development (such as
it is) is halting and contradictory; and we cannot take Garcilaso as a 'natural' beginning for its progress, or a 'neutral' backdrop which serves to throw into relief his less prudent
successors.

2. GARCILASO AND VOICE

The use of examples to develop an argument is a notoriously
unfair method of critical analysis. Within the limits of this
chapter there can be no 'representative' selection of extracts
which could do justice to the variety and sheer volume of lyric
in the Golden Age. Hence, in this chapter, as in those that
follow, I have thought it better to examine a few texts in detail
than to allude briefly to a number without submitting any to
close analysis. I have suggested that *enargeia* is a privileged
figure in poetic discourse and the texts I have chosen are

examples of its use by three major poets: Garcilaso, Herrera, and Góngora. I shall also refer briefly to a fourth (Lope de Vega) at the end of the chapter. The first three poets are generally considered to show a development of some kind. My aim is to question the nature of this development as defined by Golden Age theorists and twentieth-century critics. Each of the poems treats the theme of immortality (that is, the indefinite extension of presence) in the context of amorous hyperbole or funeral lament. And each of them employs the linguistic means discussed by Scaliger and the rhetoricians for the purpose of heightened pictorial expressiveness. In this process of representation the poems necessarily imply a particular conception of that mimetic contract by which the poet undertakes to recreate an object in language for the pleasure and profit of the audience. It is the flexibility of this contract (which may be identified with the rhetors' 'decorum') that makes it so difficult to examine, so resistant to the critical gaze.

The romantic, almost novelistic quality of the life of Garcilaso de la Vega (his love for Isabel Freire and his early death in battle) has lent force to the biographical approach of more traditional modern critics who tend to see the excellence of the poem in the extent to which it inspires a sense of intimacy between poet and reader, a sense of the poet as immediate presence or speaking voice.[4] Yet there is much evidence that, even in the case of Garcilaso, Golden Age readers had little interest in sentimental biography. Herrera's *Anotaciones* offer a minute analysis of Garcilaso's linguistic practice to the neglect of his amorous motivation. In the Golden Age, again, the Third Eclogue, relatively 'artificial', seems to have been more popular than the First, ostensibly more 'natural', and thus more popular today. Close examination of the opening stanzas of the Third Eclogue suggests that the gestural 'presence' produced by the poet is not an authentic speaking 'voice' but rather an appeal to the traditional modes and means of *enargeia*. I give the first two stanzas below, followed by my own literal version.

> Aquella voluntad honesta y pura
> illustre y hermosíssima María,

---

[4] For a refutation of the biographical fallacy see M. J. Woods, 'Rhetoric in Garcilaso's First Eclogue', *MLN* 84 (1969), 143–56.

que'n mí de celebrar tu hermosura,
tu ingenio y tu valor estar solía,
a despecho y pesar de la ventura
que por otro camino me desvía,
está y estará tanto en mí clavada
quanto del cuerpo el alma acompañada.

Y aun no se me figura que me toca
aqueste officio solamente'n vida,
mas con la lengua muerta y fria en la boca
pienso mover la boz a ti devida;
libre mi alma de su estrecha roca,
por el Estygio lago conduzida,
celebrando t'irá, y aquel sonido
hará parar las aguas del olvido.[5]

That noble and pure intention that was once mine, illustrious and most beautiful María, to praise your beauty, intellect, and courage, in spite of the fate which leads me away along another road, [that intention] is and always will be fixed in my heart as long as my soul is accompanied by my body.

And it seems to me that this duty is not mine only while I live, but rather even when my tongue is dead and cold in my mouth I intend to exercise the voice I owe to you; when my soul is free from its narrow rock, and is led through the Stygian lake, it will continue to praise you, and that sound will make the waters of oblivion stay their course.

The passage is in praise of the lady (María) to whom the poem is dedicated, as signalled explicitly by the verb 'celebrar' ('to praise'). It thus belongs to the demonstrative genus, the one which Quintilian considers most appropriate for *evidentia*. In the first stanza the use of apostrophe and the insistent alternation between first and second person engage a level of generalized, yet apparently personal, utterance: 'I will praise you until I die.' The temporal perspective moves from a state of affairs existing in the past ('solía'), to actual predicament in the present ('desvía'), to the persistence of this state into the future ('está y estará'). Herrera as commentarist notes the demonstrative, gestural force of these lines by saying that the poet shows ('muestra') the constancy of his will (note H-763, p. 566). This sense of anticipation or prolepsis, of extended or suspended immediacy of feeling is defiantly asserted in the following

[5] *Obras completas con comentario*, ed. Elias L. Rivers (Madrid, 1974), 418–20.

stanza, when the poet claims he will continue to sing the lady's praises even after his own death. The appeal to the poet's 'voice' as transcendent principle could hardly be more explicit. But it is, of course, immediately disabled by the reader's knowledge that the claim is impossible. The landscape invoked is distanced, metaphorical: the rock is the poet's body, the lake is the classically resonant Styx, and the waters of oblivion its twin river, the Lethe. Yet the image conveyed, however general, is graphically physical in character. Syntax and diction are defiantly plain, engagingly 'transparent', yet heightened by the judicious use of epithets ('estrecha', 'Estygio'). The poet thus ranges over the three modes of *evidentia* (person, time, and place), employing quite unselfconsciously the rhetorical means habitual on such occasions (exclamation, present tenses, epithesis). The graphic detail of the 'dead and cold tongue' is a fine example of that particularity of image which the rhetors claim will stimulate the audience's emotions with the greatest efficacy. And it is no coincidence that, as all the commentators note, this is also an allusion to the death of Orpheus in Virgil's *Georgics*, Book iv: Garcilaso's authority is implicitly enhanced by association with the classical hero, supposed founder of lyric. But his verse is also dignified by its echo of Scaliger's master poet, the paragon of integrity and moderation. Garcilaso, like Virgil, would rather be loved than feared, and his poetics of reticence, artlessly sophisticated, is no less effective today in stirring powerful emotion. It is the shifters in the poem (personal, temporal, topographic) which lend this sense of immediacy to it and permit the temporary suspension or dissolution of the distance which separates the poet from his reader. And as in the case of Valdés's *Diálogo de la lengua*, we find a curious inversion of the relative positions of speech and writing in this connection. For while Garcilaso appears to appeal to 'voice' as authentic, eternal utterance, he knows that the preservation of that voice is dependent on its duplication by the written word. Speech is personal but temporary, writing alienating but eternal.

Less critical readers may fancy (with Scaliger again) that the power of the imitation derives from the thing expressed rather than the manner of its expression. Love, after all, is commonly believed to be historically undifferentiated and universally apprehensible. Yet in this case the unmediated expression of profound sentiment is hard to accept as cause of the poem's efficacy. The María addressed (whoever she may have been) is certainly not the Isabel whose death inspires the poem as a whole and who has always been taken to be the source of the poet's inspiration.[6] Hence the emotion we feel in the invocation is an effect of language not of life, and of a language which even here tends towards excess. Tamayo, a contemporary commentator, attacks the conspicuous detail on which the text's immediacy depends, claiming that it is excessive and unnecessary to say that the tongue is in the mouth. Where else would it be? (*Anotaciones*, T-148, p. 652.[7]) The detail is superfluous and lacking in substance. Here poetic ornament is held to be redundant, external to plain speech: the fact that the tongue is within the mouth may safely be taken for granted. What Tamayo fails to concede is that such excess is precisely what distinguishes poetry from speech. The necessary superfluity of *evidentia* is thus present even in a relatively 'naked' passage by an habitually reticent poet. Indeed, Garcilaso's curiously emphatic 'tongue' stands as a peculiarly apposite icon of that linguistic excess on which the poet must always depend for his efficacy. The question begged by Tamayo is the same as that begged by Scaliger in his discussion of prudence and ostentation: where do we place the margin? Where do we draw the line?

Quintilian suggests that the orator introduce *evidentia* by means of a formula which will prepare the audience for what is to follow (see Lausberg, para. 814, section 2a). The most common formula, indeed the very definition of the figure, is used by Garcilaso, when he claims in one poem that the swift movement of a river seemed to be 'painted before the eyes'. The graphic ambition common to poet and rhetor has seldom been more explicit. Yet, ironically, this very example is cited by one distinguished modern critic (Dámaso Alonso) as evidence for the novelty of Garcilaso's pictorialism. He claims that the perfect precision of Garcilaso's description is totally new in the period; that he depicts movement for us like a painter; and that his ability to put before our eyes such images as the complex movement of a girl's blond hair is cinematographic in char-

---

[6] See Rivers (p. 417) for possible identifications of María.
[7] 'T' stands for Tamayo.

acter.[8] The traditional effects of rhetorical technique are here reassigned to modern technology. Alonso's response to the luminosity of the poem is as intimate and intense as Scaliger's: he says that the beauty of the landscape reaches the depths of our soul (p. 37). Yet for Alonso this sensorial representation is of a purely individual character and the poet is experienced in himself as temporal and spatial presence: he 'speaks' from beside us as our contemporary, and takes part in the language of modern times. Alonso thus reiterates unknowingly the three modes of *enargeia*: persona, place, and time are all experienced as present and immediate. On the following page the production of emotion is claimed as the goal of modern writing. Alonso says that emotion is the ultimate end of literature today, and one which Garcilaso also shares. The critic seems unaware that the production of emotion was also the goal (or one of the goals) of classical rhetoric and Renaissance poetic. What is truly modern in Alonso's exposition is the redistribution of emotion from the reader or target to the poet or source. He claims that we feel 'behind' the words an emotional disturbance, a repressed boiling or bubbling ('borboteo') as if of tears which seek to be shed (p. 38). I shall return in the chapter on the comedia to this 'hydraulic' model which takes desire to be pressurized liquid, seeking relief in whatever channel is open to it. More important here is to note the difference between Renaissance and modern critics. However moved Scaliger may be as reader he never projects his feeling on to the poet who has produced it. His awareness of the complexities of poetic language will not permit him the modern critic's easy phonocentrism, in which writing becomes voice, and voice the immediate expression of feeling. Ultimately, the problem which is repressed is once more that of the relative priority of word and thing. Alonso, like the Renaissance theorist, seeks the meaning of the poem outside the text itself, but unlike Scaliger he is unwilling to analyse those relations of art and nature which make the poetic object different from its equivalent in the world. And this wilful impressionism seems to be founded on a mistrust of writing itself: poetic emotion is identified with the *pneuma* (breath, soul, or inspiration) expelled by the poet at the

[8] *Cuatro poetas españoles* (Madrid, 1962), 36.

moment of authentic utterance. Garcilaso is said to have lent his verse a breath ('hálito') of emotion, a soul (p. 40).[9] As in the case of the Golden Age theorists we examined in the first chapter, Alonso's arguments are founded on metaphorical terms which cannot be subtracted from his writing in the quest for a supposed original substance. The advantage of the 'poetic' or 'impressionistic' criticism which Alonso offers here is that it gives the lie to the neutrality generally claimed for itself by such writing: criticism is as compromised by the wayward path of figuration as poetry itself.

Alonso's judgement on Garcilaso is not unusual. Indeed, it is a critical commonplace that Garcilaso is the poet of 'presence' and that the Third Eclogue is an artificial deviation from a natural plenitude. Thus Lapesa claimed in 1948 that the essence of Garcilaso was a primal innocence of artifice, a poetry free of complication, but with the strength of contained emotion. The Third Eclogue is an 'escape' from life and an 'evasion' of reality, experienced by the reader as an absence of personal feeling.[10] For R. O. Jones (1954) the artifice of the Third Eclogue is a means of 'distancing' emotion.[11] Even in Dario Fernández Morera's excellent study the same opposition recurs. Thus he compares the invocation of the *Polifemo* to that of the Third Eclogue: 'what . . . in Góngora would be a poetic manifesto that for all its vehemence is no less theoretical, in Garcilaso is rather a statement of his own personal condition as a poet.'[12] Garcilaso's 'evocative power' is greater than that of Góngora: 'For he conjures up both the figure of Orpheus and a rivered and cavernous landscape. And it is in such a landscape that his self-praising verses resound.' (p. 88.) Fernández Morera is well versed in Golden Age theory, but at this point at least his argument appears to be circular: the poet creates the topography and the topography, in turn, recreates the poet. The operation performed seems to be ineffable and somewhat impressionistic. Yet as Renaissance poetic teaches us, the poet is not so much a conjuror or magician, but rather a craftsman or

---

[9] p. 40. Elsewhere a more precise linguistic analysis also culminates in an appeal to atemporal presence. See 'Garcilaso y los límites de la estilística', in *La poesía de Garcilaso*, ed. Elias L. Rivers (Barcelona, 1974), 269–84 (p. 284).

[10] *La trayectoria poética de Garcilaso* (Madrid, 1968), 166.

[11] 'Garcilaso, poeta del humanismo', in River's anthology, pp. 53–70 (p. 67).

[12] *The Lyre and the Oaten Flute: Garcilaso and the Pastoral* (London, 1982), 84.

artisan who works with specific, determinate means. This is the general attitude displayed in Fernández Morera's book, which is mainly concerned with the relationship between Garcilaso and his poetic predecessors. It is all the more surprising, then, that he agrees to some extent at least with the traditional view of Garcilaso as the poet of personal presence.

An unexpectedly flexible model is given by Azorín in 1921. For him the decorative patterning of the Third Eclogue is a 'plateresque vision'.[13] There is no immediate correlation between the Toledan landscape and the superfluous ornament placed over it by the poet. Yet, Azorín implies, this linguistic excess, external to nature, is also necessary and substantial, serving as it does as makeweight in the balance between art and life. This supplementary relationship seems to recur on the final page of Elias L. Rivers's 'The Pastoral Paradox of Natural Art' (1962).[14] Nature is deficient once more: man supplies a lack in the landscape by the addition of water-wheels. The landscape itself would not exist without a poet-painter to contemplate it. The artist engages in a kind of productive consumption using 'natural materials, which have been artificially prepared, to express a vision of nature' (p. 144). Yet if art is necessary it also appears to be superfluous, alienating nature, interposing an absence between man and world, where previously the mutually constituting structure of each was the very condition of their existence: 'Thus, in the Third Eclogue, it is art which orders and simplifies nature, rendering it intelligible; it is a clear sense of artistic distance which converts grief into beauty. As this humanistic dream attains perfect verbal expression, Garcilaso's poetic achievement is complete.' There seems to be some slippage here between the twin functions of art, which both complements and alienates experience.[15] And it is surely a tautology to claim that Garcilaso's language ('verbal expression') is equal to his matter ('humanistic dream') when access to the latter is only available by means of the former. Rivers appeals implicitly, like Scaliger in the opening of his chapter on

[13] 'Garcilaso', in Rivers's anthology, pp. 35–9 (p. 39).
[14] *MLN* 77 (1962), 130–44.
[15] This problem is alluded to in Rivers's final note (pp. 143–4) on the competition between Horatian and Aristotelian ideas of art, and the possibility that Garcilaso anticipates Scaliger's resolution of the two.

'efficacia', to the priority and pre-eminence of the concept as criterion of poetic excellence. He invokes that presence of the word, the indwelling of thought and elocution, which is the siren-song of the most perceptive critics when confronted with a superlative poet (Virgil or Garcilaso). But he gestures none the less and in spite of himself at the irreconcilable and strangely asymmetrical configuration which *res* and *verba* tend to adopt.

Yet if the poem is not to be taken as the direct expression of personal feeling, this does not mean that it is purely literary or 'artistic'. Alan K. G. Paterson treats this problem at the conclusion of his study of ecphrasis in the Third Eclogue (Garcilaso's poetic description of works of visual art).[16] He suggests we should see the poem as the poet's testament or will drawn up in advance of his death (p. 92). The idea of poem as testament (both catalogue of past glory and anticipation of future death) combines communication with presence: it is only by directing his 'voice' to a reader that Garcilaso can continue to speak from beyond the grave. The association of writing and death, which will recur in later chapters of this book, is rarely more explicit than here. Hence, if Garcilaso achieves no unified sense of self (no consistent presence of meaning), then we should not be surprised if it is also lacking in Herrera.

3. HERRERA AND AMPLIFICATION

In the broad trajectory of Golden Age lyric Fernando de Herrera is often seen as occupying an intermediate position. As theorist, he is the most subtle and erudite commentator of Garcilaso. As practising poet, he anticipates much of the linguistic elaboration once thought to originate with Góngora.[17] Herrera, called 'divino' in his own time, has had less fortune in the post-Romantic era. Artifice and learning have often been seen as excessive and extrinsic, mere barriers to that immediate expression of authentic emotion which is taken to be the validating principle of all poetry. Even recent defenders of Herrera have taken such commonplaces for

---

[16] '*Ecphrasis* in Garcilaso's "Egloga tercera"', *MLR* 72 (1977), 73–92.
[17] See José Almeida, *La crítica literaria de Fernando de Herrera* (Madrid, 1976), esp. pp. 110–11.

granted.[18] Modern critics thus reveal a misunderstanding of that fundamental term of Renaissance poetics, amplification. They take it to mean not a graphic heightening of diction for the conveyance of emotion, but an empty inflation of language for the purpose of mere display. This (unconscious) critical bias has a great effect on readings of a poet such as Herrera, whose verse tends towards an increasing painterliness or luminosity. As Oreste Macrí notes, the careful revisions made over a period of years to the sonnet reproduced below reveal a progressive intensification of imagery relating to colour and precious metals.[19] The sonnet is rather similar to the poem by Quevedo we examined in the Introduction: it is a stylized portrait of the poet's lady. Herrera celebrates the woman by appealing to the universal and eternal forces of the cosmos (sun, wind, moon, stars) and by claiming that the lady exceeds them in beauty, as in cruelty. Its genus (the demonstrative) and its rhetorical structure (apostrophic) correspond to those recommended by rhetoricians for the exploitation of *evidentia*. Once more I give a literal version beneath the original.

> Roxo Sol, que con hacha luminosa
> coloras el purpureo i alto cielo,
> hallaste tal belleza en todo el suelo,
> qu'iguále a mi serena Luz dichosa?
>
> Aura suave, blanda i amorosa,
> que nos halagas con tu fresco buelo;
> cuando se cubre del dorado velo
> mi Luz, tocaste trença mas hermosa?
>
> Luna, onor de la noche, ilustre coro
> de las errantes lumbres, i fixadas,
> consideraste tales dos estrellas?
>
> Sol puro, Aura, Luna, llamas d'oro,
> oistes vos mis penas nunca usadas?
> vistes Luz mas ingrata a mis querellas?

---

[18] See Violeta Montori de Gutiérrez, *Ideas estéticas y poesía de Fernando de Herrera* (Miami, 1977), for an affirmation of Herrera's fundamental 'sincerity' and of the merely instrumental nature of his erudition (p. 169). For a rhetorical reading of selected poems, see M. J. Woods, 'Herrera's Voices', in *Medieval and Renaissance Studies on Spanish and Portuguese in Honour of P. E. Russell* (Oxford, 1981), 121–32.

[19] *Fernando de Herrera* (Madrid, 1959), 487. Arthur Terry reprints three versions of this sonnet in full in his *Anthology of Spanish Poetry, 1500–1700*, Part 1 (Oxford, 1965), 104–5. My text is from *Obra poética*, ed. José Manuel Blecua (Madrid, 1975), no. 116.

Golden Sun, who with your shining torch lend colour to the lofty, scarlet heaven, did you ever find such beauty on all the earth that could equal my serene and happy Light? Gentle Breeze, soft and amorous, who delight us with your cool flight; when my Light is covered by her golden veil, did you ever touch more beautiful tresses? Moon, glory of the night, illustrious choir of both fixed and wandering lights, did you ever contemplate two such stars? Pure Sun, Breeze, Moon, golden flames, did you hear my unwonted complaints of grief? Did you ever see a Light more scornful of my entreaties?

As in the case of Garcilaso, the direct address ('you'), verbs in the present tense, and general yet vivid topography engage the personal, temporal, and spatial modes of *enargeia*. But unlike in the case of Garcilaso, Herrera is a critic as well as a poet, and we know that he is well aware of the effect his language produces. In the *Anotaciones* he praises Garcilaso for a similar passage in terms which should be familiar by now, saying that such a noble hypotyposis expresses the object in such a way that we seem to see it more than we hear it (H-734, p. 559). As ever, the visual is said to displace the aural. For Herrera, apostrophe itself participates in this dialectic of presence and absence. He defines the figure (known in Latin as 'aversio' and in Spanish as 'apartamiento') as being when we direct our speech ('habla') to an absent person, twisting it from its straight and natural course to some other one (H-32, p. 323). It is perhaps significant that even Herrera, a highly literate poet, should still think in terms of speech when he discusses the more graphic figures.

Expressive language is here seen as a distortion of plain speech, as an unnatural perversion of its course. Yet it is quite clear that Herrera's poem, far more so than that of Garcilaso, is decked with 'plateresque' ornament and makes no pretence towards 'natural' simplicity. Theory and practice seem to contradict one another. Yet the supposed functional character of those ornaments deployed in the sonnet becomes clear on reading the *Anotaciones*. Thus Herrera the poet uses enjambment and asyndeton: 'ilustre coro / de las errantes lumbres'; 'Sol puro, Aura, Luna, llamas d'oro'. But Herrera the critic tells us when these figures occur in Garcilaso that the first is used to regain the highness of Latin epic and the second to say something with strength, vehemence, and swiftness, with anger, impetus, amplification, and nobility (H-1, p. 309; H-22,

p. 321). Language thus supplies the efficient power which (by implication) can no longer be entrusted to the persuasive force of the thing itself. The repetition in the sonnet may also be intended to bear a particular force. Herrera states that we use repetition for great effects, because it signifies the perpetuity of representation (H-618, p. 529). Verbal duplication is thus used in an attempt to ensure the indefinitely extended presence of the object. The question of whether this kind of amplification can succeed in such a mission is left unasked.

Frequently implicated in Herrera's pervasive concern for linguistic excess in its various forms is Scaliger himself, apostle of mediocrity. At times, Herrera follows his predecessor on the virtues of discrimination and modesty: the 'unnatural' mixing of languages, the attack on the 'lascivious' Catullus, the praise of prudence itself (H-132, 187, 344). I shall return to the question of prudence in my conclusion. But elsewhere Herrera goes beyond Scaliger, while still citing him as authority. This is the case with the definition of hyperbole (another of the figures used in the sonnet above), in which Herrera cites Scaliger to the effect that hyperbole means excess and redundancy and is caused when we praise a thing more than is required by its own nature (H-84, p. 346). It should be noted that Herrera still takes it for granted that the value or status of the object is extra-linguistic. But the difference in tone between Scaliger and Herrera is marked. Scaliger's sentence is plainly proscriptive, attacking the redundant verbiage which the figure entails. But Herrera's translation of 'hyperbole' is neutral ('engrandeci-miento' or amplification) and his tone indulgent. *Res* may be inflated by *verba* when the poet thinks it necessary. Herrera also cites Scaliger (the chapter on 'efficacia') in defence of another kind of replication, hendiadys, or the use of two words to represent one thing. In such cases as these, efficacy is rarely tempered by prudence and the poet is encouraged to direct his reader and transform his matter in a way which Scaliger would not have allowed. Herrera's ambiguous reliance on Scaliger is typical of the movement of Spanish *preceptiva* we saw in the last chapter: native innovation takes care to ground itself in foreign authority.

The most prominent feature of linguistic excess, the one which is most emphatic in the sonnet and which causes Herrera the critic to engage most closely with Scaliger, is the adjective, for it possesses by its very nature a dangerous tendency to become superfluous. It has been shown by R. D. F. Pring-Mill that Herrera quotes extensively from Scaliger's chapter on 'efficacia' in his discourse on the epithet.[20] Garcilaso's epithets are, as I suggested earlier, relatively discreet and few in number. Herrera's are many but by no means indiscriminate. Thus in the first stanza of our sonnet Herrera replaced the adjectives in his successive revisions. By this process the poet attempts to increase the graphic potency of his imitation. The theorist's discussion of this technique treats, as so often, the relative priority of word and thing, and the possibility of superfluous language. Scaliger begins by claiming, characteristically, that those who think the epithet is only in the elocution are wrong: it is also in the object itself, as when we say of a man that he is loyal or just. The classic example (cited later) is of course 'pius Aeneas'. Inversely, the epithet is in the speech when the poet uses it for a specific purpose: amplification, diminution, periphrasis. An example of the last would be when the poet calls a 'strong man' a 'man of marvellous strength' (p. 118). These examples recur in Herrera, and it is worth noting that, as in the case of *efficacia* as a whole, the 'natural' plenitude invoked is itself a cultural construct, based on received notions of male and female: men are essentially (and not accidentally) strong, loyal, and just, and the poet's verbal elaborations cannot affect this fundamental truth. As so often, the examples presented as 'natural' are already dense with cultural signification. Herrera also adopts Scaliger's division of epithets according to past, present, or future tense: thus 'miserrima Dido' referring to future suicide 'puts the thing before our eyes'. Both critics also draw a distinction between necessary and unnecessary epithets, the latter indulging in verbal display, the former implying logical cause or justification. Yet Herrera, unlike Scaliger, explicitly defends the use of redundant epithets in poetry: we all know that snow is white, or the sun golden, but in poetry such excess brings sweetness ('gracia'). A slip of the pen (or perhaps a failure of the memory) is relevant here. Scaliger praises the force of the metaphor 'ferreum pectus', or

---

[20] 'Escalígero y Herrera: Citas y plagios de los *Poetices libri septem* en *Las anotaciones*', *Actas del segundo congreso internacional de hispanistas* (Nimega, 1967), 489–98 (p. 496).

'breast of iron'. But Herrera lauds the efficacy of the metonym 'ferreus ensis', or 'sword of iron'. Once more the example suggests an understanding of rhetoric as a violent struggle between men. Perhaps more important is that Herrera seems more willing to permit redundant usage unjustified by conceptual change. The cause of this anxiety appears to be an emergent sense of the insufficiency of words to convey the things they claim to represent. Epithets must be used, Herrera says, when we seek strength and meaning in the names of things and cannot find them (H-82, p. 344). Plain language is now felt to lack the force which the poet seeks to convey, and the proper term must be amplified by words added on ('adjecta') to it.

Scaliger's immediate access to matter through language, his (albeit intermittent) faith in the substantial efficacy of things themselves, is replaced, in part, by a growing awareness of language as deficient or disabled, requiring the skilled assistance of the rhetor to restore its lost potency. And this sense of deficiency recurs again and again in key passages in Herrera's aesthetics. However, just as the epithet is both proper and redundant, so the status of this deficiency is undecidable, alternately and simultaneously present and absent. We have already noted some of these passages in the previous chapter. For example, in his opening remarks Herrera claims that the Spanish language is not impoverished or lacking, but rather full and abundant, loaded with all the ornaments and jewels which can make it noble and esteemed (p. 307). Yet in the same sentence he suggests that too much concern with affairs of state has left the Spanish language ignorant or naked of literary propriety and caused poetry to languish in ignorant darkness. Herrera's erudition thus both fills a gap in a deprived Castilian and constitutes an excess over and above a language already self-sufficient and integral. It is supplementary. Likewise, in the first note on the sonnet we are told that matter should be treated in plain language so as to appear 'proper' and 'native' (H-1, p. 308). Yet ordinary speech is deprived and requires the poet's art to restore its plenitude. Artifice, once again, is both essential and excessive, intrinsic and extrinsic. This leads one more time to the vexed question of 'clarity'. In a third passage we read that 'claridad' is of the essence and that it must not be compromised: if clarity is lacking, then all grace and beauty is lost too (H-78, p. 342). Yet obscurity is also to be praised, as long as it occurs *in re* rather *in verbis*: the obscurity which comes from subject or hidden meaning is praised and highly valued by *cognoscenti*; but it should not be made more difficult by verbal obscurity: conceptual obscurity is enough. The distinction between 'good' and 'bad' obscurity is rather similar to that drawn later by López Pinciano. And, as we saw in the previous chapter, the elusive difference between verbal and conceptual difficulty will be a commonplace of the controversy over Góngora some forty years later.

We seem far indeed from the transparency of diction and matter which in Scaliger ensures the greatest degree of efficacy. Yet, as I have suggested, this reflexive, reciprocal logic in which opposites 'inhabit' one another is prefigured by Scaliger's view of nature as both original source and imperfect expression of the art with which it is made to compete. Hence, Herrera's amplification, his sensorial elaboration, cannot be 'redundant' in the common sense of the term. Bernard Weinberg states of Italian theorists in the 1570s that 'increasingly, writers see as one of the necessary components of imitation a kind of heightened and vivd portrayal which appeals to the senses rather than to the intellect' (*History*, p. 633). For Herrera too, writing in the same period, graphic pictorialism is a necessity, it fills a perceived absence in a textual fabric which can no longer trust to the prestige of an immutable nature and of a moderate, prudent language. As in Quintilian and Garcilaso the linguistic means which produce *enargeia* are the essential supplement by which presence itself is figured. Herrera is like the she-bear in Covarrubias's emblem: however much he licks and polishes his poetic progeny he claims to be performing a natural rather than an artistic function. Herrera's amplification brings both presence and absence: it conveys the poetic object more vividly to the reader as it weakens our sense of the poet as an individual, speaking voice. The more brightly the cosmic lady is made to glow in the tiny, convex mirror of Herrera's sonnet, the more the writer himself (lover of the lady, author of the poem) is excluded from that same textual space. As we shall see, this problem is much intensified in Góngora.

4. GÓNGORA AND ABSENCE

If Garcilaso has been seen by traditionalist critics as the poet of intimate presence and Herrera as a 'genuine' voice distanced, nevertheless, by excessive erudition, then Luis de Góngora has often been read as the poet of the void itself, of absolute and uncompromising absence. In his influential account of the controversy of the *Soledades* and the 'new poetry' Menéndez y Pelayo claims (with Jáuregui and other seventeenth-century critics) that Góngora's error lay not in the strangeness of his ideas, but rather in the lowness and emptiness of his words.[21] This judgement relies of course on the assumption (common in all periods) that *res* and *verba* may be separated without prejudice to the character of either, and that matter must precede linguistic expression. The critic is thus free to look 'behind' the poet's words. For Menéndez y Pelayo, Góngora's poem lacks that sense of interiority essential for excellence and is reduced to a mere shadow. He claims it has no subject matter, no internal poetry, no emotions, or ideas. It is mere appearance, wholly deprived of soul ('alma'). Lack of thought and of matter is here associated with lack of emotion, the implication being that, as in Scaliger, a sufficiently prestigious object of imitation will move the reader without recourse to additional and compromising linguistic aid. Góngora attempts to remedy an absent matter by supplying it with superfluous diction. Menéndez y Pelayo claims that with extravagant language Góngora attempted to fill the absence of everything, even his previous ability to describe nature. Material absence here seems prior to the linguistic excess which seeks to fill it, and I shall suggest in my conclusion that an awareness of origin as absence is the efficient or instrumental 'cause' of any rhetoric of presence. Of course it would be easy to attack the supposed naïvety of a critic who complains that a poet lacks 'soul'. More important is to try to discover why it is that the critic feels defrauded by the poet. It seems likely that they fail to coincide in the terms each lends his own version of the mimetic contract.

The image of Góngora as the poet of personal absence persists even after his rehabilitation in 1927. Writing in 1961, Dámaso Alonso states that Góngora is no longer 'our poet'.

[21] *Historia de las ideas estéticas en España* (Santander, 1947), ii. 329.

Today writers seek the immediate reproduction of nature and the direct communication of emotion: they would rather offer life without any intermediary and move human hearts with whatever material comes to hand.[22] As Alonso had attributed Garcilaso's pictorialism to a uniquely modern temperament, so here he appropriates the traditional aim of rhetoric for a single moment in the twentieth century. Chronologically distant from Góngora, who remains imprisoned in the seventeenth century, we are also spatially removed from him, 'closer' to Fray Luis, San Juan, or Quevedo. Góngora is a great artist but cannot move readers in so far as they are capable of moral emotions (p. 250). The concept of 'moral emotion' is obscure. But it betrays the frustration felt by even the most sensitive reader when a poet seems to make himself absent from the text. However, Alonso's separation of art and feeling would, I believe, have proved unintelligible to the Renaissance theorist or poet for whom artistry was precisely that which enabled the successful conveyance of emotion. If Góngora achieved one, then the other would naturally follow.

Alonso's views are echoed and developed by other critics. For Fernando Lázaro in 1966 Góngora's verbal excess results in personal deficiency or absence: there is a hollow or void in those places where we attempt to gain access to him as a man.[23] Góngora's 'magnificence' thus precludes that illusion of intimacy sought by the psychologically biased critic. Although such critics are generally faithful to the criterion of authorial intention, they rarely stop to ask themselves if the writer who produced such complex and intricate verse could have 'intended' to offer the reader a simple or direct picture of himself. Emilio Orozco Díaz's viewpoint is slightly different. He suggests in 1969 that Góngora's art is not merely one of unnatural alienation, of pure aestheticism 'distanced' from real life.[24] Beneath the surface of the poet's language lies the organic matter of lived experience: life 'beats' ('late') even under the most artificial of Góngora's metaphors. Yet Orozco Díaz's own metaphors are contradictory. If art is above life, it is also outside it: he claims that art envelops life, but does not

---

[22] *Góngora y el 'Polifemo'* (Madrid, 1961), 250.
[23] *Estilo barroco y personalidad creadora* (Salamanca, 1966), 143.
[24] *En torno a las 'Soledades' de Góngora* (Granada, 1969), 38.

stifle it. Citing Góngora himself (perhaps unconsciously), Orozco calls the poetic text a 'peel' or 'bark' ('corteza'). This suggestion of a natural, organic interiority, denied Góngora by critics such as Alonso, is supported by *pneuma*, the metaphysical inhabitation of matter by the poet's breath or inspiration. Orozco claims that Góngora's subject matter trembles and makes us tremble when it is inspired by the soul of the authentic poet. As in the case of Menéndez y Pelayo, it would be easy to mock such criticism. What seems more interesting is to note that metaphysical effects of this kind can be produced even by a poet as difficult and 'obscure' as Góngora.

Hence for some twentieth-century readers Góngora achieves an effect of 'presence' and for others he does not. Yet this confusion is hardly surprising, when we consider that those exorbitant linguistic traits which modern critics tend to find 'distancing' are precisely those techniques recommended by Renaissance theorists for the achievement of graphic immediacy and employed for that very purpose by Spanish poets from Garcilaso onwards. It could be argued that Garcilaso and Herrera are as 'absent' from their poetry as Góngora. But this would not be to deny that Góngora's poetry is different from that of his predecessors, but rather to echo Dámaso Alonso's suggestion that Góngora's newness is one of quantity, rather than quality. Elements already present in the early works are accumulated and concentrated in the later. For Alonso, Gongorism encapsulates an entire literary tradition: it is the synthesis and intensification of Renaissance lyric.[25] The difference between Góngora and his predecessors is thus not absolute, but relative.

The tendency towards accumulation in Góngora is noted by critics of his own time. Yet seventeenth-century polemic, for all its pedantry and conventionality, sometimes reveals a more complex approach than that of modern critics, who are at once rigidly prescriptive and fluidly impressionistic. In the previous chapter I mentioned one contribution to the debate on Gongorism, Pedro Díaz de Rivas's *Discursos apologéticos*. The four major charges made against Góngora (and refuted by Rivas) all involve superfluous language: the excess of rare words, of tropes,

---

[25] *La lengua poética de Góngora* (Madrid, 1935), 219–20.

and of hyperbata, and the stylistic obscurity which results as a
consequence of these verbal resources (*Documentos gongorinos*,
p. 35). In each case the defence is based, as in Herrera, on the
necessity of the usage. In the list of minor charges, the final one
is redundancy itself. Díaz's reply is telling: he claims that
Góngora is not redundant in his language, but rather brilliant
and ornate, rivalling the most noble poets and orators in his fer-
tility, copiousness, and vividness ('pintura') (p. 65). Díaz's
catalogue of nouns, like that of Menéndez y Pelayo, reveals
those normally unvoiced assumptions and equivalences which
are the basis of any aesthetic. Where once linguistic superfluity
led to darkness, now it is brilliant and decorative. Abundance
and pictorialism are juxtaposed, an indication that, as in Quintilian, *evidentia* is always excessive. Díaz's final justification for
redundancy is the authoritative example of previous writers.
The imitation of art rather than nature which we saw emergent
in Scaliger and more developed in Herrera is here openly
dominant. Góngora's graphic excess is thus a necessary and
constitutive element of his art, the natural product of a continuing process of linguistic elaboration. As in the case of Luis
Carrillo, poetic ornament is for Góngora both decorative and
functional. It is an 'arreo': both a covering for the naked poetic
animal, and a harness to lead it where the poet wishes.

A rather similar logic (or illogic) of the supplementary occurs
in Salcedo Coronel's foreword to his commentary on the *Soledades*. He admits that many have attacked Góngora for his obscurity, and does not claim himself that obscurity is good. But
in Góngora it is to be praised, because he has 'illustrated' the
language with idioms, tropes, and figures never before used by
Castilian poets.[26] Obscurity cannot be good, but nor in some
cases can it be bad. Indeed, it leads, paradoxically, to the illustration of the language, to the supplying of a deficiency unfilled
by previous poets. As so often in critical discourse, the appeal to
half-erased metaphors based on light and dark is persuasive but
logically inconsistent. The peculiar turn of the argument is
reminiscent of Herrera on the same theme many years before.
It seems that the perceived 'gap' in Spanish literary culture remains constant however much poetic erudition (both excessive

---

[26] *Soledades . . .comentadas* (Madrid, 1636), fo. ††ʳ⁻ᵛ.

and essential) may seek to close it up. Most modern critics have tended to praise nature and clarity and to denounce art and obscurity, without examining the preconceptions implicit in both pairs of terms. The former are thought to underwrite and the latter to undermine that intimate sense of the 'real' that is assumed to be the poet's aim. In the Golden Age, on the other hand, critical terms are dangerously volatile. They cross over from one side of the paradigm to the other, increasingly so as time goes on. This instability derives ultimately from the continuing rivalry between art and nature, from the shifting emphasis attached to twin irreconcilable 'goods'. Hence, if Góngora takes art rather than nature as the object of his imitation then this need not mean that he is 'distancing' or 'absenting' himself from the real. Rather it confirms the suggestion I made in the previous chapter in relation to López Pinciano, that any simple or primary imitation of nature is an impossibility.

These questions may seem abstract, but they are not purely theoretical. They intrude directly in the poems themselves, as we shall see in the analysis which follows of the sonnet below. Like the poems I chose by Garcilaso and Herrera, this is a song of praise to a lady, in this case Queen Margaret of Austria who had died in 1611. The poet seeks to immortalize her memory by addressing her tomb. The complexity of language and density of figuration make it particularly difficult to translate.

> Máquina funeral, que desta vida
>   nos decís la mudanza, estando queda;
>   pira, no de aromática arboleda,
>   si a más gloriosa Fénix construida;
>
> bajel en cuya gabia esclarecida
>   estrellas, hijas de otra mejor Leda,
>   serenan la Fortuna, de su rueda
>   la volubilidad reconocida,
>
> farol luciente sois que solicita
>   la razón, entre escollos naufragante,
>   al puerto; y a pesar de lo luciente,
>
> obscura concha de una Margarita
>   que, rubí en caridad, en fe diamante,
>   renace a nuevo Sol en nuevo Oriente.[27]

---

[27] Text from *Sonetos completos*, ed. Biruté Ciplijauskaité (Madrid, 1969), no. 138.

Funerary engine, which tells us of the mutability of this life, while remaining motionless itself; pyre, not of aromatic wood, but built for a more glorious Phoenix; ship in whose shining tackle stars, which are daughters of a better Leda, calm the storm of Fortune, after recognizing the inconstancy of her wheel; you are a shining lighthouse which guides reason, floundering amongst the rocks, safely to harbour; and in spite of the brightness [you are] the dark shell of a Margaret [pearl] who, like a ruby in her charity and a diamond in her faith, is born again to a new Sun in a new Dawn.

The opening lines exemplify that quality of arrested motion which the rhetoricians attribute to *enargeia*: the tomb is still, but proclaims, none the less, the ceaseless mobility of mortal life. The repeated apostrophes, the present tenses and personal pronouns, and the compressed and abstracted topographia combine to engage the three modes of immediacy in a wholly traditional manner. Yet there is an extreme intensification and accumulation of the high means we saw somewhat less developed in Herrera: hyperbaton, enjambment, 'luminous' vocabulary, and epithesis. The commentaries on this poem suggest both the broadness and the specificity of reference to the natural world implicit in poetry of the period. For example, the 'stars' in the allegorical ship's mast (that is, the candles on the tomb) are both St Elmo's fire and Castor and Pollux, Christian and pagan symbols respectively of meteorological protection in stormy weather.[28] In its density, scope, and compression the poem might be seen itself as a marvellous construct ('máquina') which seeks to stay time and encompass the world with the brilliant materiality of its linguistic presence. Like Garcilaso's Third Eclogue (but in a rather different way) the sonnet can be seen as a testament: a poetic gesture which seeks in vain to supply the absence always renewed by death. And like the sonnet by Quevedo we examined in the Introduction, Góngora's poem employs the figure of metalepsis: the real candles become figurative stars, and those stars in turn become mythical heroes. But, once more, this chain of substitution or displacement offers no escape from the condition of mortal life. Just as the wheel of fortune must eventually come to rest, so the poem itself finds both end and origin in the extinction of the individual.

---

[28] *Obras . . . comentadas*, ii (Madrid, 1649), 722.

In the tercets light and dark are made to coincide when the tomb is compared to a shell with a pearl inside. The commentator explains that the shell is dark because of the sadness of mortal death,. but bright because of the certainty of the unending life to come. The essential condition of contraries (that is, the impossibility of their occupying the same space) is thus wilfully violated in the poetic expression of this paradox.[29] We have seen this collusion of light and dark (clarity and obscurity) in the theoretical defences of Góngora. But it is not peculiar to this local controversy nor indeed to Spain. In Torquato Tasso's critical works the darkness of an increasingly mannered ornament had already been granted positive value, as the necessary supplement to an insufficiently heroic language. Tasso defends his own 'strange' or 'nomadic' style by saying that if a text seems lacking in clarity it is similar to that obscurity which increases nobility ('l'onore') by means of shadow ('l'orrore'), not only in temples, but also in forests.[30] The negative value of darkness here has the positive effect of gravity, and clarity and nature are no longer unthinkingly associated. The obscurity now prized in art is perceived as constitutive of the world itself, and the noble shadows of the temple (human construct) are equally characteristic of the forest (natural phenomenon). While the traditional ends remain the same, the distinctions on which they rest are increasingly blurred. Like Pedro Mejía's *Silva*, the poetic forests of Tasso and Góngora take nature as exemplary not of order, but of proliferating disorder.

Góngora himself, of course, is Spain's greatest poet of the natural world. And as light and dark mingle in the sonnet, so nature and culture displace one another in the chiaroscuro of the *Soledades*. As critics have often noted, the 'natural' virtues of the country are praised in so far as they resemble the 'artificial' delights of the town.[31] I would suggest, then, that what we find in Góngora's career is not a progressive absenteeism, both cause and effect of an irresponsible excess of words, but rather

[29] See the *Anotaciones* where Herrera cites Hippocrates' definition of contraries as things that cannot be together (H-409, p. 469).

[30] Cited by Ezio Raimondi in 'Poesia della retorica', in *Retorica e critica letteraria* (Bologna, 1978), 123–50 (p. 149).

[31] See e.g. M. J. Woods, *The Poet and the Natural World in the Age of Góngora* (Oxford, 1978), esp. pp. 156–72.

the linguistic infilling or supplementing of a nature found increasingly to be lacking in substance. This process is related to the desire of poets to elevate 'mediocre' lyric to the heroic status of Tassesque epic, by appeal to the 'high' figures which tend to produce graphic brilliance. In Herrera, we remember, this function is precisely that claimed for such devices as enjambment. Hence, increasing linguistic elaboration is both extratextual and intratextual: it reflects changing conceptions of both the relationship between poem and world and that between one poem and another.

According to Anthony Easthope, the founding moment of English Renaissance poetry is when it attempts to repress all evidence of linguistic materiality (phonetic and semantic excess) and makes the highest aim of lyric the imitation of a speaking voice. For Easthope, this tendency is accentuated in the seventeenth century when we find an explicit appeal in poetics to linguistic transparency as ideal goal of the poet.[32] Easthope implies that this ideal is not current before the seventeenth century. As we have seen, this is certainly not the case in Spain. Indeed, the movement towards increased transparency is precisely the opposite of the one we have traced in this chapter. Easthope's study raises the possibility, however, that Góngora's practice (which greatly intensifies the reader's sense of the density and materiality of the word) may be more archaic than innovatory. It is in the medieval ballad that Easthope finds a similar surplus of enunciation over statement and of signifier over signified (pp. 88–93). It is perhaps no accident that Góngora, too, was attracted to the ballad form, albeit in a highly sophisticated and self-conscious manner. For Easthope, the apparent impersonality of the ballad (its lack of concern for the imitation of the individual's speaking voice) lays bare contradictions in subjectivity normally repressed by later lyric: our sense of wholeness or integration is founded on discursive and ideological disjunctions openly displayed in the halting and fragmentary texture of much medieval verse. It is possible to read Góngora's absence in just this way, as a denial of that 'imaginary' wholeness on which human beings rely for their sense of self. This is not to suggest that Góngora 'intended' to

---

[32] *Poetry as Discourse* (London, 1983), 110–21.

communicate such knowledge to the reader. Rather it is to affirm that the reflexivity of his poetry (its tendency to dwell on itself as a literary construct) denies readers the flattering reassurance they seek so often in the 'mirror' of art.

5. LYRIC AS SUPPLEMENT

Lyric in the Golden Age does not move from presence to absence. Rather its development is supplementary: poets seek both to add to the old poetry and to displace it by the new. As Scaliger projected in the previous century, the art of poetics expands during this period to encompass the whole body of human and natural sciences. Already in his notes to Garcilaso, Herrera treats such apparently peripheral subjects as the history of artillery, and in his commentaries on Góngora, Salcedo Coronel presents himself as geographer, astronomer, and historian. The boundaries between disciplines come under increasing pressure. Likewise, poetry itself reveals a closer engagement with the particularity of the external world, linked aesthetically with the quest for graphic detail associated with *evidentia*. Thus in Herrera's sonnet 'stars' represent the heavenly bodies in general, but in Góngora's they denote quite specifically the meteorological effect known to sailors as St Elmo's fire. The crowded landscape of the *Soledades*, with its rabbits, goats, and curious sea monsters (inconceivable in Garcilaso), is another case in point. Yet the discovery of the specificity of natural phenomena is also the revelation of its fundamentally compromised and determinate character, of its necessary collusion with art or culture. This contradiction (the prominence yet insufficiency of nature) is confirmed by that manifesto of seventeenth-century taste Emanuele Tesauro's *Cannocchiale aristotelico* (Turin, 1670). In his section on 'harmonic' or phonetic figures Tesauro cites Mario Bettino's recreation of the song of the nightingale. It begins:

> Tiùu, tiùu, tiùu, tiùu, tiùu;
> Zpè tiù zquà;
> Quorrror pipì
> Tío, tío, tío, tío, tìx . . .[33]

[33] See the facsimile edn. (Bad Homburg, 1968), 167.

And so on. Here art reproduces the sensorial immediacy of natural utterance in an apparently immediate mode of imitation. Yet, in spite of Tesauro's denials, the authentically 'natural' language of bird or beast here stands revealed as an impossibility. For it is quite literally incomprehensible: unintelligible to human beings and unbounded by the signifying practices of their culture. The song of the bird (when copied by the human) is pure phonetic excess. The anecdote which follows on the same page is quite different. Tesauro recounts how a contemporary Spaniard has constructed an artificial leather tongue, which can be moved in imitation of the natural organ. In this way he teaches mute children to speak, artfully supplying his patients with those words denied them by a parsimonious nature. Garcilaso's cold tongue, we remember, was thought unnaturally redundant by one commentator. Tesauro's leather tongue, on the other hand, is wholly artificial, a marvellous example of that human ingenuity which now completely displaces the intermittent and fallible voice of nature and a fitting analogue of a poetry which wholly supplants that nature in which it continues, nevertheless, to base its claim to legitimacy. Like the red ink in which Juan de Valdés wrote those words in his translation of the Psalms which had no Hebrew equivalent, the leather tongue stands as an icon of originary absence.

The dominance of language over matter, then, is the enabling and essential condition of literary discourse, a factor habitually repressed by many critics, especially in modern times.[34] Literature is distinguished by a surplus of phonetic and semantic value, and imitation tends inevitably to displace its supposed object or original. The true concern of the critic is the variable status of means and object within this excess. When the means are discreet (as in Garcilaso), language offers itself as transparent and facilitates the fiction of immediate access to author. When they are more emphatic (as in Góngora), then language itself is, provisionally at least, denaturalized, and its representational function can no longer be taken for granted. The knowledge of an absent origin (the

---

[34] One possible exception to this rule is Formalism, with its stress on the literarity which defamiliarizes common speech. For a critique of the relation between textual dominance and signification, see Terry Eagleton, *Criticism and Ideology* (London, 1978), 78–9.

impossibility of the author inhabiting his words) is thus concealed by the 'natural' discourse and foregrounded by the 'artificial'. Once more, the redundant has positive effect in pointing up the necessary character of writing as a whole. On the other hand, increased verbal elaboration may be experienced by an unwilling readership as the intolerable imposition of an opaque language by a tyrannical author. The virulence of attacks on Góngora, past and present, would seem to bear this out. As Scaliger warned, the poet of excess is feared rather than loved, the 'natural' style provoking a more affectionate, because less obviously prompted, response. It is no accident that Herrera's examples (borrowed from Scaliger) of epithets *in re* and *in verbis* should be 'a strong man' and 'a man of marvellous strength'. Rhetorical proficiency is a continuing struggle for dominance, a point implicitly acknowledged by Scaliger's examples of *efficacia*: the grieving mother and virile warrior. Góngora flaunts his verbal potency in the reader's face, while Garcilaso seeks to conceal it within the smooth surface of his textual body. Both walk the poetic tightrope between ostentation and languor, although their respective definitions of these terms would have been rather different. Yet if Garcilaso is more prudent than Góngora, he is no less artificial.

Yet, as we shall see in the chapter on the comedia, the virtue of prudence is as complex as that of efficacy. In his chapter on prudence Scaliger begins by defining this virtue as the anticipation of future circumstance. His first example (typically) is a military commander who draws up his troops in such a way as to ensure victory, even if his preparations are unprecedented in previous campaigns (p. 113). The transference of this model to the poet is more complex. At first Scaliger follows the traditional definition of decorum: the prudent poet can reproduce any affect (including 'lascivia') as long as he does so at the right time and in the right place. He goes on to advise that just as imitation should keep close to the object, so constancy should be the companion of imitation. However, what if the poet seeks to imitate an inconstant object? Scaliger's examples are Ligurians (notorious liars) and women (known for mutability). The first, he says, are octopuses (perhaps because of their multiplicity); the second are chameleons (undoubtedly because of their faithlessness). Scaliger solves the problem he has created by claiming that the prudent poet should be constant even in his depiction of inconstancy. But what seems more important in this passage is not the rather facile conclusion but the sense of anxious suspicion it suggests towards the volatility of the world outside the traditional conception of literary decorum: certain objects (Ligurians, women) do not submit to ordered imitation. It seems possible, then, that the increasing exoticism and extravagance of lyric after Scaliger reflects an awareness among poets that there is no proper 'fit' or adequation between poetry and nature; indeed that the more poetry attempts to reproduce the multiple diversity of the world the more it must acknowledge its failure to do so. The space of the *Soledades*, for example, radically duplicitous and shifting, marks a point at which Ligurians and women are in complete control.

It may well be true, then, that as Golden Age lyric develops art takes over to some extent from nature, ornament from plainness, obscurity from clarity, and *verba* from *res*. Yet the distinctions are problematic and the final emphases already emergent in Garcilaso and Scaliger. The same terminology seems to recur in critics of all periods. Yet the greater sophistication of some Golden Age readers lies in their refusal (or inability) to lend a restrictive or privative value to one half of the paradigm. For them, each of the terms may be good and bad simultaneously, and neither term can be wholly absent or wholly present. Hence the logic of poetics, such as it is, has to be copulative (additional), not disjunctive (alternative). As we have seen, the traditional opposites define the field of critical enquiry and poetic performance, but they provide a deficient model of both. For what is missing is the supplement of artifice or poetic making, that excess value conferred on the poem by the poet which is both essential and extrinsic and which serves to distinguish poetry from the common speech whose linguistic matter it shares. The hidden motive of *enargeia* or *evidentia* may indeed be the attempt to defer death by enforcing, in Herrera's phrase, a 'perpetuity of representation'. If this is so, then the poems treated in this chapter can be taken as exemplary of this function. But a close reading of Golden Age theory, its preconceptions rather different from those of modern critics, confronts us with truths we may prefer to ignore: that poetry is never immediate; that the relation between author, text, and reader is inevitably partial and determinate; that the rhetoric of presence aspired to by poets and longed for by readers is denied at the very moment of its proposition by the multiplicity of attempts to theorize and to practise it.

I have stressed that the development I have sketched from Garcilaso to Herrera to Góngora is necessarily halting and intermittent. But it remains, none the less, overly schematic. If we introduce a fourth poet into the picture the effect is highly disruptive. Lope de Vega was born some fifty years after Garcilaso, but even more than his predecessor Lope is considered by many to offer the most authentic and natural 'voice' in Golden Age lyric. However, a recent study has shown that this traditional view of Lope is erroneous and that his sonnets reveal linguistic and psychological contradictions similar to those I have discerned in the other poets. For Mary Gaylord Randel, Lope's ostentatious spontaneity is by no means 'immediate'. For example, Lope bares his soul to the reader, but can only do so by means of borrowed words. His appeal to personal sincerity is contradicted by the artistic self-consciousness of his verse and thus produces the troubling oxymoron of an 'imitative confession'.[35] Likewise, Lope is at once highly suspicious of figurative language (which he associates with the adulteration of the proper tongue) and fully conscious of the virile power of metaphor (the act of appropriation) (pp. 229–31). This linguistic hesitancy reduces him, the proud father of innumerable poetic offspring, to the status of adulterer or stepfather. He cannot master the texts he has produced, which prove to be embarrassingly fragmentary and discontinuous. What is more, this indeterminacy is reproduced by the reader: 'Our critical contortions seem destined to ape the textual acrobatics of his personal poetics, which keep us suspended along with his poem-children in mid-air, swinging endlessly to and fro, between the man and his masks.' (p. 246.)

Lope's failure to attain (or his unwillingness to communicate) an integrated, authentic persona is thus similar to the cases of the other poets we have examined. It also confirms the truth of the dictum often repeated by Lacan that 'Desire is desire for [or of] the Other'. The question posed implicitly by the

---

[35] 'Proper Language and Language as Property: The Personal Poetics of Lope's *Rimas*', *MLN* 101 (1986), 220–46 (p. 224).

lyric poet is not 'What do I want?', but 'What do they (the reader, the addressee, the model poet) want from me?' The rigorous conventions imposed by Renaissance lyric and the sense of pressure exerted by the works of the great masters of earlier times help to explain the apparent paradox that the genre in which presence-to-self is cultivated is also that in which alienation from self cannot be repressed. It could hardly be otherwise, when the forms of the most intimate subjectivity are dictated by external authority. Hence the poet's 'here and now' should be read as an 'always already'; amatory experience is wholly familiar territory, endlessly mapped by previous generations; its shifter is impotent, or hollow. And this is particularly the case in Spain where, as we saw in the last chapter, there is a continuing anxiety as to the relationship between local and imported culture which is still felt today. In the introduction to an anthology of traditional Spanish lyric, Dámaso Alonso claims that Garcilaso is the first modern European poet and that Lope is the first poet in Europe to fuse life and work together in experiential union.[36] Alonso's desire is still 'desire of the Other': the question he asks is not 'What does Spain want from its poets?', but 'What does Europe want from Spanish poets?' But this anxious substitution of questions is associated with a sense of extremity or marginality which is, to some extent at least, self-imposed. Alonso claims that (with the exception of Garcilaso) the genius of Spanish lyric lies in its restlessness ('desasosiego'), even frenzy (p. xvi). Thus for Alonso, Spanish lyric is at once inside and outside the European tradition: it exemplifies international qualities (modernity, authenticity), but also embodies national peculiarities (extremity, insanity). Its status, once more, is supplementary. However, the question to be asked now is how critics respond to one genre which Spain can indeed claim to have originated: the picaresque novel.

---

[36] *Antología de la poesía española: Lírica de tipo tradicional*, ed. with José Manuel Blecua (Madrid, 1969), pp. xiv–xv.

3

THE RHETORIC OF REPRESENTATION
IN PICARESQUE NARRATIVE

I. PICTORIALISM AND REPRESENTATION

THE problems raised by picaresque narrative are at once opposite and equal to those raised by lyric poetry. On the one hand, picaresque denies the reader that direct equation of voice and person offered by lyric: the 'I' of the narrator cannot be identified with the 'I' of the author. Indeed, as we shall see, one distinguishing characteristic of picaresque is that it calls attention to this fundamental division within the speaking (or more properly the writing) subject. On the other hand, the very transparency of this division elicits a new kind of identification from the reader, and promotes a new kind of 'presence' in the text. We are inclined to believe not that Alemán or Quevedo 'speak' directly to the reader (as Garcilaso or Lope are often thought to do), but that they are concerned with the reproduction of coherent and integrated speaking subjects analogous to their supposed equivalents in the real world. The perception of presence in the text (of a speaker to whom the reader has immediate access) thus shifts from the register of experience to that of representation, from life to art. But critical approaches to both genres share a bias towards the direct intuition of the 'real' in writing, and a desire to submit one's will to that imaginary lure. As is well known, Renaissance theory (following classical authority) pays little attention to prose narrative: the Horatian and Aristotelian traditions are mainly concerned with lyric and dramatic verse. There is thus more opportunity in this chapter than in the last to appeal to modern theories of writing and representation. But, as I hope to show, rhetorical conceptions of writing and reading are as evident in picaresque as they are in lyric, and the quest of modern critics for a natural language commensurate with human experience is equally doomed to failure.

One more link between the genres is that picaresque narrative tends towards excess and proliferation. According to received critical opinion, the *Lazarillo*, small in scale and modest in means, gives way to the *Guzmán*, vastly swollen in both narrative and commentary, and the *Buscón*, with its hyperbolic register and extreme linguistic complexity. Moreover, the sheer bulk of picaresque narrative produced in the Spanish Golden Age (both the number of works and their length) is matched only by the critical literature which has accumulated around them. The abundance and variety of this 'secondary' literature not only demonstrates the continued importance of the genre to a modern audience; it also suggests that picaresque narrative presents contradictions or problems which remain unsolved and which may, indeed, prove to be insoluble.

The main aim of this chapter is to propose that most critical approaches, whatever their surface allegiance (historical, linguistic, psychoanalytical), are based on certain unexamined preconceptions concerning the nature of representation in literature and that these preconceptions are often derived from what I shall call 'pictorialism': that is, an appeal, whether explicit or not, to the visual arts or the visual imagination as a privileged model for writing. I shall propose a revised model of literary representation which, unlike pictorialism, does not suppress the contradictions inherent in picaresque, falsely reducing the works to an aesthetic continuity which may be consumed without effort by the modern reader, but rather incorporates those same contradictions into the fabric of its argument. My approach will therefore of necessity be theoretical and somewhat abstract in character, without, I hope, becoming overly technical in vocabulary. The primary texts are now thick with critical accretion. The time may have come for a broader treatment of the critical enterprise itself.

My position here, as elsewhere, will be broadly anti-humanist: that is, I am in opposition to the myth of 'Man' as founding father of the text and as integrated, active subject within that society which the text is thought to reflect. In this I take my general approach from strains of modern critical theory, particularly in France, which themselves derive ultimately from Marx, Freud, and Saussure. Such a position may be accused of anachronism. But if this is so, 'humanist' critics are equally anachronistic. For the ideals they cherish belong neither to the Renaissance nor to our own time. They derive rather from a particular historical moment (the mid-nineteenth century) and the literary form most characteristic of it (the 'classic' or 'Balzacian' novel). Though many critics proclaim their adherence to the literary conventions of the Golden Age, the critical concepts they employ and the aesthetic values they propose (suggesting on the one hand a primal 'unity' or 'integrity', and on the other an 'ambiguity' or 'tension' neatly resolved by the author) are consistent with received, nineteenth-century 'humanism'. The tools of previous scholars are thus, necessarily, an object of my own critical investigation and cannot serve as the instrument of my own reading of the texts. My reading will attempt to disclose and exploit the necessary pre-conditions of writing. And I will suggest that this strategy of radical disclosure, this refusal (or inability) to conceal the labour or process of writing, is itself a defining characteristic of the picaresque as genre.

My task is made more urgent by the recent appearance in English in revised and expanded form of an influential study first published in Spanish: Francisco Rico's *The Spanish Picaresque Novel and the Point of View* (Cambridge, 1984).[1] In many ways this is an exemplary study. Professor Rico pays close attention to the historical circumstances of writing and to the formal techniques by which writers represent a speaking subject and his view of the world. And unlike other lesser critics, he gives no special privilege to the 'realist' mode by suggesting it is 'naturally' superior to such other modes as fantasy or allegory. However, the constant appeal to pictorialism in his study has certain general consequences which are widespread in the critical literature as a whole. On the one hand, the author (through the narrator) is thought to give an illusionistic 'picture' of at least an aspect of the 'real' itself, however partial or relative this may be. On the other hand, this 'painterly' depiction of the world leads the critic to seek structural symmetry in the plot and psychological unity in both character and author: perspective is identified with and justified by authorial

---

[1] The English translation is by Charles Davis with Harry Sieber.

intention. The stress on point of view, that is, on the individual as origin of vision and of speech, thus presupposes both a concrete and empirically verifiable object 'out there' (the 'real' as foundation of social practice) and a coherent and unified subject 'in here' ('Man' as source of psychic experience). Moreover, there is a pervasive movement from the purely formal or aesthetic to the overtly moral or prescriptive: thus *Lazarillo* and *Guzmán* are more 'successful' examples of picaresque than the *Buscón*, as the latter does not possess that coherent and unified perspective which the critic has discerned in the former.

What Professor Rico fails to give is a critical account of 'point of view' itself. It is invariably presented as benevolent: unifying, validating, and authentic. Yet the appropriation of knowledge and of sensation implied by the single viewpoint could equally be seen as insidious and oppressive in its enforcement of hierarchy and ruthless exclusion of deviance. Rico's own inability to address the *Buscón* is a case in point. What is more, the 'point of view' is no natural, universal phenomenon, but rather a specific, historical production: 'perspective' in the modern sense is, of course, unknown in the visual arts of medieval Europe or the Far East. The same may well be true of its equivalent in narrative. If, as Rico seems to suggest, the 'point of view' emerges contemporaneously with picaresque narrative then it is perhaps unwise to use it in any attempt to investigate that very genre in which it is so profoundly implicated.

Professor Rico's thesis rests ultimately on the possibility of a simple opposition of subject and object and of the direct operation of the former on the latter: the writer reproduces the world in the text, and the text, in turn, reproduces the writer's meaning in the reader. As we shall see in many other critics, contradictions and discontinuities in the text are said to reinforce both the illusionistic depiction of character and the intentionalist model of literary creation. For example: if the actions of Guzmanillo and the sermons of Guzmán are inconsistent, it is because Mateo Alemań intended by this contradiction to reinforce our sense of the psychological verisimilitude of his character. Whatever the complexities of this process, for Rico the dominion of character over environment and of author over text remains unquestionable.

One British critic has also tried to offer an analysis of Golden

Age prose whose starting-point is visual perception. In two articles, R. D. F. Pring-Mill gives an interesting, if undeveloped, reading of the development of picaresque and other genres in Spain.[2] Pring-Mill refers alternately to 'depiction' and 'representation', and does not seem to distinguish between the two. The first article begins with the chastening observation that 'absolute realism is unattainable', and that all representation is subject to a double compromise. The first compromise is between our chaotic perception of the world and the process of interpretation by which we reduce it to order; the second is that between the motives of the writer and the conventions within which he or she must work. Pring-Mill claims that non-naturalistic genres (which he would call 'non-photographic') such as pastoral or mystical writing are not a flight from the real, but rather an attempt to represent the world as it was 'really' thought to be beneath the surface of sensual phenomenon (pp. 20–1). The tension between essence and appearance betrayed by such writers leads to an increasing strain on the resources of photographic representation which culminates in the disintegrating 'portraits' of the *Buscón* and the incompatible 'pictures' of the *Sueños* (p. 280). In the second article Pring-Mill claims that photographic verisimilitude is a mere decoy. He quotes Wellek and Warren to the effect that there is no simple opposition between reality and illusion, only a variety of modes of each (p. 270). Hence, if Quevedo 'discards the naturalistic composition of the picture' (p. 279), it is in order to allow a reintegration of 'reality' which is achieved on the plane of intellect, not sense impression. Likewise, Gracián's 'emblematic' techniques are incompatible with photographic realism. But the *Criticón* 'still shifts before us on the page, sliding backwards and forwards between the two planes of vision [essence and appearance], yet constantly providing "signs" for the discerning eye to read' (p. 284). Hence, even the most anti-naturalistic writing is by no means divorced from the real.

Pring-Mill's study is unfinished: he presents the articles as the first draft of a book which never appeared. But it offers, none the less, some interesting insights, which derive, no doubt,

[2] 'Spanish Golden Age Prose and the Depiction of Reality', *ASSQJ* 32–3 (1959), 20–31; 'Some Techniques of Representation in the *Sueños* and the *Criticón*', *BHS* 45 (1968), 270–84.

from the critic's familiarity with rhetoric. Unlike Rico, Pring-Mill has no interest in setting up a unified individual at the centre of the fictional world, be it the author, the protagonist, or the reader. Rather he takes it for granted that the modes of representation are multiple at any moment in history. And unlike Rico again, Pring-Mill tends to refer not to the 'point of view', but to the 'eye'. There are evidently problems in transposing an 'ocular' model of perception from the world of phenomena to that of fiction, problems which are not really examined by Pring-Mill. But his perhaps unintentional abstraction of the eye or look from a particular, individual witness frees him from some of the prejudices of other pictorialist critics, who tend to present vision as a natural and unchanging criterion of verisimilitude. Thus Pring-Mill can end the first article by claiming that there may come a time when the *Criticón* is valued as highly as the *Quijote*: the modern bias towards photographic realism is as conventional as the seventeenth century's mistrust of what it takes to be a purely superficial depiction of the world. Where Rico stresses the relativity of points of view, but fails to examine the problem of perception itself, Pring-Mill stresses the plurality of modes of representation and thus (implicitly) calls into question the prestige of vision as a universal principle. Yet, it seems unlikely that Pring-Mill would have undertaken a critique of pictorialism and the conventional humanism that lies behind it, even if he had had access to the theorists I will cite myself. His concern for representation as a changing historical phenomenon does not extend so far as to question the social and subjective forces which produce Man as cultural construct.

My own starting-point is more difficult: a rhetoric of representation. By this I mean a complex of overlapping relations necessarily involved in the production of narrative. The three principal relations are those between the individual and the world as presented in the text; between the writer and the reader as implied within the text; between the practice of writing and those non-discursive practices necessarily excluded from the text. They correspond to three disciplines or areas of study (psychology, narratology, and politics) which I shall explore in connection with the three works on which Rico concentrates (*Lazarillo*, *Guzmán*, and the *Buscón*). However, unlike those of other critics, the relations I trace are not teleological but reflexive; that is, they operate not in one direction (subject to object), but in both directions simultaneously, and thus call into question the status of both terms. Hence subjectivity (the sense of being an individual) is produced by interaction with the world, and is not somehow separate from and prior to it. Likewise the act of writing is not invested solely in the author, but can only be completed by the reader to whom it is implicitly directed. Finally, literature does not simply 'reflect' or 'depict' a given social reality external to it, but rather participates in those social practices through which a sense of the 'real' is produced.

These relations will be demonstrated in the remainder of this study. But they are insufficient in themselves. What is also required is a critique of that pictorialism which seems inseparable from our perception of the 'real' in art and which conditions our sense of the 'aesthetic' in general. Jacques Derrida has recently made such a critique in his *La Vérité en peinture*.[3] While the implications of this work are wide-reaching, its relevance to my own thesis is in its proposal of a basic principle of representation which not only dissolves the unitary and functionalist aspects of the 'point of view' but is also peculiarly appropriate for the study of picaresque. That principle is the 'frame'. In the visual arts the frame is commonly considered to be extrinsic and subordinate to the image it encloses: it represents nothing and bears no conceptual or sensorial value. Yet, it is also intrinsic and necessary to the process of representation. Without the frame the image would be physically unlimited and artistically unmotivated, commensurate with the world itself. The image is deficient: it lacks finality, in the twin senses of 'completion' and 'purpose', and this absence can only be supplied by the frame. Moreover, the frame, unlike the image, is material or concrete. Yet a condition of representation (for the nineteenth-century spectator at least) is that it should not flaunt its materiality or draw attention to its own presence. Derrida cites Kant for whom the 'gilded frame' is a primary example of the 'unaesthetic', of that which detracts from artistic representation and must be excluded from it (p. 62).

[3] Published in Paris, 1978. In the paragraphs which follow I paraphrase and greatly simplify 'Le Parergon' (pp. 44–95).

The relation of image to frame in painting is thus reflexive and reciprocal: each determines and is determined by the other. And this relation may be transposed to picaresque narrative as follows: the texts offer the reader a 'picture' of contemporary society which has not failed to move and delight in all periods. But they also present a very prominent attempt to bound or frame this proliferating image with an internal representation of the necessary conditions of narrative itself: the narrator constantly addresses the reader, whether specific or general; reveals the supposed causes of his narration and the effects he hopes it will cause; draws attention to the process of story-telling and its relation to didacticism. The picaresque is a frame-tale. And this internalization of the conditions of narrative has had a varied critical reception.

An awareness of these framing devices is not new, by any means. But I would suggest that a close attention to these devices not only reminds us that all representation (in narrative as in painting) is necessarily compromised by formal and material constraints; it also tends to suspend or subvert some of the major sources of critical controversy with regard to picaresque as genre, and to which I will return in my final pages. Firstly, the question of origin and purpose (beginning and end): neither frame nor image precedes the other, but both come into being together. Secondly, the related problem of hierarchy and precedence: 'secondary' or 'extrinsic' material may prove to be as essential as that safely included within the critical convention of 'relevance'. Elements commonly excluded to the margins of discourse or society may hold the key to their respective systems as a whole. For Derrida, the frame is the primary form of what he goes on to call (after Kant once more) the 'parergon': the apparently secondary and subordinate term which is in fact essential to the operation of any practice.

The significance of Derrida's text, then, is that it offers us an opportunity to rethink the relation between language and vision without surrendering to the lure of presence or *enargeia*. But, as always, the difficulty of Derrida's writing makes paraphrase a tricky business. The very title of the book, borrowed from Ceźanne, opens up an infinite play of meaning: what does it mean when a painter promises to 'speak' the truth in painting? Cézanne's truth will be found only within the painting of which it claims, none the less, to speak (p. 13). Thus the peculiarly reflexive problem of aesthetics is that the discourse on beauty is also a discursivity in beauty. It is therefore impossible to use such terms as 'parergon' as if they were (external) instruments which serve to disclose the (inner) secrets of the work of art, for Derrida's text makes no claim to be 'outside' the hermeneutic circles of which it speaks. The first section of *La Vérité en peinture* is called 'Passe-partout'. It is typical of Derrida that he uses this term not in its common sense of 'master-key', but in its specialized sense as a slip-in mount with a detachable back. The passe-partout is not strictly a frame. Rather it is a frame within the frame, taking up a variable space between the inner edge of the frame proper and the outer edge of the picture itself (p. 17). It thus points to the inadequacy of those binary oppositions (picture and frame; ground and figure; form and content) which neglect or repress the necessary asymmetry of the relation between language and vision: the inner edges of the passe-partout are often bevelled, cut at an oblique angle (p. 18). The action of the parergon, we might add, is equally oblique.

The main question posed by this discourse on the frame is 'What is extrinsic to the work of art?' As so often in Derrida's readings, the examples offered by the model author (in this case, Kant) serve merely to undermine the coherence of the author's argument. We have seen that one example of the parergon is the frame which surrounds a picture. The other two are the clothing which covers statues and the pillars attached to the façades of buildings (p. 62). We saw in the previous chapters that clothing is the traditional example of ornament in poetics, and that it serves, as Derrida notes in the case of sculpture (p. 66), both to decorate and to veil the naked body. Likewise, it is not immediately evident to the spectator if a pillar serves a structural or an ornamental function in a building. Derrida argues that it is precisely the difficulty of subtracting these 'external' items from any 'internal' substance (their very closeness to the main work or ergon) which defines them as parerga. They fill a lack in the ergon, a lack of 'outside' (p. 69). According to Derrida, the further question posed by such examples is how we can account for 'energeia' (*sic*), the vital force of the aesthetic effect (p. 83). We cannot do this by pro-

posing new frames for the represented object, nor by seeking
the (impossible) abolition of the frame (p. 85). Derrida seems at
one point to hint at an alternative in a fragment which speaks
of a 'theory on rollers' (p. 62). But he later reveals that this
image is stolen, once more, from Kant, who uses it as a metaphor for the examples inserted by the philosopher to help the
weak-minded understand his argument (p. 91). The curious
status of examples is thus that, like rollers, they both support
the body of the text, and enable it to go forward. But this sense
of a lack in the philosophical text is also found in the aesthetic
sense itself. In a later section of his work, Derrida treats at
length two more curious examples given by Kant. The first is a
wild tulip. The essence of its beauty derives from a 'finalité sans
fin' (p. 97), a coherent organization of means that is, none the
less, wholly gratuitous in effect. The second example is a prehistoric axe that has lost its handle (p. 101). This object bears
witness to a finality which has come to an end: it can no longer
perform the operation for which it was intended, and is therefore unaesthetic. Derrida glosses the examples as follows:
beauty is determined by the cleanness of the cut which severs
the object from specific purpose. The artistic object must display no trace of the process by which it was severed from the
real. Hence art is not simply redundant or lacking: it must display that lack as pure and unmotivated (p. 107). If the tulip is
considered for its biological function of reproduction it loses its
aesthetic quality; but if the stone implement is viewed in the
ignorance of its original function it gains the status of art previously denied it. I will return to the distinction between pure
and impure severance in the conclusion of this chapter when I
treat the difference between the canonic picaresque novels and
a little valued outsider, *La pícara Justina*.

Derrida's text is concerned with the aesthetic in general; but
it is surely no accident that the images which 'illustrate' the
discussion of the parergon are drawn from sixteenth- and
seventeenth-century sources: designs for ornamental doorways,
architectural façades, and decorative cartouches. For all the
questions he treats are historically specific. The 'gilded frame' is
secondary, inferior, and excessive to Kant, but not perhaps to
viewers and thinkers of other periods. Indeed, evidence of the
historicity of the frame is provided by the illustrations to early

editions of the picaresque novels themselves. Thus two of the original editions of *Lazarillo* (1554) depict characters from the narrative on their frontispiece: Lázaro is shown with the blind man and the *buldero* respectively.[4] But in both cases the characters are enclosed by a dense and elaborate frame, frequently omitted in modern reproductions. The frontispiece to López de Ubeda's *La pícara Justina* (1607) is equally well known. It depicts a number of picaresque characters on board an emblematic ship, which is itself towed by Lazarillo in a rowing boat. It bears a more slender, but no less prominent, frame, within the space of which is depicted a variety of objects associated with the genre: food, musical instruments, and so on. This 'ajuar de la vida picaresca' is made to enclose and delimit the space of representation. However, the illustrations to a late edition of Quevedo's *Buscón* (1699) are quite different.[5] They are by no means completely illusionistic: successive episodes are represented within the same picture. But the frame itself has completely disappeared, and the image can present itself as unlimited and unmediated, appearing to offer the spectator immediate access to the scenes depicted.

It may be that this progressive disappearance of the frame corresponds in some measure to the rise of a system of literary representation which aspires to 'realism', suppresses the narrative 'framework', and thus appears to write itself. Picaresque might then be seen as a midpoint in this transition. The passage 'from Aristotelian mimesis to bourgeois realism' is too large a project to be dealt with here.[6] It is enough to suggest that while the former pays equal attention to the means, medium, and object of imitation, the latter concentrates on the object alone. More relevant to our purpose are the ways in which modern critics (like realist novelists before them) tend to conceal the labour they have expended in the assimilation of Renaissance texts and present the unitary, pictorialist qualities they have projected on to the text as the intrinsic and immutable nature of the text itself. We may now trace this invisible or self-erasing labour in critical approaches to *Lazarillo de Tormes*.

[4] Reprinted most recently in Antonio Rey Hazas's edn. (Madrid, 1984), 50.
[5] Reprinted in A. A. Parker's *Literature and the Delinquent: The Picaresque Novel in Spain and Europe 1599–1753* (Edinburgh, 1967).
[6] See the article of this title by J. Bruck in *Poetics*, 11 (1982), 189–202.

2. *LAZARILLO* AND SUBJECTIVITY

Any reading of the *Lazarillo* will suggest two areas of uncertainty or possible disagreement. The first is formal: what is the significance (if any) of the evident disproportion between the length of the first three *tratados* and the brevity of the remainder, between the leisurely detail of the first half and the extreme compression of the second? The second is epistemological: what value (if any) can we attribute to the disjunction between the predicament of the character and the protestations of the narrator? How can we 'know' what is happening at any particular point? As we shall see, the two questions become one in the work of modern critics who seek to uncover both artistic and psychological continuity beneath what they take to be a merely 'superficial' fragmentation of the aesthetic and conceptual registers of the text.

It is hardly surprising, therefore, that the article which has been acclaimed as 'the foundation of all serious criticism' on the *Lazarillo* is F. Courtney Tarr's 'Literary and Artistic Unity in the *Lazarillo de Tormes*' (1927).[7] For pictorialist critics unity is perhaps the highest good, and its innate prestige is rarely subject to question. Tarr begins by attacking those critics of a previous generation (such as Chandler and Bonilla), who saw in the *Lazarillo* 'a poorly sustained and even unfinished piece of work' (p. 404). He proposes instead an 'unmistakeable continuity' beginning in the first three *tratados*, based initially on theme or motivation (Lazarillo's increasing hunger), but later located in the guiding intention and increasing proficiency of the unknown author, 'a definite plan and a steady growth in artistic ability on the part of the author' (p. 412).

The unifying force of the author in this scheme is absolute, but somewhat contradictory: he both implements a preexistent pattern with effortless certainty and grows to the artistic 'maturity' of realism as he does so. In other words, the text both reflects his unvarying intention and reproduces his variable proficiency. The argument becomes increasingly circular: if the fourth *tratado* is short it is because 'this is an adequate picture of the restless friar' (p. 413). The friar receives

---

[7] The evalulation is by A. D. Deyermond in *Lazarillo de Tormes* (London, 1975), 102; the article itself in *PMLA* 42 (1927), 404–21.

little space because he lacks narrative relevance (and vice versa). The very brevity and inferiority of the later *tratados* is 'intended' by the author to enhance the relative superiority of the first three (p. 421). Formal inconsistency is thus resolved and reduced to a seamless, 'aesthetic' integrity, hermetically sealed from social practice and remorselessly policed by authorial intention.

Subsequent critics take the 'unity' of the *Lazarillo* for granted, though the justification they give for it may vary. Thus Claudio Guillén (1957) resolves the 'apparent' discontinuities of the narrative by appeal to its status as 'relación', that is, as a story told by an individual.[8] The narrator projects himself in time, and having achieved a personal integrity or presence in the third *tratado*, it is only 'natural' that he withdraw, discreetly, from a self-depiction which has now achieved its purpose. The 'unity' of the *Lazarillo* is thus cumulative and progressive, and may be perceived only in the diachronic movement of time or narrative, not in the synchronic moment of image or picture. Raymond S. Willis is more purely pictorialist (1959), and reduces a dynamic narrative to a series of symmetrical tableaux.[9] Thus *tratados* 4, 5, and 6 form a 'triptych': 'a large central panel with two smaller ones at the sides, which counterbalance, or mirror, one another neatly in length, tempo and style' (p. 277). Or again, Lázaro's position at the end of the narrative is the 'inverse' of what it was with the squire, the text having swung around 180 degrees on the smooth 'hinge' of the fifth *tratado*, redundant in early criticism, but now claimed as essential (p. 279). Here difference becomes symmetry, and symmetry unity, in an ingenious movement of pictorialist rationalization. For Bruce W. Wardropper (1961), the *Lazarillo* is also governed by a kind of symmetrical inversion, in that it portrays ('retrata') the moral reversals of its subject.[10] As late as 1975

---

[8] 'La disposición temporal del *Lazarillo de Tormes*', *HR* 25 (1957), 264–79. For a recent view on Lázaro's 'relación' and its dangers for the reader, see M. J. Woods, 'Pitfalls for the Moralizer in *Lazarillo de Tormes*', *MLR* 74 (1979), 580–98. For a new theory of the possible circumstances of the 'relación' and its consequences for the reader, see Robert Archer, 'The Fictional Context of *Lazarillo de Tormes*', *MLR* 80 (1985), 340–50.

[9] 'Lazarillo and the Pardoner: The Artistic Necessity of the Fifth *Tractado*', *HR* 27 (1959), 267–79.

[10] 'El trastorno de la moral en el *Lazarillo*', *NRFH* 15 (1961), 441–7 (p. 441).

these points are echoed by Howard Mancing, who revises Willis's graph plotting the simultaneous rise of Lazarillo's material fortunes and decline of his moral status and proposes the '*Subir/bajar* dichotomy' as a 'succinct and complete framework within which Lázaro's entire life unfolds'.[11] These symmetrical schemes are of course imposed retrospectively. They are undisturbed by the frequently disorientating process of reading the text, but assume a transcendental 'viewpoint' from which all its divergent and conflicting moments may be safely ranged and classified. The critic's role seems to be to construct by careful selection an ideal paradigm which will explain and correct the deficient and inconveniently material syntagm which is the narrative processus itself.

Of course, paradigmatic critics do not offer this pictorialism as a direct imaging of the real: masters such as Bataillon and Castro had warned against such naïveties long before.[12] But the vigour with which they defend the plastic virtues of unity and symmetry is matched by the certainty with which they seek to resolve the inconsistencies of the narrative by subordinating them to the figures of narrator and author. This reduction is achieved by the presupposition of a 'real' situation exterior and anterior to the text itself, of which the text is somehow a necessary, but deficient, reflection. For example, critics have speculated at length as to the exact nature of the relation between Lázaro and the Vuestra Merced to whom he writes, and appealed to the 'case' mentioned in the Prologue as both motive and explanation of the details of the narrative that appear excessive and subordinate. Or again critics have offered a variety of readings of the final *tratado*, each of which competes for the status of 'genuine' truth: Lázaro is the innocent victim of a cruelly arbitrary predicament; the disillusioned subject resigned to a status quo over which he has little control; the malevolent cynic who succeeds in procuring an immoral but advantageous position. To choose any of these interpretations as the 'real' one is to presuppose the author's interest in the illu-

---

[11] 'The Deceptiveness of *Lazarillo de Tormes*', *PMLA* 90 (1975), 426–32 (p. 430).

[12] See Marcel Bataillon, *Défense et illustration du sens littéral*, Presidential address of the MHRA (Leeds, 1967), 18–19; *Pícaros y picaresca: La pícara Justina* (Madrid, 1969), 203, 214. Américo Castro, 'El *Lazarillo de Tormes*' (first published 1948), in *Hacia Cervantes* (Madrid, 1967), 143–9 (p. 143).

sionistic representation of character, in the creation of a three-dimensional narrator with a single, unified, and authentic psyche. But equally, to claim, with other critics, that the *Lazarillo* is a purely 'open' text, the product of its author's (successful) attempt to reproduce a moral and evaluative ambiguity, is to assert what might be called a 'dogmatic relativism'. That is, the libertarian free-play of the text is in fact superseded and 'framed' by the supposed authorial perspective, which invariably transcends and invalidates the inferior and subordinate propositions of the voices it creates. For Rico, Lázaro's fortunes tell us that 'there are no values, only lives—individuals' (p. 29). But this supposed disclaimer of transcendent value is in fact a proposal of the unitary individual himself as validating principle, the 'touchstone' by which the real itself acquires significance. A fixed and unquestionable subjectivity is thus proposed as the 'universal equivalent' of both narrative and narration, the gold standard by which all value in the fictional economy is enforced. The supposed 'deceptiveness' of *Lazarillo* is invariably subject to rigorous curtailment by the humanist critic, and the ironic narrative framework is confidently enlisted for illusionistic purpose.

Yet, there are hints in the criticism that subjectivity in *Lazarillo* cannot be taken for granted, that its status is more radically precarious and discontinuous than the relativists might suppose. Thus Castro had suggested in 1948 (in a study which explicitly denies *Lazarillo* the status of 'painting' or 'drawing' of the real) that the apparently unmediated intimacy we feel for Lázaro the narrator is illusory and that his identity as character is founded on negation: he is not the subject of action, but the object of his masters' attention, and his social being is not so much formed as unformed. The narrative enacts not the integration of a coherent viewpoint or subject position, but rather its annihilation.[13] For Guillén, Lázaro, as existential hero, creates himself in the struggle with time and the world. But this supposed 'triumph of the will' finds a radically ambiguous source in time, its position both integrated and elusive, present and absent.[14] Lázaro's identity has no essential unity, no primal origin. For Stephen Gilman (1966) the only moment of integ-

---

[13] 'El *Lazarillo de Tormes*', pp. 146–7.
[14] 'La disposición temporal', p. 277.

rated presence in Lázaro's career is the 'sepulchral utopia' of his first night with the squire, when he curls up at his master's feet, like a stone dog on a sarcophagus. Hence Lázaro's achievement of selfhood has no plenitude, but is predicated on a vacuum: the inevitable and omnipotent absence which is death itself, and which is revealed through the very act of narration.[15]

A revised model of subjectivity in the novel is offered by a recent full-length study, Harry Sieber's *Language and Society in 'La vida de Lazarillo de Tormes'* (Baltimore, 1978). In spite of his title, Professor Sieber is concerned with language as semiotic rather than social practice, as a symbolic system somewhat removed from the specificities of historical determination. Thus the first *tratado* is seen as representing the initiation into a 'language' of blindness, or repression; the second, a subjection to the 'sacramental' discourse of the Church; the third a confrontation with the secular, visible 'language' of the honour code (p. xii). Lázaro learns first to constitute his own 'reality' through speech, and then to suppress it through self-censorship. But, unlike the 'point of view', language here is no site of unification for the individual. Lázaro's lesson in silence is based on a primal division intrinsic to the practice of story-telling or fabulation which itself constitutes our social being: 'that space between Lázaro as narrating subject (writing self) and finalized product of his narration (written self)' (p. x). The subject who speaks is never the same as he who is spoken: in linguistic terms, *énonciation* and *énoncé* fail to converge.

One example within the narrative of this founding disunity of language and self would be the '¡Madre, coco!' episode of the first *tratado*: Lazarillo's half-brother fails to recognize that his own colour is identical to that of his black father. Previous critics have debated the relative precedence or hierarchy of discourses in this scene and thus produced a specific (though variable) meaning. The child's cry is invalidated by Lazarillo's sententious commentary: 'How many people in the world cannot see themselves as they really are!' But this utterance itself is seen as subordinate to the author's global perspective, within which Lázaro fails to recognize the inconsistencies of his own

[15] 'The Death of Lazarillo de Tormes', *PMLA* 81 (1966), 149–66 (p. 166).

position. Moreover, readers who laugh at either child or narrator and neglect to consider the possibility of their own selective
blindness may also be subject to the author's serenely ironic
gaze. Three or four perspectives are thus set in motion, each of
which is discrete and subordinate to the one above itself: actor,
narrator/reader, author. The problem of subjectivity itself, of
the coherence or integrity of each of these 'viewpoints', is
simply ignored.

Professor Sieber's approach is quite different. He takes this
scene as a representation of the 'mirror stage' familiar from
psychoanalysis (pp. 2–6). The new-born infant exists in a state
of narcissistic and self-pleasuring immediacy, unable to distinguish between self and world. The reflection of self in the
mirror or in the projection on to external object precipitates the
first stage of subjectivity proper: the sense of self as at once subject and object (same and other). Yet this identification is more
properly 'misrecognition': the image or object both is and is not
the self. More particularly in the scene above, the white mother
is the 'image of a similar being through which integration takes
place', while the black father is the 'object of foreclosure', the
third term which shatters the narcissistic transference of the
mirror stage (p. 5). The scene enacts the moment of initiation
into the 'symbolic', that is, the cruel and alien world of social
differentiation articulated through language (p. 6).[16]

This theory has two consequences. Firstly, subjectivity is
closely linked to representation, to the imaging of self in
language. Secondly, if subjectivity has an origin, it is not in
unity but in division and dispersal. Hence we may extend
Sieber's suggestion by stating that if Lazarillo as character
achieves a certain measure of identity it is through the projection on and misrecognition of self in objects which he
encounters and desires. His often noted concern for clothes is a
case in point. But this primal division is not merely represented
in the narrative as the varied and often contradictory experience of a fictional protagonist; it is also reproduced by the narration in the inconsistent texture of its representative process.
As many critics have noted, the first *tratado* is the most 'communal' in style, in its appeal to folk motifs expressed in tradi-

---

[16] See Jacques Lacan, 'Le Stade du miroir comme formateur de la fonction du Je', in
Écrits, i (Paris, 1966), 89–97.

tional terms. The third is the most 'original' in its naturalistic depiction of place, dialogue, and a new literary type (the squire). The other *tratados* occupy intermediate positions between these extremes. Hence the position (or positions) from which the author writes is curiously mobile and contingent, and the reader is confronted with a plurality of mutually exclusive codes of representation, a patchwork of heterogeneous fragments. The *Lazarillo* is, in Maurice Molho's word, a *cento*, a linguistic scrapbook.[17] For Bruce Wardropper (again), the *Lazarillo* presents the 'seamy side of life', in the twin senses of low milieu and inverted morals (p. 441). But I would suggest that it also reveals the 'under-side' of subjectivity and of fiction: in its ignorance of the consistency we associate with 'classic' realism, it lays bare the devices of both identity and narration, the 'seams' of the psychological and literary garment which are conventionally repressed.

But if the origin of the sense of self is in division, then the condition of its persistence is in subjection. The 'imaginary' relations by which the child is constituted are duplicated in the individual's engagement with society as a whole.[18] And subjection, like division, both 'speaks' and 'is spoken' in the *Lazarillo*. It is depicted in the passivity of the character's career, in his habitual role as recipient rather than initiator of action, from the moment he is delivered into consciousness by the first blow from the blind man. The objects of his identification or misrecognition (such as the clothes, once more) are prescribed by social values which precede and envelop him. And these identifications are not so much a distorted representation of a 'real' predicament, as an empiricist might suppose; they are rather the actual relations of a society as it is perceived by its subjects. Thus the question of to what extent Lázaro is 'really' aware of his position is strictly unanswerable, for (as the narrative reveals) the very condition of social identity is its denial of access to the 'real', its pervasive prohibition of authenticating self-knowledge.

In an introduction to his essay on the mirror stage, Lacan

---

[17] *Introducción al pensamiento picaresco* (Salamanca, 1972), 29.
[18] For the application of Lacanian psychoanalysis to social practice see Louis Althusser, 'Ideology and Ideological State Apparatuses', in *Lenin and Philosophy*, trans. Ben Brewster (London, 1971).

hints at this point when he states that the only real to be found in the primary process is 'the impossible', and that any mechanism ('appareil') of the real we may attribute to the subject is a mirage (*Écrits*, i. 82–3). He also warns against collapsing the mirror stage with the physical capacity to see: even a blindman will go through the same process, as long as he knows himself to be the object of a look (p. 85). And if we examine Lacan's paper itself more closely, we note that, in spite of the apparent privilege accorded the act of seeing, everywhere it undermines the presuppositions of pictorialist (and humanist) critics. For example, Lacan begins by stating quite explicitly that his theory is wholly opposed to any philosophy based on the *cogito* (the active autonomy of human thought and perception) (p. 89). And if he claims that the mirror stage is an 'identification' then his definition of that term is far from the humanists' 'identity': identification is the transformation produced in subjects when they assume their image (p. 90). This transformation situates the ego in a line of 'fiction' or discordance which can never be resolved by the individual. Indeed, the very permanence of our sense of self is proof of our alienation (p. 91). The development of the subject is a drama: caught from the beginning by the lure of the spatial image, the child proceeds to experience fantasies of a fragmented body, before finally assuming a rigid totality, an 'armour' of alienating 'identity' (p. 93). Hence the 'stade du miroir' (invariably translated as 'stage') is also a stadium or arena (p. 94), in which conflicting images battle for control. When, as it must, the specular self twists or turns into the social self, then alienation becomes paranoiac: following the desire of the other, subjects form their objects only in so far as those objects conform to the rival wishes of other people (p. 95).

Even at this early stage of his work, Lacan's thought is highly dense and intricate: like Derrida's parergon, Lacan's imaginary does not respond to simple definition. But it is not difficult to see why the imaginary has proved so popular with literary critics: Lacan's own references to 'fiction' and 'drama' seem to encourage us to borrow his terms. It is tempting to relate this description of the evolution of the subject to Lázaro's career as fictional character. Most of the points seem to coincide. I have already mentioned the impossibility of access to authentic knowledge of the real. The inconsistency of Lázaro's career (the way he changes with each master) also suggests that the story is a sequence of 'identifications', images of self assumed by the character which transform his very being. The way in which this early fragmentation fixes or congeals into the rigid armour of social identity is also clear in the story, as is the alienating nature of this identity, which prevents the character from satisfying his needs at the same time as it claims to have done so. Lázaro's psyche is a battlefield, torn between desire and Law, and his adult experience is paranoid in Lacan's technical sense: the only knowledge of the world to which he gives credit is that dictated to him by other people. It is not simply that social success is bought at the cost of personal failure, but that Lázaro has no personal space, no authentic desire uncompromised by alienation.

As I said, it is very tempting to make such readings of literary characters. But if the imaginary forms the very basis of human mind then it is perhaps more applicable for an analysis of the reading process than of the characters within the text. The great mass of *Lazarillo* criticism testifies to the willingness with which readers surrender to a mirage of the real, and the urgency of their desire to assume the image of the other. As in the case of the child's fantasies of the body, disintegration and fragmentation give way to a spurious, yet seductive, unity: both character and work take on a substantial 'presence' lent them by the readers themselves. This process is not peaceful; rather it takes the form of a battle in the critical arena, where readers struggle to construct a textual identity which will be ratified and recognized by their fellow critics. For, as in the case of Lázaro, once more, if the satisfaction of their needs is not confirmed by others, then it is no satisfaction at all.

Lacan calls the specular image the 'threshold' of the visible world. Like Derrida's parergon, it takes up its place in or on the margin of representation. I shall return to the mirror stage and Lacan's later elaboration of the symbolic in the chapter on the comedia. But the concept of 'identification' in Lacan's sense has a particular significance in the *Lazarillo*. The central irony is that it is Lázaro's perception of himself as a free agent capable of autonomous action which is the most illusory of these delegated and internalized representations of self. For he is the recipient not only of action, but also and primarily of inspection. He is not the subject but the object of the 'point of view', and of a perspective not personal and authentic like that proposed by Rico, but generalized and pernicious, the condition and instrument of power. The cause we are given for the narrative as a whole is surveillance: Lázaro's ménage is observed by others and he is obliged to give an account of it. Thus the speaking subject is determined by its relation to power and its utterance is a reactive gesture to the menace of alterity. Hence if we 'read out' the implications of the narrative and the contradictions of the narration by appeal to authorial intention we merely reproduce the trajectory of Lázaro's own subjection, by internalizing external authority as both censor mechanism and validating principle. The representative 'frame' of the *Lazarillo* (its avowed concern for the origin and purpose of its own enunciation) should be read not illusionistically, as a necessary (but self-erasing) aid to the depiction of a coherent, if complex, individual, but critically, as the (unintended) pointer to the reflexive and contingent relation of self and world and the deficient status of the social subject. This 'critical' reading does not linger in the narrative space, speculating on the relative 'truth' of fictional propositions which must, finally, remain unanswerable. It is deflected back to ourselves. But there is no direct 'mirroring' of reader in the text. The story is not 'about' us.[19] Rather it reminds us in exemplary fashion of the provisional nature of all representation, of misrecognition as the absent origin from which all sense of self is derived.

   This inconsistency of narrative process may be historically specific, and I shall treat this problem in social or political terms with respect to the *Buscón*. But one unique aspect of the *Lazarillo* is essential here, and that is its anonymity. Critics have always tried to identify a particular author and thus reduce the text to an original authority. But it remains a text whose author, as Harry Sieber notes (p. 97), has rejected its paternity. The author's ambivalent position itself bears witness to the origins of subjectivity. The *Lazarillo* is produced by the combined negative and positive forces of power and knowledge: as a disinherited text it reveals (like the character represented within

---

[19] As Deyermond claims in the conclusion to his *Lazarillo de Tormes* (p. 98).

it) both the fear of surveillance and the urge to testify. For it is
the potential imposition of censorship which produces the partial exposition of identity.[20] It is highly appropriate, then, that
the emergence of a modern subjectivity should be marked by
such a marginal text, deprived of fixed origin or distinction,
and whose value goes unrecognized on its first appearance. But
it is also significant that the representation of the individual in
this fiction is based not on the speaking but on the writing subject, an emphasis which will assume its greatest importance in
the case of the *homo scribens*, Guzmán de Alfarache.

3. *GUZMÁN DE ALFARACHE* AND WRITING

The *Guzmán* is concerned explicitly, if intermittently, with the
process of representation itself. The work as a whole is 'framed'
by two well-known anecdotes which treat differing aspects of
the problem.[21] In the first, two artists are required by a patron
to paint a portrait of his favourite horse. While the first confines
his depiction to the animal itself, the latter fills in the rest of the
pictorial space with a landscape and other details. In spite of
the second painter's claims that he has 'illustrated' and
'enriched' the principal theme by these adornments, the patron
chooses the first, plainer version: he had not requested the
'excess' material. This story thus raises the problem of pictorial
relevance or integration: what is intrinsic to representation and
what extrinsic? What should be included and what excluded
from the constrictive but necessary limits of the frame? The
question of superfluity (which I have suggested as characteristic of the picaresque as genre) will be a constant preoccupation
of the *Guzmán*. But the author also raises, perhaps unknowingly,
the problem of direction or audience: artists do not work in a
vacuum, but rather 'direct' their work to a historically determinate public. In other words, painting and text are both 'dialogic': aesthetic production is originally implicated in and
finally completed by the active consumption of the witness. The

---

[20] For the role of surveillance, testimony, and confession in the creation of the
modern individual, see Michel Foucault, *Surveiller et punir: Naissance de la prison* (Paris,
1975), *passim*.

[21] In Francisco Rico's edn. (Barcelona, 1983), I i. 1 (pp. 107–9) and II iii. 9 (pp. 892–
3).

source and target of the artistic message (in so far as we can distinguish between them) are not discrete and unitary, but reflexive and mutually constituting. And narrative 'relevance' is the battlefield on which the two forces meet.

The second anecdote is that of the spectator confronted by a painting which is upside-down. He cannot tell what it depicts until it is turned the right way up. The problem here is in interpreting the pictorial message: conventional perception, Alemán tells us, is distorted by inversion. In particular, his protagonist fails to recognize his ostensible position (the 'cumbre de miserias') as the depths of depravity from which grace and repentance may still save him. But the general hermeneutic question remains for the reader: given the constrictions of narrative illusionism, how do we interpret the action, read the 'picture' offered to us by narrator and author? The 'marginal' status of these anecdotes itself dramatizes the questions they raise. Placed before and after the action proper, they both assume the precedence and finality implied by their respective positions, and deny the authority they seem to possess by their exclusion from that same action. Pictorialism is at once intrinsic and tangential to Guzmán's career and Alemán's enterprise.

These two questions of integration and interpretation have been the main concerns of modern critics. But, as in the case of the *Lazarillo*, the two fields (formal and evaluative) tend to coincide. For if critics seek, as we shall see, to establish the narrative 'relevance' of the didactic interludes in the *Guzmán*, it is by reassigning them to an illusionistically 'integrated' narrator, whose testimony (paradoxically) is validated by its supposed unreliability. Aesthetic and psychic continuity are thus retrieved from the precarious instabilities of the representational process.

The critical history of the *Guzmán* is well known. Eighteenth- and nineteenth-century readers and translators succumb to the supposed 'picture' of contemporary society it offers, while excluding or excising the narrative 'framework' radically different in tone from the story it encloses. Guzmán's commentaries on the action and apostrophes to the reader are held to be subordinate and excessive to the main body of the plot. Twentieth-century critics vindicate the 'necessity' of the didactic elements by appeal to the pictorialist or schematic virtues already 'discovered' in *Lazarillo*: unity, symmetry, inversion. Thus, moral reflection and immoral action are said to complement each other by virtue of their very contrariety. As in *Lazarillo* once more, contradiction is resolved by authorial intention and integrated narrative persona. For A. A. Parker, Alemán exploits the polar opposites of sinner and penitent in order to dramatize the Catholic dogma which it is his purpose to demonstrate. Illusionist narrative is thus the vehicle for universal 'truth' (*Literature*, pp. 21–23). For Francisco Rico, all inconsistencies are resolved by the exemplary smoothness and unity with which narrating and narrated self come together at the essential and inevitable moment of (genuine) conversion (*Point of View*, p. 45). Each moment of the account (cruel or kind; active or reflective; sensuous or sententious) finds its organic and 'natural' place in this flexibly accommodating yet rigidly unifying 'perspective'.

The question of hierarchy or precedence is much debated: if the *Guzmán* is a moralized fiction, then its primary action is disrupted by secondary reflection; if it is a fictionalized sermon, then its essential moralities are interspersed with the intrusive pleasantries of the plot. Critics have generally asserted the priority of one or other of these terms. Yet such prescription seems unnecessary, for Alemán himself seems to suggest the mutual dependence of the two terms in his writing. Thus at one point the fiction is described as the soft fruit of the melon which can only be reached through the bitter skin of didacticism which surrounds it; and at another it is the 'gold' coating the pill of morality which lies invisible and original beneath it (pp. 92, 490). In these two conflicting metaphors, inside and outside (intrinsic and extrinsic) are curiously mobile, each substituting for the other. Which is not to say that they are fused organically; they are simply unstable.

As we shall see, such contradictions may be related to the act of writing itself. However, in the last decade many critics have indeed rejected as inadequate the moral and perspectival unities of Parker and Rico, and stressed not the coherence but the discontinuities or 'fissures' of the text. Thus Joan Arias has called attention to the unresolved contradiction between narrative and narration: the glee with which the supposedly reformed galley slave presents the evil deeds of his younger self.[22] But this inconsistency is perceived by Arias not as a gap in the representational process, but as a flaw in the testimony of Guzmán himself as character, 'the contradiction between the reality he sees around him and what he says the reality is' (p. 87). However, as Professor Arias herself admits, the question of our access to this 'reality' is somewhat problematic since the first-person narrative offers only what he says. Guzmán the 'unrepentant' narrator is thus reinstated as a 'fully rounded' personality, and Alemán's supposed concern for illusionistic depiction of character and relativist depiction of truth go unchallenged. Hence, traditional and heretical critics tend to converge: for Rico the moral of the *Guzmán* is 'the self as measure of all things' (p. 49); and for Carroll B. Johnson it is that 'man is the being through whom value exists in the world'.[23]

Such readings, ostensibly 'objective', remain philosophically naïve, at once idealist and empiricist. Idealist in that they posit an eternal and unchanging subjectivity ('the self', 'man') immune to the rigours of history and which the reader may scrutinize through the medium of the author's words. (I have already questioned this belief with reference to *Lazarillo*.) Empiricist in that they suppose a concrete and discrete object, divorced from, yet freely accessible to, the critical gaze. It is significant that Professor Johnson defends his use of twentieth-century critical 'tools' (Marxism and psychoanalysis) by appeal to astronomy: now that men can fly to the moon, they no longer need examine it with an outmoded telescope (p. 9). But the text is not material in the sense that a heavenly body is, and still less is the figure represented within it a three-dimensional psychic space which will open for the reader to probe 'inside'.

If the *Guzmán* seems contradictory and discontinuous it may be not because it betrays the deceit of the character it represents (or alternatively the subtle, ironic design of the author who produced it), but because it reproduces contradictions in the practice of writing which are both general to that practice and specific to a historical instance of it. Almost twenty years ago Edmond Cros published a massive study of the *Guzmán*'s

---

[22] *'Guzmán de Alfarache': The Unrepentant Narrator* (London, 1977).
[23] *Inside 'Guzmán de Alfarache'* (Berkeley, 1978), 10.

relation to the contemporary practice of writing, a study whose
radical implications Spanish and Anglo-Saxon critics have
failed to recognize or chosen to ignore.[24] And it is no accident
that this grammatological study should uncover in the *Guzmán*
not the seductive but spurious unity of psychologism, but the
multiple elaboration and differentiation of literary language
itself.

Professor Cros begins not with the author, but with the relation of the text to its public. The *Guzmán*'s first readership sees it
not merely as a mirror but also as a theatre of the world, a spectacle with Guzmán as the protean actor, which both represses
the artifice of its production 'behind the scenes' and foregrounds it in acknowledging its own status as distorted and distorting representation ('leurre', p. 94). If this mode of
representation seems excessive, Cros reminds us that for the
seventeenth century verisimilitude was associated with 'amplification', that is, the use of a language rich anough to convey a
significant theme with appropriate elaboration (p. 128). Contemporary writers have no naïve faith in a 'transparent'
language which will correspond 'naturally' to the object of imitation. Rather they appeal to 'parascholasticism': the technical
vocabularies and techniques derived from rhetoric and the imitation of classical models (p. 161). Such knowledge is rightly
marginal to the intellectual culture of the age, but will prove
intrinsic to the development of the novel.

Indeed, the linguistic excess of the *Guzmán* may be related
directly to the prestige of rhetoric as discipline (p. 179). Cros
shows in detail how the 'places of invention' (genus and species,
part and whole, and the rest) both form and frame the proliferating movement of Alemán's prose. Such questions may seem
technical. Yet the rhetorical distinction between, say, intrinsic
and extrinsic 'places' (that is, topics derived directly from the
matter in hand and those based on external authority) is essential to our understanding of the dynamics of the text. For in
Alemán, the 'extrinsic' places tend to invade and take over the
narrative space as a whole. External and subordinate in the
traditional discipline, they become internal and dominant in

---

[24] *Protée et le gueux: Recherches sur les origines et la nature du récit picaresque dans 'Guzmán de Alfarache'* (Paris, 1967). Much of this material is condensed and simplified in the same author's *Mateo Alemán: Introducción a su vida y a su obra* (Madrid, 1971).

the 'new' novel. In particular, *exemplum* is the privileged place of the *Guzmán*, its very status exemplary of a 'marginal' genre, insecure of its position in the traditional hierarchy of writing. For although the *exemplum* is (by definition) unrelated to the principal *res* or matter of the oration, it is also considered to be more efficacious in the communication of feeling than the intrinsic or artificial places for which it substitutes (p. 185). The frequent use of both the place definition and the trope metaphor is also due to their peculiar efficacy. They serve in the 'sermons' to both animate and circumscribe the endlessly expanding narration (pp. 247–58). But if rhetoric is a 'frame' ('cadre'), it cannot be detached from the 'picture' it confines, but is essential for the development of the heterogeneous elements within, because without it they could not have come into existence (p. 242).

The rhetorical frame thus suspends teleology: it creates a free yet determinate space in which the habitual combatants of the novel (reader and writer, subject and object, language and society) may perform in relatively autonomous yet disciplined display. The author is no longer the single origin of the text, nor is the narrator its unique focus. For the anonymous yet prestigious discipline precedes the first and relativizes the second. If (as Cros suggests) the techniques of representation are seen themselves to be conventional, then there can be no immediate access to the writer who employs them or the character who is produced by them. Which is not to say that rhetoric produces the text: the art precedes the artists, but is itself subject to their practice of it.

But I would go further than Cros, and suggest that the distinction between intrinsic and extrinsic places sheds new light on the question of truth or interpretation in fiction of the period. In rhetorical theory truth is invested in the 'authority' of the speaker, in the 'inartificial' statement which (as in *exemplum* or citation) requires no linguistic skill to convince the audience. 'Magister dixit' is the motto of Alemán the didacticist, as for generations of rhetorically trained writers before him. In the twentieth century, the mechanisms for the validation of truth have changed. In accordance with the rise of the natural sciences (such as the astronomy invoked by Johnson), truth is revealed not by appeal to authority but by demonstration of

empirically verifiable context.[25] It is this empiricist epistemo-
logy which leads modern critics to seek the significance of the
Guzmán in the coherence or disparity of the action represented
within it. It is perhaps ironic that the didactic tone of the text
they investigate should reveal its author's habitual appeal to
the external presence of a truth quite immune to this kind of
critical investigation. In other words, if the textual register of
the *Guzmán* seems inconsistent, it is because its author juxta-
poses the individual and deficient testimony of the character
with the universal and authoritative commentary of the narrator with no concern for illusionistic pictorialism or empiricist
evaluation.

Hence, the site of unification (if one were needed) is not in
the author or narrator, but in the reader. The *Guzmán* contains
within itself a constant and ever-changing projection and
representation of the public to whom it is addressed. But the
readership is shown to be as multiple and fragmented as the
narrator. Divided initially and uncompromisingly into the
common and the disabused reader ('vulgar' and 'discreto'), it is
unceasingly imaged throughout the narration. Thus the very
first sentence expresses the fear that some pedantic logician will
reproach the narrator for not proceeding in traditional manner
from 'definition' to 'thing defined'. In spite of a recent study
which argues to the contrary,[26] the *Guzmán* has all the qualities
of written, as opposed to oral, language; albeit of a literacy still
deeply marked by orality. Firstly, the hesitant and provisional
entry into discourse, preceded by multiple addresses and *tasas*,
a mass of preliminary matter which seeks to define and con-
strict the wayward movement of the pen. Secondly, a constant
qualification of utterance, a habitual checking of the progress
of speech, manifest most strikingly in the proliferation of subordinate clauses. Where the characteristic feature of *Lazarillo* is
parataxis, the unexplained juxtaposition of discrete narrative
fragments, that of the *Guzmán* is hypotaxis, the attempt to order
a dangerously expansive body of fiction and doctrine by

---

[25] For the evolution of 'truth' from authoritative utterance to experimental deduc-
tion, see Michel Foucault, *L'Ordre du discours* (Paris, 1971).

[26] See George Peale, '*Guzmán de Alfarache como discurso oral*', *JHP* 4 (1979), 25–57.
Compare Walter J. Ong, *Orality and Literacy: The Technologizing of the Word* (London,
1982).

reducing it to grammatical and evaluative hierarchy. Thirdly, the love of logical structure (proposition and syllogism), impossible in oral discourse. Finally, a pervasive, even neurotic, concern for the reader as target of the fictional message (a possible discomfort at the moral digressions; an improper delight in the immoral anecdotes), and also for the end of the narration itself, which (unlike the *Lazarillo*) promises its own indefinite extension at the very moment at which it draws to a close. If, in Walter J. Ong's phrase, 'the writer's audience is always a fiction',[27] then Alemán's represented public is more emphatically projected and hence more resonantly absent than many before or since. And this agonistic concern for the readership and the consequent refusal to assume a posture of flattering yet deceptive intimacy with it may be related to the historical moment at which Alemán wrote, to the relative novelty of the represented, novelistic dialogue which he set in motion.

The *Guzmán* suggests that writing is always predicated on absence: the reader, unlike the listener, is never 'there'. Alemán's habitual distance, his didactic authoritarianism, is a product of his inability to repress that absence, and is a characteristic unpalatable to many modern readers, accustomed to the recreation of a democratic familiarity between novelist and public. But this sense of absence is perhaps also the origin of the endless extension of Alemán's fiction. Its proliferation seeks to 'bridge the gap' between writer and reader, to defer death through the interminable displacement of narrative incident: the reader, like Guzmán, moves desiring but unfulfilled along a metonymic chain which can have only one conclusion, however long it is deferred. A contemporary emblem shows a skeleton holding up a mirror to the spectator: death is the final imaging of life, and artistic representation must always be deficient.[28]

Comparable images of radical negation are found throughout the *Guzmán*, and they are signs not so much of a historical 'pessimism', as of an insistent linguistic circularity. Alemán's own favoured emblem, the spider which descends along its web to kill a snake, is an appropriate symbol of undifferentiated,

[27] See the article of the same name in *PMLA* 90 (1975), 9–21.
[28] In Sebastián de Covarrubias Orozco, *Emblemas morales* (Madrid, 1610), ii. 182.

mutually reflexive negation.[29] If the celebrated 'watchtower' ('atalaya') of the title may be read as the sign of an active moral perspective, it is equally a passive icon of the reader's oppression. The texture of the *Guzmán* is uneven: even Rico has some difficulty in assimilating the interpolated novels to a single, unificatory design. The *Guzmán* thus tends to draw attention to the process of its own writing. And behind this heterogeneity we might glimpse (as in the case of *Lazarillo*) not vision but surveillance, the human being as object rather than subject of perspective. The watchtower, at once anonymous and multiple, scans the reader from its privileged viewpoint. We are subjected by its persistence and subdued by its indifference. Yet this exercise of power is not purely negative: it produces, as we have seen, a wide spectrum of different readings, each defined and individualized by the invisible authority of the text itself. And it is this positive effect of a textual tyranny which I hope to disclose in the final work to be examined, Quevedo's *Buscón*.

Michel Foucault has suggested that the watchtower plays a crucial role in the development of modern society.[30] His study of 'panoptisme' (the tyranny of vision) begins with the rules drawn up for a seventeenth-century town in the grip of the plague: divided into minute sections, subject to constant surveillance by the forces of order, the plague town is the model ('dispositif') of the disciplinary society which is already starting to form (*Surveiller et punir*, pp. 197–9). In previous times, marginal subjects (such as lepers) were expelled from society; now this simple separation of pure from impure is supplemented by the minute observation of all citizens (p. 200). For Foucault the emblem of this surveillance is the 'panopticon', the architectural model drawn up in the eighteenth century by Jeremy Bentham, which also has antecedents in the previous century. The panopticon consists of a central watchtower surrounded by a continuous circular structure in which the subjects are housed. The classic example is the prison, but the model is also appropriate for hospitals, schools, or factories. Here the amorphous crowd of earlier times becomes a collection of separate individuals, each caught in the trap of visibility (p. 202). While

---

[29] Reproduced and discussed by Cros in *Protée et le gueux* (p. 309).
[30] For the role of the watchtower in the surveillance and differentiation of the individual see Foucault on the 'panopticon' (*Surveiller et punir*, pp. 197–229).

the prisoners (patients, workers) know they can be seen in their compartments, the presence of the watcher inside the darkened tower cannot be verified (p. 203). Thus a genuine subjection is born of a 'fictive' relation: there may be no one inside the tower, but that does not reduce its effect, for those who feel themselves to be observed internalize their relation to power (pp. 205–6). Hence, while the pestilent town is the example of an extraordinary and violent exercise of discipline, the panopticon represents a generalized and immaterial climate of surveillance, in which discipline leads to the production of useful individuals (pp. 209–12). If Antiquity was a society of spectacle, in which it was necessary to make a small number of objects accessible to the inspection of the multitude (as in the triumphal march of the emperor or the sacrificial rite of the high priest), then the nature of modern society is quite the opposite: the multitude is made visible to a small number of people, or even to one individual (p. 218). This reversal is provoked in part by demographic changes in seventeenth-century Europe, in particular the increase in the vagrant population (p. 220). And one precedent for this 'technology of individuals' (p. 226) which is also pre-eighteenth century is the Inquisition. Just as the inquisitorial process of investigation has its counterpart in the rise of the empirical sciences (the close observation of the world), so the later codes of discipline are reflected in the growth of the human sciences (the interrogation of Man himself) (p. 227). The main difference between the two regimes is their relation to the body: while the *ancien régime* had as its greatest punishment the torture of the prisoner until death, the disciplinary society's most potent weapon is an interminable interrogation, a file which is never closed (p. 228). The disciplinary model, less blatant and more insidious than previous organizations of power, spreads throughout society: we should not be surprised that factories, schools, and hospitals all resemble prisons.

The relevance of this schema to the *Guzmán* is not immediately evident. Foucault is concerned with the heritage of the Enlightenment and, indeed, makes much of the irony that the 'light' of the reformers should have become a means of repression. Yet Foucault states that the eighteenth century sees only an acceleration of tendencies already present before; and I would argue myself that Alemán anticipates many points made by Foucault in his practice as a writer. Thus much of Foucault's analysis of power can be related to Guzmán as character. His marginal position (like that of Foucault's deviants) is twofold, or alternating: at times he is branded like the leper and expelled from society; at others he is allowed entrance but is in constant fear, like the plague carrier, that his invisible shame will be brought to light by the forces of order. Like the prisoner of the panopticon, he is one of a multitude, but wholly separate from his fellow men, never achieving lasting contact with any of them. He is caught in the trap of visibility: wherever he moves he will inevitably be identified and humbled by the omniscient gaze of power. And if Guzmán's experience is ever more bodily (in, for example, the obsessive recurrence of hunger and excrement), then the power which surveys him is curiously immaterial and unverifiable. Guzmán claims, as we have seen, to speak to the reader; but the supposed motive of his testimony (to warn us of spiritual danger) is inconsistent with the obsessive detail with which he narrates his evil actions. Ultimately, the addressee of his confession must be God, the immaterial, unverifiable being *par excellence*. We are reminded of the engraving reproduced by Foucault (no. 20), which shows a convict at prayer in a model prison: we cannot be sure if he is praying to the Deity or to the shadowy watchtower which rises up before him. Similarly in the *Guzmán*, the destination of the message is uncertain. It is enough to know that surveillance leads (as in the *Lazarillo*) to confession when the relations of power are internalized.

We might see the *Guzmán* (like the panopticon) as a laboratory which serves to fragment and magnify human productivity: in each tiny incident (each graphically illuminated cell) the subject is 'caught' in a posture which requires praise or blame, reward or punishment. In its role as witness, the readership holds a privileged position. The multitude is made visible to the single person in a spectacle of surveillance: we observe Guzmán, who is aware of his own visibility. As I suggested earlier, the critic's gaze is often inquisitorial: we are tempted to make 'empirical' judgements as to the 'facts' of Guzmán's case. But it is also humane: we seek to understand the psychological 'truth' of his condition. And just as the narrator's testimony is never finished (the second volume is not written), so the critic's investigation is interminable (the interpretations and hypotheses multiply). This indefinite surveillance re-enacts the endless monotony of incident in the *Guzmán*: just as the school, hospital, and prison are all alike beneath superficial variations, so the pleasant variety of Guzmán's adventures gives way (long before the end) to a wearying repetition of incident.

I shall return to Foucault's critique of sight in the chapter on Cervantes. But it should be noted here that although Foucault's panopticon (like Derrida's parergon and Lacan's imaginary) is associated with the faculty of vision, it avoids all the traps associated with pictorialism. And by setting up an opposition between the bodily torture of the *ancien régime* and the more subtle surveillance of the technological state, Foucault also suggests a way of distinguishing between the *Guzmán* and the *Buscón*: for in the latter we find, quite simply, the flagrant and outdated operation of aristocratic power on the rebellious body of the deviant.

4. THE *BUSCÓN* AND POLITICS

As has often been noted, criticism of the *Buscón* has tended to fall into one of two camps. One school (which includes A. A. Parker) sees Quevedo's work as a morally serious enterprise in which the truth of Catholic dogma is demonstrated by the inevitable misfortunes of a 'rounded' character placed within a setting which is recognizably 'real', albeit dramatically intensified.[31] The other follows Fernando Lázaro in seeing the *Buscón* as a comic exercise in linguistic aestheticism, a display of verbal ingenuity which betrays little or no concern for either psychological verisimilitude or exemplary didacticism.[32] Both schools might be seen as 'pictorialist' in ways I have already noted above: the psychologist, in its bias towards illusionist representation; the aestheticist, in its concern for 'balanced', decorative sensualism. And each prizes unity in its own way. The first, the unity of character through which the writer dictates his chosen moral to the reader; the second, the continuity of expression

[31] See *Literature*, pp. 56–72.
[32] See 'Originalidad del *Buscón*' (first published 1961) in *Estilo barroco y personalidad creadora: Góngora, Quevedo, Lope de Vega* (Salamanca, 1966).

through which the author expresses his unvarying linguistic invention. Such unreflective praise of the novel's supposed unity and symmetry occurs even in a recent and relatively experimental reading by Gonzalo Díaz-Migoyo.[33]

Francisco Rico's dissenting position owes something to both schools. The *Buscón* fails as a picaresque novel, because it offers no coherent and unified perspective which may be assigned to its central character. Lacking in both psychological veracity and formal unity, Quevedo's use of picaresque conventions is redundant and superfluous: residual 'framing' techniques, such as the intermittent address to the reader in the foreword and within the narrative, have no necessary function in the text. Quevedo's conspicuous punning, which cannot be attributed to the narrator/protagonist, is a redundant intrusion of authorial voice. In short, the *Buscón* is a useless and vacuous object 'like a frame separated from its picture' (p. 72), and Quevedo's verbal superfluity, although the work of an artistic genius, is compromised by plagiarism (p. 81).

As in the cases of *Lazarillo* and the *Guzmán*, numerous critics have vindicated the symmetry of the *Buscón*'s plot and the unity of its form. Yet others have noticed the heterogeneous nature of its various components: Pablos's own narration (with or without authorial intervention); his uncle's letter; the soliloquy of such characters as the *arbitrista* and the impoverished nobleman; the mock proclamation against poetasters. For there can be no doubt that Quevedo's language, with its constant hyperbole and multiple diversity, tends far more to excess and redundancy than that of previous texts; and that the divergence between author and narrator (and between the varied constituents of the text) is more apparent than in the *Buscón*'s antecedents. I will suggest, firstly, that this linguistic superfluity and narrative discontinuity are essential to an understanding of the *Buscón* and its place in the picaresque canon; and secondly, that these two features may be related to the political questions raised by the narrative: the status of individuals in society and their relation to the power invested in that society. Indeed, it may be that both moral and aesthetic schools of *Buscón* criticism represent an anxious, liberal retreat from the author's uncom-

---

[33] *Estructura de la novela: Anatomía de 'El buscón'* (Madrid, 1978).

promising aristocratic ideology and its (apparently direct) reflection in the novel's anti-Semitism, misogyny, and scorn for
the socially inferior.

The 'rey de gallos' episode is a good example of the ambivalence of critics' response to such problems. Pablos, carnival
king for the day, attempts to halt the hail of vegetables aimed at
him by an angry mob, by claiming that the aggressors have
mistaken him for his mother, who had been paraded through
the streets as a witch. His nag then throws him into a dung-
heap, the first of many descents into scatology. Where Parker
(p. 66) had seen this as a primal scene of guilt and alienation,
many subsequent critics have taken it as evidence of Quevedo's
lack of concern for continuity and verisimilitude, which are
subordinated to a cruel and gratuitous comedy of class: it is
implausible that Pablos should betray his shameful origins in
public, unless obliged to do so by Quevedo, the tyrannical
puppeteer.[34]

Recent critics have paid increasing attention to the 'ideology' of the *Buscón*, as implicit in such episodes. Constance Rose
and Michel and Cécile Cavillac tend to see the text as the
unmediated reproduction of orthodox class interests: Quevedo
is determined to subdue Pablos, pitifully deprived representative of a struggling and repressed bourgeoisie.[35] This view is
similar to that given earlier by Marcel Bataillon, for whom the
Buscón quite simply 'symbolizes' the social state of Spain at the
time it was written.[36] However, other critics have seen contradictions within this ideology and have sometimes related
them to the gaps or inconsistencies in the work's narrative
'framework'. Thus for Richard Bjornson (1977) Quevedo's
anti-illusionism (his refusal to give a 'realist' depiction) results
from a class-based ideology which cannot permit its characters
the relative autonomy of the more liberal naturalist mode.[37]
Or for Edwin Williamson in the same year, the conflict
between author and protagonist reveals (in spite of Quevedo

[34] For the lack of clear distinction between the viewpoints of Quevedo and Pablos,
see B. W. Ife's introduction to his edition of the text, *La vida del buscón llamado Don Pablos*
(Oxford, 1977), 13–15.

[35] See 'Pablos' *Damnosa Heritas*', *RF* 82 (1970), 94–101; and 'A propos du *Buscón* et de
Guzmán de Alfarache', *BHisp.* 75 (1973), 114–31.

[36] *Défense et illustration*, p. 30.

[37] 'Moral Blindness in Quevedo's *El buscón*', *RR* 67 (1976), 50–9.

himself) the existence of a dominant and oppressive ideology to which the author merely gives voice. Quevedo's excessive political power (or rather that of his class) results in a correspondingly excessive language which (paradoxically) through the very flagrancy of its own presence betrays the absence of that which it represses, the persistence of social or material deficiencies which are unsaid or indeed unsayable.[38]

As in the case of the *Guzmán*, it is perhaps Edmond Cros who gives the most sophisticated analysis.[39] For Cros the ideological 'frame' ('cadre') of the *Buscón* is an element we have already seen in the 'rey de gallos' episode, the carnivalesque: the conventional discursive space within which social value is at once asserted and inverted. The unusual prominence of Quevedo's language discloses the necessary 'margin' of literary discourse, as his attention to a subordinate class reveals the essential yet marginal status of his character. The peripheral becomes central (and vice versa), in the extended yet ironic treatment of a socially insignificant milieu. In the final analysis, however, the *Buscón* remains imprisoned in its historical circumstance, the production of a single class at a particular moment of its history. More recently Anthony N. Zahareas has suggested (1984) that the inconsistencies of the *Buscón* both enable the reader to dismantle or historicize the ideology which speaks through them and promote a 'subtle integration' of form, which denotes a coherent intention on the part of the author.[40]

Yet if narrative inconsistencies are no longer taken as increasing the psychological 'interest' of a rounded character, how might they be seen? One answer may be developed from hints in Spitzer's classic essay of 1927.[41] Quevedo's narration is contradictory because Pablos is both active and passive, both subject and subjected. And this reflexive relation is also that of the individual to society and of the reader to the text. Pablos is

---

[38] 'The Conflict between Author and Protagonist in Quevedo's *Buscón*', *JHP* 2 (1977), 45–60.

[39] *L'Aristocrate et le carnaval des gueux: Étude sur le 'Buscón' de Quevedo* (Montpellier, 1975), see pp. 45, 53, 58, 105, and 118.

[40] 'The Historical Function of Art and Morality in Quevedo's *Buscón*', *BHS* 61 (1984), 432–43 (p. 442).

[41] Sobre el arte de Quevedo en el *Buscón*', in *Francisco de Quevedo: El escritor y la crítica*, ed. Gonzalo Sobejano (Madrid, 1978), 123–84. For a defence of psychological interest see Ife, p. 29.

subdued by his adventures, as is the reader by Quevedo's inexorable invention; but he is not so much puppet as puppeteer, interrupting and recommencing the narrative apparently at will. Quevedo thus reproduces in his text both the oppression of individuals by social constraints and their illusory freedom of action within those constraints. And he does so (inadvertently) by precluding the reader's identification with his character, by presenting us with an excessive and superfluous fictional 'world' which refuses to pass as 'lived' experience.

I would go further. If the constant humbling of Pablos and the oppressiveness of Quevedo's narrative demonstrate a fixed position to which the author's class and politics confine him, then the extreme volatility of Quevedo's language and his evident inability clearly to distinguish between his own voice and that of his character reveal no less decisively (if unintentionally) that both writing and society are more mobile and less constrictive than linguistic and social oppressors might suppose. Quevedo's obsessive puns and metaphors are not (or not merely) examples of a gratuitous linguistic aestheticism. They also testify to the inherent libertarian tendency of writing, which exceeds the conscious aims of the author, however tyrannical he may be. Hence the apparent paradox that the *Buscón* promotes freedom through excessive restraint. Gonzalo Díaz-Migoyo ends his study by comparing the *Buscón* to Velázquez's *Meninas* (p. 166). The latter, he implies, is an open or libertarian work within which the spectators may 'freely' adopt their own favoured position. Quevedo's supposed 'pictorial' qualities have led critics to produce many such analogues.[42] Yet I would suggest that what the *Meninas* offers is a masterful depiction of the illusionistic space proper to 'classical' representation; and that for all its novelty, it imposes a single perspective or subject position which the viewer must inevitably adopt. It thus hints at the rise of bourgeois individuals distracted from their subjection by an increasingly sophisticated (yet increasingly illusory) sense of liberty.[43] The *Buscón*, I would argue, allows no such flattering and familiar consolation. It denies the

[42] See e.g. James Iffland's study of the 'portrait' and 'anatomy' in *Quevedo and the Grotesque*, i (London, 1978), 71–111, 134–74.

[43] My interpretation of the *Meninas* follows Foucault's in *Les Mots et les choses* (Paris, 1966), 31.

equation of subject and object (we cannot recognize ourselves or our lives in Quevedo's world) and collapses illusionistic space (at the very moment at which its potential is being explored by other writers and artists). Quevedo oppresses the reader as he does the character with his relentless and obsessive discipline.

Why then does the *Buscón* seem to give up so easily the conditions of its production, where other works do not? Because in its overt oppression and surveillance of reader and character (far more emphatic than in *Lazarillo* or *Guzmán*) it reproduces the social relations of feudalism in an age of incipient capitalism. We have seen in *Lazarillo* an internalization of censorship (Lázaro is watched by characters within the fiction, not by the author), linked to a nascent psychological interiority which will become fully developed in bourgeois realism. The *Buscón* harks back to an already outdated period of naked oppression by the ruling class, and to a literature concerned more with the perpetuation of external hierarchy than with the exploration of internal consciousness. The hidden contradiction of the *Buscón* is that the literary practice it employs fails to coincide with the social practice it claims none the less to represent. It looks not forward to the novel, but backward to the allegorical fantasy, and thus testifies through its very conservatism to a truth with radical implications: the historicity of fiction and of politics. Quevedo's 'failure' to achieve the realist mode discloses the historical and literary preconceptions inherent yet invisible in realism itself.

I suggested in my analysis of *Lazarillo* that the imaginary relations by which the child is constituted are reproduced in the relations of the individual to society. This application of psychoanalysis to politics derives from a well-known essay by Althusser, reprinted in *Lenin and Philosophy* (pp. 127–86). If we look more closely at this essay, it points to a more subtle understanding of both politics and history than has been offered by critics of the *Buscón*. Althusser is concerned with ideology, a term as elusive and contradictory in his usage as parergon, imaginary, or panopticon in other theorists. Like the other terms, ideology is situated at the edge or margin of human thought: the question of whether Althusser can claim scientific objectivity for his critique of social relations is one he poses himself. He begins, typically, by admitting that it may be impossible to raise one's point of view to the level not of production (the making of commodities), but of reproduction (the production of the conditions under which commodities are produced) (p. 128). However, it is at this level of reproduction that ideology operates (p. 133). The use of the term 'level' is quite deliberate. As Althusser is quick to point out, the traditional model of social process offered by Marxism is topographic in character: the infrastructure of the material base supports the superstructure of culture, including ideology (p. 135). For Althusser the advantages of this traditional model are that it suggests the relative autonomy of culture from production (ideology relies on the base, but is separate from it); and the reciprocal action of the two (each affects the operation of the other). The disadvantage of the model is that it remains metaphorical, merely descriptive. Here Althusser suggests the possibility of a neutral, non-figurative language which later aspects of his theory would tend to contradict. Althusser's new theory of the state calls attention not to the overt tyranny of the Repressive State Apparatuses (the army, prisons), but to the more subtle action of the Ideological State Apparatuses (the Church, education) (pp. 142–5). The latter institutions serve to reproduce the relations of production (that is, the conditions under which production is possible). In feudal society the Church was the dominant ISA, serving to inculcate those values of piety and obedience required by society of its subjects; in modern society, education has taken over the same role (pp. 152–2).

So far Althusser's argument is almost empiricist in method. With the introduction of a new definition of ideology, however, the tone changes. For Althusser, ideology can no longer be understood as a system of ideas dominant in a social group at a particular time (p. 158). On the contrary he claims that ideology has no history (although this does not mean that there is no history in it). This somewhat elusive distinction is followed up by the definition of ideology as 'a "representation" of the imaginary relationships of individuals to their real conditions of existence' (p. 162). Hence, ideology is not so much illusion as allusion: it points to historical circumstance but does not correspond to it (p. 167). Just as in Lacan there is no simple opposition between imaginary and real, so in Althusser there is no simple opposition between ideology and history. And, as in Lacan once more, one condition of the imaginary (of ideology) is that there is no space 'outside' it: both the writer and the reader of Althusser's essay live 'naturally' within ideology, even when they attempt to resist the dominant order (p. 171). But how does this global ideology operate? Like the imaginary once more, it retains its position through the other. Our existence as subjects is purely relational: if a friend asks 'Who's there?', we are bound to reply 'It's me'; and if a policeman calls out 'Hey, you there!' we always know it is us he is addressing (pp. 172–4). Like the unborn child who will be thrust into a particular family and forced to bear the father's name, we are always-already subjects, never innocent of ideology (p. 176). Through more subtle forms of address ideology fosters specular illusions, imaginary identifications whose role is to 'tell' us that we are the centre of the world: for example, the Holy Family of Christ is reflected in the sanctity granted the bourgeois family (and vice versa) (p. 180).

How might this theory underwrite a political reading of the *Buscón*? First, it suggests we should attempt to raise our 'point of view' to the level of reproduction, not production. We should ask not 'How does the text reflect reality?' but 'What conditions enabled such a text to be produced?' If we seek evidence of historical process in the work we should look not at the objects Quevedo represents but at the very texture of his writing. The old model which assigns ideology to superstructure is not very helpful here: it tells us there is no immediate connection between writing and history but gives no help in analysing the mediations it claims to have identified. The distinction between R S A and I S A is more fruitful: the *Buscón* is repressive in so far as it serves as a blatant instrument of the aristocratic class to which Quevedo himself belongs; it is ideological in so far as it subtly reconciles its readers to the 'naturalness' of social relations in general. Thus when Quevedo has the upstart Pablos mutilated by the aristocrat Don Diego's henchmen, he 'repressively' reaffirms the traditional definition of ideology as a fixed system of belief belonging to a particular historical class. But when he lends Don Diego a surname known to be common to *conversos* in Segovia he more subtly reconfirms the social hierarchy by flattering the reader's unmerited sense of self-importance. Quevedo thus sets up his highly coloured narrative against an apparently neutral 'ground' which is in fact composed itself of unexamined differences (men and women; rich and poor; Christian and Jew) whose appeal is all the more convincing because it is unstated. Hence for Quevedo and the contemporary reader ideology has no history: the state of affairs he describes is eternal and natural. But for those modern critics who repress Quevedo's ideological load and offer 'psychological' readings of the *Buscón*, ideology has no history in it: they, as modern readers, claim immediate access to an unchanging human nature. Of course, this is not to say that Quevedo's 'vision' is simply false or unreal: it points to the same historical circumstances that it fails so conspicuously to reproduce. It is not illusion, but allusion. Thus Quevedo's fantastic depiction of poverty and hunger reproduces both the real squalor of material conditions in the period and the ideological attitude through which the aristocracy saw them. Indeed, it implies that there is an intimate connection between the two. Even within the fiction Quevedo suggests that there is nothing 'outside' ideology: Pablos's attempts to resist a dominant order (unlike our own) are not even dignified with the appearance of autonomous action; they are inevitably doomed to failure.

Pablos, like the subject of ideology, is always constituted by address: like the other *pícaros*, his discourse is one of confession elicited by an absent master. The unstated question which provokes the narrative is 'Who do you think you are?'; and Pablos is compelled to answer, even when (as so often happens) he ends up incriminating himself. Burdened with a spectacularly degraded genealogy, Pablos serves as an excessive, parodic example of the alienating imposition of identity suffered by all individuals. The world which centres on him is a mirror image of the celestial one, an Unholy Family which focuses all its venality on its offspring. But, once again, the process is reflexive. For we are also constituted as subjects by Pablos's own address, and as equally immoral subjects. The *Buscón* assumes an implied readership as brutal and prejudiced as the characters represented within it. And it also offers the more subtle flattery implicit in any depiction of low life: the suggestion that we (the author, the reader) are outside or above the milieu in which we take such vicarious pleasure. This, then, is the final significance of the picaresque's most enduring innovation, the first-person voice which addresses the reader. As specular image of ourselves, it invites us to take up a position outside the frame, assume the imaginary fantasm, adopt the position of power. It is not easy to accept that invitation while retaining a certain measure of disengagement. It is the work initiated (the position occupied) by the parergon.

5. PICARESQUE AND PARERGON

Critics have often tried to define the picaresque genre by listing the formal characteristics considered essential to it; the corrupted innocence of the hero; the autobiographical viewpoint; the 'low' milieu presented in comic style.[44] However, there is now widespread unease at such attempts. They appear both reductive and proscriptive. Reductive in that they 'level down' a variety of works to meet a unitary standard derived from one work alone (generally either *Lazarillo* or the *Guzmán*); proscriptive, in that they forbid analysis of works and characteristics which fail to conform to this abstract, founding type. The *Buscón*, rarely taken as 'typical' of the genre, has suffered particularly from such preconceptions.

Other critics have sought the source or origin of picaresque: in social tensions associated with the *conversos*, in a new moralism fostered by the Counter-Reformation, in the resentment of a bourgeoisie repressed by the dominant aristocracy.[45] But whether the 'origin' is located in race, religion, or class, the model remains unreflectively positivist and mechanistic. Social circumstance does not 'produce' writing in any direct sense. The very variety and proliferation of picaresque texts (which can only be hinted at in this piece) is proof enough of this perhaps unpalatable fact. If a moment in history can be characterized by unitary movements of this kind (and this itself is by no

---

[44] Recent general treatments of picaresque include Harry Sieber, *The Picaresque* (London, 1977); Richard Bjornson, *The Picaresque Hero in European Fiction* (Madison, 1977); Peter N. Dunn, *The Spanish Picaresque Novel* (Boston, 1979). See also Dunn's 'Problems for a Model of the Picaresque and the Case of Quevedo's *Buscón*', *BHS* 59 (1982), 95–105.

[45] These theses derive respectively from Castro, Parker, and Molho.

means self-evident) then writing is manifestly multiple, not conterminous with, but relatively autonomous from, the social practices within which it finds its meaning.

The most recent general study proposes a new genesis for the picaresque. According to B. W. Ife, the genre can be read as a response to the attacks on fiction made by contemporary Platonists.[46] The three major picaresque texts 'break the illusion' of narrative and representational coherence and thus enlist the rigorous pleasures of an active, disabused reading in an attempt to disclose the enervating rapture of a passive absorption in the text. We are at once involved by the picaresque's first-person narrative and distanced by the wilful inconsistency and unreliability of its perspective. This is a welcome advance on Rico's stress on the necessarily unified and 'organic' status of the 'point of view'. As Ife concludes: '[The reader's] natural engagement with the text ... is countered by the equal and opposite sense of disengagement that comes with a recognition that he has, as a reader, been made to work hard at his reading, to interpret difficult and conflicting evidence, to judge complex issues and ultimately to submit himself to judgement.' (p. 173.)

This is an original and suggestive thesis. However, it raises certain theoretical problems. For example, surely the reader's involvement and detachment cannot be simultaneous as Ife suggests (e.g. p. 127), but can at best be alternating? What is more, this (intermittent) alienation of the reader can have no fixed or permanent status. The denaturalizing 'frames' praised by Ife must begin at once to lose their potency through their very enshrinement in popular and prestigious texts. The history of any genre is composed of a dialectic between transgression and recuperation: the breaking of rules and their subsequent revision in the light of a changing practice. Finally, if Ife cites, like myself, such modern critical concepts as the distinction between 'énonciation' and 'énoncé' or the Lacanian 'mirror-stage' (p. 98) he is unwilling to accept the broader implications of linguistics or psychoanalysis. For Ife, as for earlier critics, the essential unity of the human subject (whether writer or reader) remains unquestionable. Indeed, implicit in his argument is the assumption that it is only by reference to this 'natural' unity

---

[46] *Reading and Fiction in Golden Age Spain* (Cambridge, 1985).

that the picaresque representation of disunity may be recognized. Hence, for Ife the act of reading, however complex it may be, cannot be freed from authorial intention and the possibility of an authentic experience of the world.

My own thesis is at once more simple and more complex. It is that the picaresque, more perhaps than any other genre, reveals the action of the parergon; that is, the element in any system which is at once essential and superfluous, dominant and subordinate, inside and outside the confines of relevance; and which (as I suggested in my Introduction) may be seen as analogous to the 'frame' which surrounds all representative space. Thus *Lazarillo* reveals the emergence of subjectivity (a 'sense of self') to be a reflexive process, neither the effect of the internal on the external (or vice versa), but a toing and froing (projection and internalization) which takes place on the margins of the body. *Guzmán* traces the reflexive relation between writer and reader, and its role in the constitution of a genre (the novel) which inverts the traditional textual hierarchies by moving marginal or liminary elements (apostrophe; parascholasticism) to a central and prominent position. And, finally, the *Buscón* asserts the subordinate place of the individual in society, yet discloses, by the very attention it pays to that individual and by the inconsistency with which he is represented, his necessary role in defining the society which excludes him. Only from his marginal position can Pablos reveal the centrality within the text of class conflicts repressed by the author himself.

If we follow the movement of the parergon, then traditional topics of critical controversy are shown to be undecidable by the very texts in which they are felt to be posed. To ask whether Lazarillo is sincerely deluded or cynically hypocritical is to assume the existence of a 'true' psychic unity immediately accessible in the fiction, and to ignore the history of alienation and misrecognition revealed by the narrative itself. To ask if the *moralités* of the *Guzmán* are superfluous or essential is to confine oneself to a proscriptive model of writing belied by the universal prolixity of Alemán's text. And to ask if the *Buscón* is a 'libro de burlas' or a moral tract is to presuppose a coherent intention undistorted by the ideological mediations in fact disclosed by the inconsistencies of Quevedo's technique. But if I suggest that such questions are properly unanswerable, this is not to imply that they should no longer be asked. Rather, that critics should be reflectively aware of the necessary limits to the 'empirical' analysis of literary space.

Hence, by saying that the picaresque is formed and framed by the parergon we do not explain the potency of the genre or resolve its plurality. The parergon is not the 'tension' or 'ambiguity' of the pictorialist critic, which finds a satisfying resolution in psychic or aesthetic unity. For it tends not to unify but to problematize subjectivity, writing, and politics: each has its origin in absence; each tends to subvert hierarchy or privilege; each blurs the confines of narrative relevance. The reader is left with not unity but difference: the difference between life and fiction, but also that between time past and time present. The 'framing' devices of picaresque, its authors' internalization and dramatization of the very conditions of narrative, alert us to the distance between the Renaissance and the twentieth century. This demystifying alienation highlights the volatility and subversiveness of the emergent novel as genre: its ambivalent position both inside and outside the prevailing ideology; the complex status of the objects it represents, both present and absent, known and unknowable. Such literate self-consciousness exposes the seductiveness of an illusionism which the Golden Age, with its deep mistrust of the mendaciousness of fiction, knew only too well. The fictional mirage tends to suspend thought and defer intuition until death. As in the emblem I cited before, pictorialist critics see their faces in the textual mirror, but are blind to the skeleton which supports the image. What is needed is a textual *desengaño*, a disciplined and liberating acknowledgement of the necessary confines of the fictional world.

But if picaresque makes us question the relation between fiction and 'reality', then it also leads us to examine the relative positions of 'primary' and 'secondary' literature, of creative writing and scholarship. We can no longer approach the picaresque with innocent eyes. Criticism has transformed not only the way we see the texts, but (through editorial work) the very substance of the texts themselves. To become aware of a rhetoric of representation in picaresque narrative (a set of specific, material relations inherent in it) is also to reflect on the nature of our own labour and to question its effect. The story is no longer 'about' us. But it may yield up the secret of how we came to see ourselves as we do.

As in the case of lyric poetry, the development I have traced in this chapter (from the *Lazarillo* to the *Guzmán* to the *Buscón*) is halting and compromised. And, once more, if we introduce a fourth work into the picture the 'line' is further disrupted. *La pícara Justina* (attributed to 'López de Ubeda') is a work not generally admitted to the picaresque canon, except as a subordinate or marginal work. Yet it shares many characteristics with its more famous rivals, even if those characteristics are somewhat exaggerated. It has an unusually cursory narrative, with the protagonist shifting rapidly and with little motivation from peasant, to pilgrim, to plaintiff. It offers the reader highly emphatic framing devices: each chapter begins with virtuoso rhymes in a variety of metres and ends with an often irrelevant 'aprovechamiento' or moral. It calls frequent attention to the act of writing, from the very beginning, when Justina makes a mock heroic address to the hair that is stuck to her quill pen and threatens to erase her words.[47] Finally, and more unusually, it calls into question the status of its own narrative: Marcel Bataillon believes it to be a *roman-à-clef* in which contemporary figures masquerade under more or less transparent disguises (*Pícaros y picaresca*, *passim*). The space of *La pícara Justina* is in between: neither pure fiction, nor historical document; neither illusion nor reality. It is this indeterminacy (the product of contradictions latent in other picaresque novels) which has proved so resistant to pictorialist 'resolution' and thus reconfirmed the marginality of the work. The distinction between the canonic picaresque novels and *La pícara Justina* is the same as that between Kant's twin examples of the aesthetic and the non-aesthetic to which I referred in the introduction to this chapter. The canonic texts are like a wild tulip: they seem to offer the reader a coherent organization of means which is, none the less, wholly arbitrary in character. The cut which severs them from the real leaves no trace behind it (or at least, no self-evident trace), and they may stand as pleasant examples of a natural process ('life' itself) to which, however, they reveal

---

[47] Barcelona, 1968 (p. 15).

no specific connection. *La pícara Justina*, on the other hand, is like the prehistoric axe which has lost its handle. It, too, is severed from the real whose purpose it serves, but in a way which calls attention to the lack which has deprived it of its function. As a *roman-à-clef* it gestures too plainly to its real function as a weapon in literary polemic, a function which it cannot serve today. The impurity of the cut which severs it from the real thus denies it the aesthetic value accorded the other works.

One contradiction absent in the canonic texts is that between the male author and female protagonist. Marcia L. Welles suggests that 'The lack of identification [between authorial and narrative voice] allows for a "gap" between enunciating "I's" that can result in the notorious irony of the *Lazarillo*. The innate duality of first-person narration is exaggerated to duplicity by the male impersonation of a female voice.'[48] The particular instance of a female narrator in *La pícara Justina* thus has a general significance for picaresque as genre. It opens the way for a feminist critique of subjectivity and representation, which is also relevant to the other novels we have seen in this chapter and the other theories we have used to interrogate them. For Luce Irigaray, any theory of the subject is always appropriated to the masculine (*Speculum*, pp. 165–82). The privilege of the (male) subject is based on his dominant perspective: he adopts the vertical position of the sun in relation to another (earth, matter) which is the mirror image of his own brilliance and potency (pp. 166–7). This sense of the Other (woman) is the guarantor of a universe always identical to the male subject. In his isolation, man takes up tools to explore the object beneath him, bending the other to the same model of representation by which he images himself, the flat, polished mirror of identification (p. 170). The female subject is thus at once unknowing and insensible (like matter) and a travesty or mimicry of man (like the mirror image) (pp. 172–4). Both same and other, she is 'framed' ('encadrée') even by the would-be libertarian structures of psychoanalysis (p. 175). Her only possibility of resistance lies in a radical disruption of language, which exploits the blanks, shifts, ellipses, and eclipses of patriarchal discourse (p. 176). Woman's sex is like the concave mirror of the specu-

---

[48] 'The *pícara*: Towards Female Autonomy, or the Vanity of Virtue', *RQ* 33 (1986), 63–70 (p. 64).

lum: it concentrates light to allow vision, but also produces the distorted reflections of anamorphosis (p. 179). Furthermore, the speculum need not be a mirror at all, but simply an instrument which opens up internal space for the gaze (p. 180). The final question, then, is whether any critique of male discourse ('despecularization') is possible, since that discourse, stretching back from Freud to Plato, offers the only model of representation to which we have access (p. 182).

The value of Irigaray's critique of vision is multiple. It is not simply another theory of representation, but is rather a challenge to all the theories to which I have referred in this chapter. Irigaray suggests at least three things: a new attention to the conventionality of representation (as male construct); a new valorization of discontinuity (as female strategy); a new suspicion of metalanguage (as phallomorphism). However, we cannot simply adopt the speculum as a more sophisticated model of representation than the (flat) mirrors of previous critics and theorists. For, in Irigaray's treatment of the motif, the curved glass sometimes serves to denaturalize patriarchy with its distorted images and at other times serves to investigate and thus subdue woman through its concentrated rays. Like Derrida's passe-partout, it is both a flexible frame and a penetrating instrument. This fluidity is typical of Irigaray's refusal to offer the reader 'useful' or 'functional' terms analogous to earlier critical concepts. Elsewhere she offers the female lips or labia as the exemplum of an imaginary which cannot be reduced to either unity (the phallus) or binarism (mirror and image).[49] She thus points to the possibility of a revised understanding of the plural perspective, different from that of the (male) relativists who fail to examine the process by which 'points of view' come into being.

But how does *Speculum* relate to *La pícara Justina* and to the picaresque genre as a whole? First it suggests a reading of the female characters in these novels. As we shall also see in the case of the comedia, women serve mainly as objects of exchange within a male system: Lázaro exchanges his wife for protection from the archpriest; Guzmán and Pablos swap one woman for another and (in spite of the former's marriage and the latter's

---

[49] See the title essay in *Ce sexe qui n'en est pas un* (Paris, 1977), 21–32.

final association with a prostitute) pay little attention to any single one of them. In *La pícara Justina* there are passages which are overtly feminist: for example, the maiden Teodora gives a vigorous defence of the pleasure women take in dancing (II. i. 1; p. 92). But such speeches are subverted by the reader's knowledge that it is the male author who 'speaks' through the woman's mouth. But Irigaray would suggest that this is not a special case, but the general condition of women who are always subject to the dominant, male perspective, always constrained to adopt a travesty of the feminine which is both the mirror image and the final guarantor of the male universe. Teodora (and Justina) remain 'framed' by an omnipresent phallomorphism. On the other hand, the curious shifts of López de Ubeda's language and the inexplicable ellipses of his narrative prevent his text passing for a polished, flat mirror, a simple imaging of the real. As a concave mirror, it serves both to shed light on woman's darkness (to explore her inner nature) and to offer the spectator anamorphic distortions of the world (to undermine our belief in external reality). Hence, from her marginal position on the fringes of psychoanalysis and philosophy, Irigaray points to the inadequacy of even those theorists (Lacan, Foucault) who are most sophisticated in their approach to the question of vision. And equally, from its marginal position on the fringes of the picaresque canon, *La pícara Justina* points to the inadequacy of even the most sophisticated models of the genre which fail to examine the problem of representation itself. And the relative lack of critical subtlety we have seen in the picaresque recurs in the case of the comedia, the genre which raises perhaps the most complex theoretical problems, but has elicited the most ingenuous criticism.

4

THE RHETORIC OF INSCRIPTION
IN THE COMEDIA

I. INSCRIPTION AND PRESCRIPTION

THE great Spanish dramatists are famed for their copiousness. Lope de Vega is known to have written at least 300 plays and Calderón some 120 comedias and seventy autos sacramentales. Any approach to Golden Age drama will at once be confronted by the sheer volume of material to be considered and the massive problems of attribution, composition, and performance which this material poses. However, as in the cases of lyric poetry and picaresque narrative, there is a received chronological trajectory in Golden Age drama which imposes a certain retrospective coherence on an unwieldy critical object. Thus scholars trace a movement from a relative simplicity to a relative complexity, even excess, of language and of thought. The canonic distinction is between Lope as a 'prodigy of nature' and Calderón as a 'prodigy of intellect'. A standard literary history still praises Lope's 'spontaneity and naturalness' which is followed by Tirso's 'subtlety of mind' and Calderón's more rigorous formalism and intellectualism.[1] No critic today would deny Lope's artistry or Calderón's ability to move the emotions of an audience. But the presupposition of a broad development in Golden Age drama from a spontaneous 'nature' to a self-conscious 'culture' remains fundamentally undisturbed.

Drama appears at first to resolve those theoretical problems we have seen in lyric and picaresque. Drama offers direct access to the visual and material presence of the human body sought in vain by readers of lyric. And in doing so, it appears to circumvent the excessive yet necessary 'frame' of verbal representation which is so problematic in picaresque. The dramatic body is not re-presented in language, but is simply 'there'. Yet

[1] Edward M. Wilson and Duncan Moir, *A Literary History of Spain: The Golden Age: Drama 1492–1700* (London, 1971), pp. 43, 89, 102.

this presence does not transcend the two contradictory relationships we have noted in lyric and picaresque: that between art and nature and that between the means and object of representation, respectively. Drama continues to call into question the integrity of the subject and the prestige of representation because the performer is at once equal to and greater than the presence of the body on stage. The actor, unlike the author, is present to the audience and material to their perception. But that presence is determined by a supplementary or surplus value which is itself immaterial: the actor's status as 'character' or fictional agent. Drama thus reproduces in the very conditions of its possibility the necessary excess common to writing as a whole.

What is more, the status of drama as institution is equally disconcerting. It is at once a potent medium of social regulation and a dangerously subversive threat to political stability. Classical and Renaissance attacks on the inauthenticity and immorality of theatre are well known. More important perhaps for a modern audience is the way in which Golden Age drama, more than most, displaces or undermines the twentieth-century bias towards writer as origin of the text. Plays are written by an author, performed by actors, and staged by a manager ('autor' in Golden Age Spanish). The confusion implied by this etymological slippage is reinforced by the historical circumstances of drama in the period, by the rapid turnover of plays and their frequent anonymity. Generally, there can be no possibility of access to an 'authentic' or 'primary' text, for any printed version of a comedia will be to some extent a palimpsest, bearing the trace of radical emendations at each stage of the dramatic process. And the primacy of audience in a popular drama such as the Spanish must also shift critical emphasis from source to target, or from production to consumption. It is hard to see the dramatist as the isolated genius of Romantic imagination. Indeed, the overtly communal nature of the dramatic text and process points in an unusually explicit manner to the communality of writing in general. Lyric and picaresque are equally (if less self-evidently) 'dialogic'. Hence, although I refer in shorthand to 'Lope', 'Tirso', and 'Calderón', the names denote not a historical subject and his individual utterance, but a body of text and its multiple determinants.

Golden Age staging is decidedly non-naturalist. The comedia was performed on a jutting, apron stage (with a balcony above), in daylight, and in the open air. The audience was heterogeneous and frequently restive. Much valuable research has been carried out on staging.[2] But it is curious how criticism tends to swing from the minutiae of dramatic performance (such as actors' wages and the cost of props) to the abstractions of a textual formalism, profoundly hostile to historical determination. This formalism has been exemplified by the 'British school' of criticism, led by A. A. Parker. The latter is the author of a brief, but highly influential, study, *The Approach to Spanish Drama of the Golden Age*.[3] The use of the definite article in the title here is no accident: Parker's schema is univocal and rigidly hierarchical. For Parker, character is subordinate to action, action to theme, and theme to moral purpose. The principle of unity so dear to the New Criticism (and so plainly lacking in the comedia's proliferating plots) is perceived at the 'deep' level of theme and associated with the operation of poetic justice. Parker's close attention to the 'words on the page' marks a necessary corrective to the loosely psychologist and historicist criticism which was previously dominant. But in its inexorable ascent from formal to moral excellence his approach serves merely (like his treatment of picaresque) to reaffirm without question the dogmas of both the New Criticism and the Counter-Reformation: hermetic aestheticism and orthodox Catholicism.

Parker's hierarchical vision has been under attack for some time now. Indeed a recent critic invokes the Marxian terms of production and consumption as a critical antidote to formalism and moralism.[4] Yet historical readings of the comedia have often been equally reductive, if not more so. Another recent metacritical study traces the development of a 'committed' socio-criticism under the aegis of Américo Castro and Noël Salomon, and attacks its proponents for the rigidity and dogmatism which others have seen in the British school.[5] While the

---

[2] The standard work remains N. D. Shergold's *A History of the Spanish Stage from Medieval Times until the End of the Seventeenth Century* (Oxford, 1967).

[3] First published in the Diamante pamphlet series (London, 1957).

[4] Walter Cohen, 'Calderón in England: A Social Theory of Production and Consumption', *BCom*. 35 (1983), 69–77.

[5] Charlotte Stern, 'Lope de Vega, Propagandist?', *BCom*. 34 (1982), 1–36.

New Critic floats the text free from its historical base and suffuses its aesthetic structure with a purely moral imperative, the vulgar Marxian snatches the text from from its cultural context and reduces a richly varied ideological process to a mechanistic propagandism. In my discussions of Lope and Calderón I shall return to these revisions of the socio-critical and formalist heritage. It is enough here to suggest that in their equal enthusiasm for moral exclusiveness and interpretative fixity both critical schools merit the name of 'prescription'.

Classical and Renaissance theory of drama, however, has no such confidence. Indeed, it tends to betray irreconcilable contradictions which may ultimately be derived from the curiously unstable status we have noted in the dramatic body itself. As George Kennedy has recently suggested, one main distinction between Aristotle's *Rhetoric* and his *Poetics* is that the former takes for granted the mastery of the orator and his success in enforcing his will on the audience; while the latter presupposes an intertext or series of mediations by which the dramatist's message is itself constituted.[6] A respected modern commentator on the *Poetics* shows that for Aristotle rhetoric disposes a person *towards* action, while drama re-presents the person *in* action.[7] The dramatic process is thus necessarily more oblique and deviant than the rhetorical.

One particular problem for Renaissance readers is Aristotle's proposal of two simultaneous and partially overlapping taxonomies of the dramatic poem: qualitative and quantitative. Thus, on the one hand, tragedy is composed of plot, character, diction, thought, spectacle, and song (and each of these qualitative parts is assigned to either the means, manner, or object of representation); and on the other, it is divided into various sections: prologue, episode, exode, and choral song. It seems at first that the qualitative classification is purely paradigmatic and the quantitative syntagmatic. That is, each of the former elements may occur at any given moment, while each of the latter must take its place in a fixed order or sequence. But 'song' is both a means of representation (qualitative or paradigmatic)

---

[6] 'Authorial Intent in the Aristotelian Tradition of Rhetoric and Poetics', an unpublished address to the Fifth Biennial Conference of the International Society for the History of Rhetoric (Oxford, 1985).

[7] William M. A. Grimaldi, *Studies in the Philosophy of Aristotle's Rhetoric* (Wiesbaden, 1972), 27, n. 17. I am indebted to Professor Rosalind J. Gabin for this reference.

and a division of the performative sequence (quantitative or syntagmatic). Likewise, plot ('mythos') would seem to encompass all the quantitative parts, but is confined to a single qualitative part, and assigned to the object (rather than the means) of representation. The two systems are incommensurate. Of course, the meanings of these terms have been argued over for centuries. What is important here is to note that even in the most lucid and prestigious of classifications there exists a certain confusion between dramatic structure (text) and dramatic performance (context).

As Weinberg has demonstrated for sixteenth-century Italy, the name of Aristotle and the ideas associated with him are invoked in dramatic theory to support both traditionalism and innovation.[8] Thus conservatives see Aristotle's 'nature' as a static, unchanging entity which justifies the perpetual validity of artistic forms; but progressives stress the variety and adaptability of nature as precedent for an understanding of literary genre as local and provisional. Likewise, the appeal to Aristotle's 'usage' may be understood in two mutually exclusive ways: as an adherence to eternal human values or an attachment to temporary social custom. The corpus of Horatian commentary is no less volatile. If pleasure and utility are the acknowledged ends of poetry, then the relative status of each is constantly changing. And if the role of the audience is dominant in determining the art, then that audience may be perceived as an undifferentiated, Aristotelian multitude or a cultured, Platonic élite. What is more, the central concept of Horatian poetics is decorum (Latin 'aptum'; Greek 'prepon'). In a recent study, Victoria Kahn has suggested that literary decorum and its ethical cognate prudence are essential to any study of Renaissance culture.[9] For although both theorists and moralists are undivided in their claims to recognize decorum or prudence in operation, they are equally united in their failure to provide an adequate theorization of these terms. The overwhelming attention paid to decorum thus decentres or displaces any facile opposition between theory and practice

---

[8] 'Aristotle becomes, simultaneously, the authority for traditionalism and the authority for change. . . . Nature, like Aristotle, serves both sides of the conflict. . . . As a result of this ambivalence, the terms in the debate will be constantly shifting.' (*History*, pp. 712–13.)

[9] *Rhetoric, Prudence, and Skepticism in the Renaissance* (Ithaca, 1985).

(idealism and pragmatism). The 'aptum' offers itself as an infinite number of possible options available to individuals, in so far as they are capable of aesthetic or moral choice. Hence if, as we shall see, an appeal to shifting conceptions of nature and usage is frequent in dramatic preceptiva of the Golden Age, then the presence of a dynamic principle of decorum (or 'discreción') is equally pervasive in the action and characterization of the Spanish comedia.

Ironically, then, the ethico-aesthetic term 'decorum' may serve in part to replace the Parkerian schema which also aspires to both moral and formal authority, but tends to erase the ideological assumptions on which its duality is based. In the subtle indeterminacy of its terms 'preceptiva' transcends modern 'prescription'. Yet, to confine an interpretation to critical concepts contemporary with or previous to the text in question is to promote a false historicism whose logical result must be the mere reduplication of the critical object. One modern concept as mobile and flexible as Renaissance decorum is what I shall call 'inscription' (broadly corresponding to the French 'écriture'). In three influential texts Derrida has suggested that writing itself is a privileged metaphor which precedes the 'authentic', oral utterance to which it is commonly thought to be subservient.[10] First, the anthropological texts of Lévi-Strauss explicitly mourn the passing of an Edenic orality in 'primitive' societies, which is lost on the introduction of writing. Yet in the complex systems of names, clothing, and kinship described by Lévi-Strauss in these oral societies, Derrida discerns an alienating social inscription always already in place and prior to any knowledge of the written word. Second, the autobiographical works of Jean-Jacques Rousseau manifest an overt preference for the 'natural' presence of the speaking voice and a disdain for the 'dangerous supplement' of writing, predicated as it is on absence and difference. Yet Rousseau states himself how the presence of the beloved renders his own discursive or sexual performance impossible. Only in writing and masturbation does he experience that subjective integrity which he attributes

---

[10] The three texts are 'La Violence de la lettre: De Lévi-Strauss à Rousseau', and '"Ce dangereux supplément"', both in *De la grammatologie* (Paris, 1967), 149–202 and 203–34; and 'Freud et la scène de l'écriture', in *L'Écriture et la différence* (Paris, 1967), 293–34.

none the less to oral communication and sexual consummation. Finally, and most importantly, Derrida treats a text by Freud in which the memory of the unconscious is compared to the 'magic writing-pad' still familiar to children today. Past inscriptions remain invisible to the naked eye, yet leave an enduring impression on one 'sheet' of the pad. In the same way, events lost to conscious memory remain present yet immaterial in the unconscious. Thus, for Derrida, psychoanalysis (which proclaims itself 'the talking cure') is profoundly compromised by psychic inscription. The magic writing-pad is not simply a metaphor; it points to an originary role for 'writing' (in Derrida's extended sense) in the constitution of the human subject. Thus inscription is endemic at the levels of communal practice (Lévi-Strauss), intersubjective relations (Rousseau), and intrasubjective experience (Freud). The difference and alienation of writing are implicit in all spheres which are accessible to our perception, that is, which are human.

The main term associated with inscription in the essay on Freud is the 'trace'. The trace is both motion and residue: the act of making one's way ('se frayer un chemin') and the trail left behind ('frayage'). The action of the trace is devious. The pen leaves a remainder on that 'sheet' of the magic pad which it has not touched directly. And the remainder, once erased, retains a ghostly presence. We might add that the English 'writing' in its common sense refers both to the act of tracing characters and to the residue of characters left behind when the pen has moved on. It may seem perverse to use the scriptural motif of the trace for the treatment of the supposedly oral medium of drama. Yet the trace may be related to both individual performance and theatre in general as each is perceived in time. Actors are material bodies, but they are inscribed only in the memory of the spectator; and theatre is the communal or social art-form, but its cultural presence is above all in the moment of performance. The experience of watching a play is one of continuing and simultaneous inscription and erasure as character and action 'write' on the spectator's memory. And the experience of 'following' theatre as an institution is of a sequence of dramatic events in which each performance of the same or a different work displaces but does not entirely erase the memory of those which preceded it. It is this inscriptional

quality which invalidates prescriptive formalism and problematizes the relation of text to perception, and institution to
history. But inscription also provides a theoretical basis
through which the empirical fact of performance may be incor-
porated, at a suitably generalized level, into a conceptual
model of dramatic fiction. Indeed, the magic writing-pad is
associated by Freud himself with the theatre. The unconscious
is 'ein anderer Schauplatz', rendered by Derrida (and Lacan in
his frequent references to this passage) as 'une autre scène'.

At times Golden Age 'preceptistas' use the word 'traza' in
their definitions of drama. Thus Carlos Boyl states in a text
published in 1616: 'La comedia es una traza / que, desde que se
comienza, / hasta el fin, todo es amores, / todo gusto, todo
fiestas'.[11] The modern editor warns us that here 'traza' is
equivalent to 'maraña' (the complex interweaving of the plot).
In modern Spanish the word more commonly refers to a 'plan'
(that is, either a map or a project). Yet, like the English and
French 'trace', the Spanish 'traza' derives ultimately from the
vulgar Latin 'tractiare', 'to drag'. It is the path left by a body as
it makes its way through space and time. My aim in this
chapter is to plot this movement in a single play by each of the
three major dramatists of the period (Lope, Tirso, and Calderón); and to relate the plays to three major areas of critical
interest (nature, desire, and honour). These areas correspond
respectively to the social, psychological, and cultural spheres of
inscription. The conclusion will deal with two perennial questions for critics: the definition of the comedia and the relation of
the comedia to history. My discussion of the single plays will be
preceded in each case by the analysis of a passage of 'preceptiva' by the dramatists themselves. For it is the shuttling
between theory and practice which defines the space, or reproduces the movement, within which Golden Age drama
develops.

2. LOPE AND NATURE

Lope de Vega's *Arte nuevo de hacer comedias* (1609) is the best-

---

[11] Cited by Federico Sánchez Escribano and Alberto Porqueras Mayo in the intro.
to their *Preceptiva dramática española del renacimiento y del barroco* (Madrid, 1965), 24.

known work of preceptiva by a Golden Age dramatist.[12] It touches with a certain irony on the uneasy relation between Spanish dramatic theory and its European counterparts and is thus characteristic of its author in tone and of its period in substance. Lope claims to write without 'art': the very idea of an *ars poetica* is superfluous in a country such as Spain where all dramatic practice goes against the precepts (135). Yet if Spain is 'outside' any theoretical influence, Lope cites none the less Aristides and Cicero and refers the interested reader to the commentaries of Robortello (143). Lope's model of drama is pragmatic: it is determined by the (vulgar) audience. Yet, as we have seen, audience is a prime concern of Horatian poetics. And Lope's recommendations are couched in explicitly rhetorical language: the author seeks to persuade or dissuade the audience (251); and vital to this persuasion are the 'figuras retóricas', especially those based on duplication or uncertainty: 'repetición', 'anadiplosis', 'anáfora', 'adubitación' (313–17). Thus although Lope claims, no doubt humorously, that France and Italy will brand him as ignorant for yielding to the desires of his audience (366), his rhetorical bias is by no means incompatible with the mainstream of dramatic theory. Indeed, rhetoric (as art of persuasion) is inseparable from a pragmatic concern for audience. The supposed dichotomy between theory and practice (like that between Spain and Europe) is thus covertly deconstructed at the very moment of its overt proposition.

Lope's other main theme is decorum, again a traditional theme of Horatian poetics. Speech must be appropriate to character and verse to subject matter (269–312). In the polymetric comedia particular verse forms are to be used for particular purposes. The stress here is on efficacy once more. But the oscillation between the responsibilities of the dramatist (decorum) and the demands of the audience (rhetoricity) creates an aporia or radical uncertainty finally resolved by appeal to the empirical fact of performance: only by hearing a play can one gain true knowledge of the theatre (387–9). Any indecision is thus curtailed (provisionally at least) by an aggressive tautology (the comedia *is* itself), and by sheer

---

[12] My text comes from Sánchez Escribano and Porqueras Mayo's anthology, pp. 125–36. Numbers in brackets are line numbers in this text.

copiousness of invention: Lope claims to have written no less than 483 plays (369).

The single play I treat here is *Peribáñez y el comendador de Ocaña*, written around 1605–8 and first published in 1614.[13] Of course, this one play could hardly be 'representative' of Lope's massive œuvre. Indeed, as we have seen, multiplicity of invention is perhaps Lope's defining characteristic. However, *Peribáñez* would seem to be a test case for any 'inscriptional' reading of Lope. For, on the one hand, it is typical of those plays (thought most characteristic of Lope) in which the dichotomy between town and country (art and nature) is held to be essential to the dramatic structure. And on the other hand, it is thought to be one of Lope's most 'finished' or unified works, less hasty and inconsistent than many others. Thus it should prove particularly difficult in the case of *Peribáñez* to propose (as I will) that a 'natural' orality is preceded by a complex cultural inscription; and that the discontinuities of this inscription are revealed in the halting and asymmetrical progress of the dramatic trace. My reading thus addresses two preconceptions of Lope criticism: the primacy of nature as thematic origin, and of unity as aesthetic end.

The plot of *Peribáñez* is relatively simple. Indeed, it lacks almost entirely the comic sub-plot, radically different in tone from the main action, which is so characteristic of the comedia. The outline is as follows. Peribáñez, a rich farmer, has recently married the beautiful Casilda in the small town of Ocaña. The noble comendador, lord of Ocaña, conceives a passion for her, and attempts during Peribáñez's enforced absences in Toledo (the second of which is procured by the comendador himself) to seduce the virtuous wife. The suspicious Peribáñez returns, slays his rival, and gains pardon from the king for his action.

Here the dichotomy between town and country (culture and nature) seems at first to be clearly drawn. According to J. M. Ruano and J. E. Varey, the married couple at first live 'in direct communion with nature' (p. 16); Peribáñez's later decision to donate to a religious institution the rich hangings he had requested from the comendador is a rejection of 'external signs of status in favour of the solid virtues . . . expressed in the

---

[13] The edition I use is by J. M. Ruano and J. E. Varey (London, 1980).

opening scene of Act I' (p. 25); and the language of the comendador derives its imagery from literature 'rather than arising,
as with Peribáñez, from a close association with Nature' (p. 40).
Central to this system of binary oppositions is the contrast
between the peasant's rough cloak and the comendador's richly
embroidered equivalent, which features in the copla or traditional song which inspired the play as a whole and is cited within
it: 'Más quiero yo a Peribáñez / con su capa la pardilla / que al
Comendador de Ocaña / con la suya guarnecida' (1594–7).

The paradigm is easy to draw up. On the one (negative) side
we have town, vice, and literature; and on the other (positive)
side, country, virtue, and orality.[14] Yet the distinction is not
quite so simple. For example, in Peribáñez's wedding speech to
Casilda he compares his bride to the artificial products of husbandry: olives, fruit, oil, wine, and wheat (46–65); and she
compares him to the delights of rural society: the dances, songs,
and processions of popular festivals (86–110). One image for
her husband is the bull (112). And if the bull is an icon of
natural virility it is also a primary example of the artful exploitation of that same naturalness for vicarious and sophisticated pleasure. Psychologically biased critics will claim that
Casilda's catalogue of pleasures denotes merely the lack of a
maturity she will acquire later in the play. But it must be con-
ceded that from the very beginning of the play both husband
and wife speak both from and of a nature already overrun by
the cultural codes of agricultural labour and religious ritual.
Ocaña is the place of 'cultus' in the twin senses of the Latin
noun: the tilling of the soil and the worship of the deity. What is
more, when next husband and wife address each other at
length it is to give their respective versions of the ABC of matri-
monial virtues (408–87). Here the use of the alphabet to structure formal oration makes quite explicit the inevitable reliance
of a 'spontaneous' orality on the conventional inscriptions of an
original literacy. Hence, even before the dramatic action
proper begins, with the alienating intrusion of the perverted
noble, writing is shown to precede speech.

In contrast, the comendador begins his first lengthy speech
on Casilda with an appeal to the unharnessed natural forces of

---

[14] See Edward M. Wilson, 'Images et structure dans *Peribáñez*', *BHisp.* 51 (1949),
125–59.

the sun, dawn, and the snow-peaked mountains (524–7). And when he turns to the 'primary' culture of the peasant he identifies it quite explicitly with the (sexual) reaping and tilling of the woman's body by the male. Thus unmediated or untrammelled nature (the exorbitance of the comendador's passion) is a dangerous supplement to a peasant culture; but that culture itself is underwritten by an invisible economy of sexual exploitation (which will be rendered visible by the action of the play). The comendador claims he would be willing to exchange his 'golden knife' for Peribáñez's hoe and the whole of Ocaña (his patrimony) for Casilda's little house (552–5). This is only one of many occasions in the play in which we find asserted the reciprocity of the tokens of social status. Yet it reminds us that the island of peasant idyll (such as it is) is entirely surrounded by the ocean of noble influence; and that the town/country dichotomy is founded not on true 'opposites' in the logical sense, but on 'relatives': mutually defining or dialectical terms. The paradigm functions only as a cultural inscription always already in place; and the mutual dependence of town and country underlies both social practice and dramatic text.

Three areas of social inscription are prominent in *Peribáñez*: food, kinship, and clothing. Thus Casilda's description of the joys of married life (703–61) centres on the provision of suitably plain and wholesome food for her husband, the 'garlic and onions' of the peasant's table. Yet such food, however plain, is not of course neutral or natural. As contemporary sources reveal, it has a positive value as a supposed antidote to the 'alien' delights of Jewish or Arab cooking, or to the newfangled spices imported from the Orient.[15] Likewise Peribáñez refers frequently to the social position and 'purity' of blood which he shares with his wife and which thus serve to underwrite the propriety of their marriage. Their union is not natural but 'naturalized': it is a celebration of conventional practices and values which present themselves as inevitable and invariable. Inversely, the comendador's transgression of that code is offered as a particular exception whose disastrous consequences demonstrate the 'natural' prestige of Law. A historically specific code of kinship is thus endowed with 'universal' relevance

---

[15] For the cultural significance of these foodstuffs see Francisco de Quevedo, *Poesía original*, ed. José Manuel Blecua (Barcelona, 1974), no. 146.

through appeal to both positive and negative examples. The very names of the characters, signs imposed on them when they come into being, stress the existence of a signifying system which precedes them and over which they have no control. Peribáñez is the rock ('piedra') of natural, material presence; and Casilda, the house ('casa') of feminine domesticity. It does not matter that the characters deviate from the emblematic tags with which they are introduced. For they require a certain backdrop of conventional values in order to be visible at all. As in the oral societies studied by Lévi-Strauss, food, kinship, and onomastics are social determinants which form a primary inscription independent of the written word, but prior to the spoken.

But the cultural code dominant in *Peribáñez* is that of clothing. All critics have noted the precision and elaboration of this code which defines subjects according to their class, gender, profession, and marital status. Perhaps less obvious is the frequency with which such clothing or accoutrements are characterized by the superimposition of different levels, the interweaving of different strands, or the decorative addition of potentially superfluous items. Thus, if we consult Ruano and Varey's notes we find that one peasant woman has 'braids of silk or linen woven into a band and containing some silver or gold decoration' ('pasamanos', 670), while Casilda herself has a dress edged with braid ('vivos', 689). The comendador would offer a noble lady 'small jewels attached to small chains and pinned to a woman's dress' ('brincos', 808); and he has Casilda painted with 'a necklace made by stringing together smaller pieces of jewellery' ('sartas', 1027). Peribáñez has 'sargas' hanging on his walls ('coarse woollen cloths with religious scenes or landscapes printed on them', 865) and foolishly exchanges them for the comendador's tapestries threaded with gold. Finally, associated with Peribáñez after he becomes a knight are a lance with a gilded point ('jineta', 2224) and a sword with golden ornament (2883).

The problem posed by such motifs is at once socio-historical and representational. They point (as in the cases of food and kinship) to a minute system of difference which offers a pre-existent range or paradigm of options within which the social subject (character or dramatist) has a limited freedom of choice. What they call into question is their own essential substance or integrity. Most of the items are 'decorative' or superfluous. Yet, it is their very redundancy which makes them potent. Indeed, 'coverings' have an essential role in the plot: it is Peribáñez's concern for the lack of proper adornment necessary to decorate his own cart and the image of the local saint which causes him to visit the comendador and to be absent from his home. When designs are superimposed ('sargas') or when threads are interwoven ('pasamanos') the common distinction between ground and figure (essence and ornament) is wholly subverted. For the totality of social practice in the play is figured in these redundant ornamentalisms. The action takes place within the shifting yet inevitable confines of a necessary symbolic and performative excess. When Peribáñez refuses to ask the comendador for a hat for his wife, the latter asks him doubtfully '¿Es exceso?' (782). The question is emblematic of a radically unstable conception of propriety or decorum in which redundant circulation or ritual exchange makes up the very substance of communal experience.

The principal motif of this kind is of course the comendador's cloak, with its richly embroidered decoration. Yet, Peribáñez's rustic cape, though unembroidered, is nevertheless woven, and is indeed shot through with cultural signification. Its very absence of colour ('pardo' is a dark grey or brown) is not neutral but (once more) 'relative', in its unspoken opposition to the comendador's more ostentatious equivalent. We might compare the status of the copla in the midst of Lope's textual fabric. Previous critics have tended to state quite simply that the insertion of popular verse into the play leads to a sense of 'authentic atmosphere' in the work as a whole (see, for example, Ruano and Varey, p. 15). Yet this 'authentic', oral quotation can also be seen as a kind of graft superimposed on the body of the text (or even a parasite feeding off its host). For if the copla is chronologically previous to the written text, it is as much the effect or end of the play as it is its cause or origin. For we read each of the moments of the action (both before and after the citation) as links in a chain of causality leading forwards or backwards to it. The intrusion of the lyric into the dramatic and of the traditional into the contemporary tends to destabilize the representative coherence of the work as a whole. The very authenticity of the fragment (a genuine testimony to the heroic Middle Ages which the play seeks merely to represent) destabilizes the sophisticated, seventeenth-century drama which seeks to absorb it. An indefinite play of recursion is set up between host text and parasite.

More particularly, the oral fragment itself betrays a verbal redundancy in the words 'su capa la pardilla'. The definite article is unnecessary in both Golden Age and modern Spanish and the diminutive ending on the adjective is ostentatiously familiar. Thus oral authenticity is reified as linguistic perversion and popular archaism is defined by its deviance from a more neutral 'ground' of written text. At this compositional level also, nature is supplementary to culture. Moreover the very prominence of this quotation alerts the spectator to the possible mediation of those intertexts which (according to Aristotle) distinguish the art of the dramatist from that of the rhetor. And in the case of *Peribáñez*, the most notable and intrusive precedent is a written one, the chronicle of Juan II, a passage of which occurs in lightly versified form at the beginning of Act III (see Ruano and Varey, p. 15). Here the orality of drama relies on the literate authority of historical narrative. Even oral or traditional precedents draw attention to their own duplicity. For example, a Spanish proverb glimpsed by the editors beneath the surface of Lope's text states that 'a good cloak reveals more than it conceals' (see note to line 1507). While the overt meaning appears to be that dignity of rank draws attention to a man, the proverb provides a succinct definition of the intermittent play of presence and absence (discovery and dissimulation) provoked by a literate, citational text such as *Peribáñez*. The play is an artificial work, directed to (and elicited by) a sophisticated, urban public. Indeed, when adapted for a rural audience it was shorn of those ornamental subtleties, properly superfluous to the workings of the plot, which are thought by critics to embody the essence of Lope's supposedly spontaneous and natural art.[16]

But if nature and text are 'scriptural', then so are the characters themselves. A recent study by Peter W. Evans treats '*Peribáñez* and Ways of Looking at Golden Age Dramatic Char-

---

[16] José M. Ruano de la Haza, 'An Early Rehash of Lope's *Peribáñez*', *BCom.* 35 (1983), 5–29.

acters'.[17] Evans anticipates many of the points I have made here: that costumes and names can suggest the imposition of personal identity (p. 140); that the received image of rural idyll is already deflated by the commerce and cowardice of the peasantry as depicted in the play itself (p. 142). And he goes on to stress that, although there are inconsistencies in Peribáñez's language at different points in the play, his opening marriage speech to Casilda is already saturated with rhetorical ornament (p. 144). Evans seeks ultimately to suspend the binaries of form and content with regard to the play's structure, accident and essence with regard to its characters, and history and author with regard to its composition. However, his persistent faith in the original presence of the subject as both character and author leads him to smuggle back these dichotomies with a traditionally prescriptive bias. Thus names are conferred on individuals who are assumed by Evans to exist already; and the author 'plays' with ideologies by which he remains uncompromised (p. 148). Evans claims at the end of his piece that 'distance, not nearness, of vision lends clarity to understanding' (p. 151). But this seems to assume an ideal viewpoint outside textual and social inscription from which the Olympian author can direct the disinterested spectator.

My own thesis is that Peribáñez's career, in its discontinuities and contradictions, exemplifies the movement of the dramatic trace. Peribáñez's speech changes with his social status: fluently discursive as a humble farmer, he becomes gravely sententious when dubbed a knight. Indeed, he comments himself on this new-found gravity as he leaves for Toledo at the head of his troops (2394–5). On his final reversion to peasant, speech changes once more with clothes, and he adopts that aspirate peasant 'h' which is the redundant sign of a marked orality (3013). Peribáñez as character is made up of a sequence of such superimposed and partially erased impressions inscribed in the memory of the spectator and projected on or from the body of the actor. His role is contradictory because, like the trace, it is both a plurality of moments (action) and the impression left by those moments (residue). He has no 'essential' status, for as the plot quite clearly demonstrates, his career is underwritten by a

<hr/>

[17] *RR* 74 (1983), 136–51.

cultural inscription which anticipates and precludes any intrinsic nature. Thus he is not simply trapped in a web of social practices and discourses; he is actually constituted by those practices and discourses in all their multiplicity and incongruity. Lope leaves no space for either idealist or empiricist conceptions of character. And this multiple constitution (quite different to the New Critical 'ambiguity' found by others in Lope[18]) may be identified in its radical uncertainty with artistic decorum and ethical prudence. Lope thus has Peribáñez speak as is appropriate to his status at different points of the action, but it is that status which is properly undecidable from beginning to end.

However, this is not to say that Lope is 'outside' contemporary ideology. Charlotte Stern has claimed that Lope is not a propagandist because there is no reductive social engineering in his work, such as we might find in modern television drama. Other critics have claimed to glimpse a sympathy for oppressed minorities in Lope's mobile affections.[19] But if we take 'ideology' in its broad, Althusserian sense, then the contradictions of Lope's perspective are as much an ideological effect as the inconsistencies of the character created by him. Ideology need not be univocal. Indeed it may reproduce 'resistances' to the dominant order, which serve finally to enforce that order's prestige. Such is the case with Lope's peasant rebellions, always already inscribed within a flexible aristocratic ideology.

At a rather different level, Henry W. Sullivan has identified Calderón with the 'symbolic' sphere of socio-linguistic Law and alienation and Lope with the 'imaginary' realm of subjective identification.[20] This is also perhaps to impose a somewhat exclusive definition on psychoanalytic terms no less slippery than those of the structural Marxists. Indeed, Lacan himself (from whom Sullivan borrows these terms) insists repeatedly that it is the symbolic which takes precedence in the constitution of the subject. Hence, if *Peribáñez* demonstrates, in spite of itself, the

[18] See José M. Ruano, 'Malicia campesina y la ambigüedad esencial de *Peribáñez y el comendador de Ocaña* de Lope', *Hispanófila*, 84 (1985), 21–30.

[19] See Louise Fothergill-Payne, '*El caballero de Olmedo* y la razón de diferencia', *BCom*. 36 (1984), 111–4.

[20] In 'La razón de los altibajos en la reputación póstuma de Calderón', an unpublished paper delivered to the Congreso anglo-germano sobre Calderón (Cambridge, 1984).

primacy of culture over an absent or deficient nature, then it also suggests the primacy of the symbolic over the infantile dependence of the imaginary. Peribáñez's hoe is the signifier which hollows out the space in which the subject takes form. And similarly, the other phallic motifs which proliferate in the play (swords, knives, and sickles) prove, like the Lacanian phallus itself, to be empty markers of difference, not substantive totems of presence. Thus, when the comendador dubs Peribáñez a knight and buckles on his sword, the ritual denotes not addition but subtraction: the symbolic castration by which the subject submits to the cruelties of social and linguistic inscription.[21] Yet Sullivan's example has shown that the Lacanian model is well adapted for the intricacies of the Golden Age theatre. And it is to Lacan (amongst others) that I shall appeal in the reading of Tirso de Molina which follows.

3. TIRSO AND DESIRE

Tirso de Molina is often considered to occupy an intermediate position in Golden Age drama. For Ruth Lee Kennedy, the 'flowering' of Tirso's drama occurs in the 'soil' prepared for him by Lope de Vega.[22] And for A. K. G. Paterson, Tirso's theatre is 'a bridge that spans the early efforts of the comedia and its fuller development in the hands of Calderón.'[23] As Kennedy has demonstrated in her studies, the historical reality of Tirso's relations with both his predecessors and his successors is highly complex. However, even within received critical opinion there are elements which tend to disrupt the smoothly organic or functionalist models (garden or edifice) which are so often used to figure the development of drama in the Golden Age. Two elements in particular serve to displace or remove Tirso from a continuous historical progression: first, his female characters, more prominent and perhaps more sympathetically portrayed than in other dramatists; second, his association with a single character who transcends the boundaries of the

---

[21] The terms of this debate will become clearer when I return to them at greater length in the next section of this chapter.

[22] *Studies in Tirso*, i: *The Dramatist and His Competitors, 1620–6* (Chapel Hill, 1974), 152.

[23] Intro. to *La venganza de Tamar* (Cambridge, 1969), 5.

Spanish comedia, namely Don Juan. Lope and Calderón thus differ from Tirso in their representation of women and in their failure to produce a type of universal renown.

In his miscellanea *Los cigarrales de Toledo* (published 1621), Tirso touches on both the national and the international questions we have seen to be current in Spanish dramatic theory of the period: the problem of his own relationship to Lope and that of the comedia's relationship to Europe and the Classics.[24] Tirso denies Lope's repeated claims that the comedia defies classical precept solely because of the demands of a vulgar Spanish audience. On the contrary, Lope has created in the comedia a perfect artistic form: the master's modesty lies behind such excuses. Those writing after Lope need only appeal to his authority as the 'Cicero of Castile' to justify their own practice. The play thus becomes less the imitation of an action than the imitation of an author, and dramatic representation is founded on a textual authority which precedes and legitimizes the work in progress. This redefinition of imitation demands a corresponding shift in the dramatist's conception of nature. Tirso claims at first that nature is unchanging, while art or culture is constantly shifting: thus the pear-tree will continue to produce pears and the oak-tree acorns. Yet the diversity of nature is the product of human artifice: the great variety of gourds, marrows, and cucumbers all derive from a single vegetable ancestor. Or again, one fruit may be grafted with another to produce a third which is superior to both its parents. Tirso places the terms 'artificial' and 'natural' in quotation marks, and thus calls into question the permanence of their status. The first is inevitably volatile (we no longer wear the animal skins of the first men); but the second proliferates everywhere (the variety of plants and trees is infinite). In a similar way, the theatre must not be bound by prescriptive models of art or nature. Tirso's appeal to the traditional exempla of clothing and husbandry thus tends to obscure rather than 'illustrate' his explanation of dramatic practice. The two parameters of the comedia (art and nature) remain essential for critical debate, yet stubbornly resistant to definition.

The relationship between art, nature, and Tirso's *comedia*

---

[24] See the selections in Sánchez Escribano and Porqueras Mayo (pp. 182–7).

nueva has been examined in detail by David H. Darst. He claims
that drama is concerned not with the material products known
as 'natura naturata', but with the metaphysical teleology of
'natura naturans'.[25] But both views may be kept in play at the
same time if we turn once more to the dramatic 'trace'. For the
material product may be seen as the residue of nature, and the
metaphysical process as its movement. And this complex
'frayage' lies behind other well-known images by means of
which Tirso attempts to 'illustrate' his practice. Thus in *El vergonzoso en palacio*, a character claims (after Horace) that, as the
poet must feel the emotion he seeks to communicate, so the
actor must experience the passion he seeks to represent.[26] Yet
this image of the immediate expression of feeling is rendered
more complex in a passage from the dedication to the 'third
part' of Tirso's comedias, a text probably written by Tirso himself.[27] Here the writer is compared to a silkworm. He has spun
the webs of some four hundred plays from the substance of his
own body, without once borrowing material from others and
passing it off as his own. Once more, drama is associated with
the integrity of the individual's experience and language. Yet
while the process of 'spinning' does indeed bring the internal to
the surface it also serves to conceal (indeed to entomb) the
author-worm as he continues to work. The moving thread of
dramatic action becomes the frozen cocoon of printed text, a
deadly monument to its author. Tirso thus hints, unknowingly,
at that fatal stillness which the dramatic movement seeks to defer, and at the mortal knowledge of absence and difference
which precedes any act of writing.

The action of the play I treat here is also based on death. It is
the first major treatment in any language of the Don Juan
legend, *El burlador de Sevilla* (first published 1627–9).[28] This
play offers especially difficult problems of attribution and composition which I shall not summarize here. For the aim of my
reading is broader and somewhat novel. It is to suggest that the

[25] *The Comic Art of Tirso de Molina* (Chapel Hill, 1974), 13–15.
[26] Cited by Antonio Prieto in the intro. to his edn. of *El vergonzoso en palacio* and *El
condenado por desconfiado* (Barcelona, 1982), p. ix.
[27] See Berta Pallares's intro. to her edn. of *La huerta de Juan Fernández* (Madrid,
1982), 9.
[28] I refer to the eleventh edn. of Américo Castro's text (Madrid, 1980).

play reveals, albeit obliquely, that a psychic (and social) inscription underlies the experience and representation of sexual desire; and that the most 'natural' of human instincts, as embodied in the most famous of its icons, is preceded by an original linguistic trace, which may be identified with the unconscious. Many critics have applied self-proclaimed 'psychological' theories in their readings of *El burlador* and of Tirso in general. A subsidiary aim of my study is to examine this critical trend and to confront its loosely archetypal or ego-based models with the more rigorous revisions of Freud offered by Derrida and Lacan. Hence the desire I treat is exemplified by both the protagonist and the critics of *El burlador de Sevilla*.

Unlike in the case of *Peribáñez*, the versions we have of Tirso's play are hasty and unpolished in style. Indeed early critics such as C. V. Aubrun and María Rosa Lida de Malkiel attacked the work for its careless and scrappy construction.[29] As in the case of the picaresque novel, however, scholars with a New Critical bias have attempted to reduce the text to structural and linguistic uniformity. Thus Daniel Rogers claimed to discover a 'fearful symmetry' by which the final retribution performed by the statue refers back to the unavenged offences committed by Don Juan.[30] And in the same year that Rogers praised Tirso for his 'satisfying ending', C. B. Morris claimed that Tirso's 'purposeful' use of imagery made 'metaphor and action blend in close harmony'.[31] These unitary, prescriptive readings are justified to some extent by the broad movement of the plot as a whole, which might be seen as transcending the flagrant inconsistencies of detail found throughout the play. Thus Don Juan seduces (or attempts to seduce) four different women in four different places, with courtly and rural settings alternating. He tricks the noble Isabela in Naples and the fisherwoman Tisbea outside Tarragona; the high-born Ana in Seville and the rustic Aminta in a village on the road to Lebrija. The statue whom Don Juan invites to dinner (and who returns his invitation) is Don Gonzalo, father of Ana, whom Don Juan has killed after attempting to seduce his daughter. There remains, however, a

[29] See Charles V. Aubrun, 'Le Don Juan de Tirso de Molina: Essai d'interprétation', *BHisp.* 59 (1957), 26–61; and María Rosa Lida de Malkiel, 'Sobre la prioridad de ¿*Tan largo me lo fiáis?* Notas al *Isidro* y a *El burlador de Sevilla*', *HR* 30 (1962), 275–95.
[30] 'Fearful Symmetry: The Ending of *El burlador de Sevilla*', *BHS* 41 (1964), 141–59.
[31] 'Metaphor in *El burlador de Sevilla*', *RR* 55 (1964), 248–55.

dissonance in structure and tone between the catalogue of jokes or 'burlas' which form the body of the play's action and the supernatural wager with which it closes, two independent folk motifs which Tirso has brought together in his play. For Margaret Wilson the play exhibits none the less a 'natural progression without any disconcerting change of mood'.[32] But this is perhaps to 'discover' (like subsequent critics) a 'rationality' in the play which is in fact imposed by the critics themselves, projected on to a text which is overtly summary and discontinuous.[33]

Indeed, from the very beginning of the play, it is the rationality of both action and audience which is called into question. In the opening scene it is dark and Isabela, believing Don Juan to be her fiancé Octavio, is helping him to leave the palace where he has treacherously enjoyed her. As Joaquín Casalduero has suggested, this opening is highly implausible: surely Isabela could recognize the voice of her own fiancé? Casalduero claims that such questions are improper: we must take the fiction at face value.[34] However the fact that as readers or spectators we do not ask such questions reminds us that by Tirso's time the comedia was tracing its action on a complex background of dramatic inscription which made up the conventions of the genre. The opening of the play is thus 'dramatic' not only because it presupposes a body of preparatory action before the actors take the stage; but because it engages triggers of recognition which ensure an immediate and responsive reception by a relatively sophisticated or 'competent' audience. And if *El burlador* begins *in medias res*, it is because the dramatic process (like its amorous equivalent) has no representable source or origin. Play and protagonist are equally nomadic.

In this opening scene Don Juan defines himself as the undifferentiated male subject: he is 'a man with no name'. And his seduction of Isabela is quite simply the 'natural' conjunction of the two sexes. When asked who is there by the king he replies, 'A man and a woman' (1. 23). Likewise, later in the act when

[32] *Tirso de Molina* (Twayne World Authors Series, 445) (Boston, 1977), 110.

[33] See Alfonso López Quintás, 'Confrontación de la figura del hombre "burlador" (Tirso), el "estético" (Kierkegaard), el "absurdo" (Camus)', *Homenaje a Tirso* (Madrid, 1981), 337–80 (p. 380).

[34] See the intro. to his edn. (Madrid, 1982), 13–14.

the shipwrecked Don Juan regains consciousness and asks where he is, Tisbea replies teasingly, 'in the arms of a woman' (1.583). Such lines imply a universal simplicity of gender: woman and man are reduced to the 'essential' distinction of sexual difference. Yet the action of the play as a whole tends to decentre these essentialist binaries: Octavio claims that inconstancy is the essential condition of woman (1.358), but it is Don Juan not Isabela who has deceived him; and when the disabused Tisbea laments the treachery of men (III.408), the misogynist commonplace is reversed. And as in *Peribáñez* the country versus town dichotomy is also subject to a curious inversion. The courtly characters speak for the most part in an urgently rapid and pared-down language. The peasants, however, deliver finely wrought orations. As Tisbea enters she makes a lengthy and elegant speech on her scorn for those who love her; and she compares the struggling Don Juan and *gracioso* Catalinón to Anchises and Aeneas on the fall of Troy (1.375–516). Her lament on the departure of Don Juan is thick with such ornamental patterning as chiasmus: 'fuego, fuego, zagales, agua, agua' (1.1043). The rustic fiancés of Act II also speak a strangely *culto* language.

The wilful perversity of this lack of correlation between character and speech betrays the anti-naturalistic bias of Tirso's comedia and the volatility of his concept of decorum: Tisbea's language belies her social status as it asserts her improper desire to transcend that status. But Tirso also suggests more generally that desire itself is cultural rather than natural in character. As many critics have noted, unlike later Don Juans, Tirso's hero is motivated less by sexual than by social concerns. His defining characteristic ('hábito antiguo') is trickery, not seduction (1.892); and his greatest pleasure is not to enjoy but to deceive ('burlar') a woman (II.270). Indeed the object of this deception is almost indifferent, and the duping of male rivals is an essential part of this process. What is more, the trickery must be broadcast in public: 'burla de fama' (II.432). Thus, as Melveena McKendrick has noted, Don Juan's 'success' depends not on his own qualities but on those of others, in particular the weakness and stupidity of the women he happens to encounter.[35] Previous critics have taken this knowledge to be

[35] *Woman and Society in the Spanish Drama of the Golden Age* (Cambridge, 1974), 159.

local or specific to the play itself or to bear a general significance of an ethical order: Tirso is attacking the prevalence of
immorality in contemporary Spain. Yet the play's overwhelming stress on a social phenomenon (the 'burla'), highly characteristic of the time in which it was written but wholly divorced
from modern views of sexual passion, suggests a much more
radical truth: that all desire is underwritten by social inscription and no passion uncompromised by cultural and historical
determinants. Indeed, sexual desire is superfluous to the character's actions and author's plot: social esteem or disgrace are
the primary considerations of both men and women. Hence the
seductive immediacy of such phrases as 'a man and a woman',
with their implicit claim to universal, prescriptive truth, is
revealed as a pose or imposture, a naturalizing strategy by
which a particular social practice would enforce its own
ubiquity.

The idiosyncrasies of Don Juan's career call constant attention to the arbitrary, yet inescapable, confines of social inscription. Don Juan's habitual role is that of substitute: he takes the
place of Octavio in Isabela's bed and of Mota in Ana's home.
However, as they are yet to marry their respective fiancées,
each of the men displaced by Don Juan has as little right as the
trickster to venture where he goes. Don Juan does not simply
transgress a fixed social law. Rather it is the transgression of the
law already performed by others (Mota) or latent within them
(Isabela) which opens the space within which he may operate.
Likewise it is Tisbea's reprehensible scorn for a socially equal
partner which ensures her seduction by the socially superior
Don Juan: he both substitutes for the rustic suitor and improperly exceeds him in cunning and status. This 'supplementary' social position is most obvious in the case of Aminta, whom
Don Juan seduces on the night of her wedding to the peasant
Batricio. Here, as an uninvited guest at the festivities, Don Juan
is quite literally a 'para-site', in the original sense of the word.
He sits next to Aminta at the wedding feast, holding her hand
and taking food from the bridegroom. His presence is disruptive: it is considered improper that a noble take part in a
peasant's wedding (II. 735). And this parasite substitutes for the
host by performing the sexual function unattempted by the
bridegroom. He displaces the 'proper' partner as defined by the

social code; but ensures this displacement within the code itself by appeal to social (not sexual) potency: he promises to make Aminta his wife. Just as the play appeals implicitly to dramatic convention to further its effect (the audience's unconscious memory of past plays and performances), so the lover appeals quite openly to social inscription to facilitate his conquest (the woman's awareness of the relative value of low and high birth). By making his way through the gaps and along the margins of a social or 'socialized' desire Tirso's Don Juan makes us question the authenticity of both human affections and the individual's image of self. For if desire is bound up with cultural or linguistic determination then any theory of consciousness or of the affects which aspires to general significance must be highly circumspect in both character and application.

Unfortunately, 'psychological' criticism of Tirso, although extensive, tends to be rigorously prescriptive. Everett W. Hesse makes unusually explicit the preconceptions of Anglo-Saxon 'ego-psychology'. He claims that 'the choices the ego makes are multiple . . . in any mature delineation of a character there are numerous choices all struggling for the dominant position in a character's psyche.'[36] In this quote we find a typical bias towards voluntarism (the sovereign will of the ego makes 'choices'), evaluative organicism (one psyche is more 'mature' than another), and evolutionism ('choices' struggle for supremacy like beasts in the jungle). The purpose of fiction is purely instrumental, and subservient to the ego: 'If the primary function of art is to use symbolic manipulation to reconcile competing pressures, then this is a regression in the service of the ego' (p. xii). This theory leads in practice to speculative diagnoses of the characters which serve merely to reinforce the humanist faith in an 'essential' psychic nature: '[Don Juan's] refusal to acknowledge the indivisible oneness of his personality may be a part of his attempt to flee that aspect of it that fears the termination of his pleasure.'[37] Or again, 'Don Juan suffers from a fragmented personality' (p. 65). This love of unity and coherence and the tendency to move from description to prescription (from quality to value) link the ego-psychologists to the pictorialism and moralism of the New Critics. Hesse con-

[36] *New Perspectives on Comedia Criticism* (Potomac, 1980), p. xi.
[37] *Theology, Sex, and the Comedia* (Potomac, 1982), p. xv.

cludes that 'Tirso's play read thus implies a psychological dimension hitherto unexplored' (p. 69). But I would suggest that this dimension is not Hesse's eminently accessible vision of an 'opposing self', but the more disturbing notion of the Lacanian 'imaginary'. Tirso's arbitrary and summary characters deny psychologist critics the illusion of authentic plenitude they require from fiction. This representational gap or fissure elicits a pseudo-medical prescription from the critic which will restore unity to the character and peace of mind to the reader. It is the critic (not the character) who is 'unable to cope with his problem' (p. 69), and that problem is not a specific instance of fragmented personality, but the general condition of subjective discontinuity and alienation.

I have argued, then, that the plot and characterization of the play (each as sketchy and deficient as the other) depend for their effect on dramatic and social inscriptions always already in place which elicit a particular response from the audience which will itself, none the less, vary greatly from one historical moment to another. While ego-psychology rationalizes and indeed promotes this 'imaginary' contribution (both instrument and effect of the spectator's 'identification' with the character), psychoanalysis proper offers a technical vocabulary capable of examining that founding inscription while remaining within it. For this vocabulary is not a metatext, aspiring to the 'scientific' mastery of prescriptive psychologism. Rather, like the critical object itself, it is linguistic or grammatological in character. We have seen that Freud compares the unconscious to the residue of graphic traces on the magic writing-pad. There can be no doubt that any response to Tirso's Don Juan is profoundly compromised by unconscious memories of similar tricksters both before and after him. But, at a deeper level, the Lacanian theory of desire and subjectivity corresponds at a number of points to the career of Don Juan as represented by Tirso: in its linguistic constitution, arbitrary social determination, and complicity with death, castration, and Law. I shall take each of these rather complex questions in turn.[38]

---

[38] I have referred to the following essays in *Écrits*, i (Paris, 1966): 'Le Stade du miroir comme formateur de la fonction du Je' (pp. 89–97); 'Fonction et champ de la parole et du langage en psychanalyse' (pp. 111–208); 'L'Instance de la lettre dans l'inconscient ou la raison depuis Freud' (pp. 249–89).

For Lacan, famously, the unconscious is structured like a language. And that language is based, in Saussurian style, on both the 'horizontal' progression of metonym or syntagm and the 'vertical' associations of metaphor or paradigm. Lacan maps this distinction (somewhat irregularly perhaps) on to the equally basic principles of Freud's dreamwork: substitution and condensation, respectively. For Lacan, substitution is metonymic or syntagmatic in its continuous displacement of one term by another; and condensation is metaphoric or paradigmatic in its fusing together of alternative terms which exist at a single moment. Where the metonymic chain is arrested, we find the fetish: the frozen instant of desire 'caught' on a random object. When the metaphoric function is confounded, we find the symptom: the alogical testimony to psychic disruption as it registers in the body. This linguistic model has at least two major implications. First, desire (like language) is arbitrary or conventional in the Saussurian sense. Lacan's favourite example of language as signifying inscription is not a picture of a tree with the word 'tree' printed above it, but a picture of two identical doors with the words 'ladies' and 'gentlemen' printed above them ('L'Instance de la lettre', p. 256). The arbitrary relation between sign and referent is thus traced back to gender as original (that is, linguistically constituted) difference. Second, desire is not (as the ego-psychologists believe) 'hydraulic', seeking to relieve libidinous 'pressure' in the service of 'mature' equilibrium. For the movement of desire is always already inscribed within the shifting webs of linguistic structure. The Lacanian model is thus hostile to prescription. Indeed, it is the role of neither critic nor analyst to 'restore' a unified, affective ego to the human subject (character or patient), for that original source of thought and mastery is itself a pernicious illusion.

In Lacanian terms, *El burlador de Sevilla* is the drama of metonymy. As we have seen, Don Juan serves himself as the 'substitute', endlessly displaced from one woman to another. His career, as presented in the play, has no beginning and ends only in death. Like the signifying function of language it is properly interminable. This displacement is structured only by the primary difference of gender: the subject is male and the objects female. Yet the arbitrary status of this paradigm is self-evident: desire corresponds to no essence inherent in the very disparate female characters and satisfaction offers no relief to the exorbitant passions of the male lover. Indeed, as we have seen, the victims of the 'burlas' are both male and female. As Lacan suggests, the very gender of the object may be indifferent in the process of subjective constitution and gratification ('Le Stade du miroir', p. 92). Desire is thus both arbitrary and insatiable; and subject and object are equally lacking in psychic integration. Critics such as Margaret Wilson have stressed the spectator's lack of 'sympathy' for the characters (p. 123). And this acedia may be related to their status as conventional markers of social, sexual, and linguistic difference.

In a similar vein, Joaquín Casalduero remarks on Don Juan's 'sterility' which he derives from the character's lack of continuity and dependence on the instant (p. 25). However, this by no means conflicts with my own view of the play as one of ceaseless metonymic substitution. For at certain moments the signifying chain is frozen into fetish. The most obvious example is that of the hands: Catalinón wishes to kiss the icy hands of Tisbea (i. 564), and Don Juan desires the white hands of Aminta (ii. 743). The burning hand of Don Gonzalo pulls him down to Hell (iii. 948). The repetition of this detail takes on a peculiar prominence amid the extraordinarily rapid movement of the action as a whole. The leitmotif of the hands is cited by Morris as proof of the 'fusion' of metaphor and action in the play (p. 253). Yet if desire itself is linguistically constituted, then the distinction between language and plot (metaphor and action) is no longer tenable: for both are underwritten by the structures of psychic inscription. The subject of the fetish is dispersed: both Don Juan and Catalinón share a weakness for white hands. Hence the psycho-linguistic operation is communal rather than individual in character. But if we take the motifs and figurative language in the play as metonymy rather than metaphor then the conventionality of Tirso's diction and characterization need no longer prove an embarrassment to critics. Morris claims that 'Tirso does not let the metaphors he chooses ... stiffen into lifelessness, but makes them supple and suggestive, giving them a point and purpose' (p. 255). But it is precisely the strategic mastery of the ego over language which is called into question by both the action of the

play and the implications of psychoanalysis. Tirso no more con-
trols his own destiny than does Don Juan. Each is caught in the
linguistic web. Indeed, it is the petrification of language when
desire is arrested which is dramatized in both Don Juan's
encounter with the statue and Tirso's confrontation with traditional literary commonplaces.

We may go further. The somewhat rigorous pleasure offered
by *El burlador de Sevilla* lies in its resolute prohibition of metaphorical transcendence. The play contains little 'striking' or
imaginatively resonant language and Tirso does not permit
Don Juan that vestigial concern for humanity in general we
find in Molière's version. The play is a sequence of linguistic
acts which offer few paradigmatic associations, a representation of desire bereft of broader subjective inflections. Hence the
difficulty of assimilating the ending. The chain of loves is shown
to be indefinite, the final invitation conclusive. Desire can only
be curtailed by the arbitrary closure of death. The play's
genuine structural incoherence thus reproduces the enabling
conditions of the human psyche. It need not be explained
away.

Yet the simple opposition of desire and death (transgression
and Law) is hardly sufficient in this case. For Lacan, desire
cannot be extricated from the socio-linguistic Law which determines subjectivity.[39] Desire and Law are mutually constituting
because the entrance into language (the 'symbolic') requires
both the deferral of pleasure and submission to the Father. This
process is known as 'castration'. It involves the separation from
a presumed nature (the narcissistic mirroring of mother and
child) and the setting up of a network of differences (such as
male and female, self and other) which permit meaning and
representation. The complicity of Law and desire is quite evident in *El burlador*. The king of Naples wrongly blames Octavio
for Don Juan's seduction of Isabela, and the king of Castile
grants Don Juan privileged status that he may marry her. Don
Juan's uncle procures his escape from Naples and his father is
willing to defend his son's honour with his sword. Yet the very
representation of this complicity tends inevitably to undermine

---

[39] Compare Foucault's treatment of this psychoanalytical theme in relation to his
own rejection of the 'repression hypothesis' as cause of the modern interest in sexuality:
La Volonté de savoir (Paris, 1976), 107–8.

the prestige of the patriarch. It is perhaps no accident that
there is some confusion in the two versions of the play as to the
name of Don Juan's father.[40] For if desire is underwritten by
Law, then both are predicated on the original lack or absence
of death. The father is as impotent and deficient as the son.

Don Juan's career is thus (in Derrida's phrase) an 'arrêt de
mort': both a stay of execution and a death sentence. The
dramatic space is composed of an endless deferment and an
inevitable termination, each of which is implicit in the other.
This reminds us once more of the trace, which is at once movement and remainder. Throughout the play Don Juan has
remarked on the extension of 'credit' granted him: he has time
enough to make amends for his sins. And at the conclusion the
chorus takes up the financial metaphor and sings that debt
must be paid for in kind. It may not be stretching the metaphor
to suggest that *El burlador de Sevilla* is based on an 'economy'
which is at once theological, literary, and psychic. According to
Henry W. Sullivan the theme of the play is the conflicting demands of free will and divine grace.[41] Sullivan associates this
sovereign will of Tirso's characters with the 'freedom' of the
author to create and modern conceptions of an autonomous
desire (pp. 169–72). Yet, as Tirso himself admits, his artistic
freedom is inevitably compromised by allegiance to those authorities (such as Lope) who precede him; and as Sullivan's later
work was to acknowledge, all desire is based necessarily on a
symbolic debt to the Father. And the severity of Tirso's psychic
inscription recurs in the more elaborate and more uncompromising drama of Calderón de la Barca.

4. CALDERÓN AND HONOUR

Like Góngora and Quevedo before him, Calderón de la Barca
was once criticized for his 'excessive' language and style. In the
lectures he delivered in 1881 on the two hundredth anniversary
of the dramatist's death, Menéndez y Pelayo attacks Calderón
for his wordiness ('palabrería') and the unnecessary complexity
('enredo') of his plots. These excesses, he suggests, make Cal-

[40] See Xavier A. Fernández, '¿Cómo se llamaba el padre de don Juan?' *REH* 3
(1969), 145–59.
[41] *Tirso de Molina and the Drama of the Counter Reformation* (Amsterdam, 1976), 39.

derón incapable of psychological analysis or the expression of 'human' emotions.[42] This inhumanity is most obvious in the wife-murder plays, in which Calderón's position is radically immoral. For Menéndez y Pelayo, Calderón condones the slaughter of innocent women and thus fails to transcend the ethical limitations of the time and place in which he wrote (p. 229).

Later critics, particularly those of the British School, sought to resolve both stylistic and moral problems by proclaiming Calderón's language to be 'poetic' or 'functional' and by proposing the existence of an implied authorial viewpoint in the plays different from (and superior to) that of the jealous husbands represented within them. Calderón's status as both dramatic craftsman and humane moralist was thus vindicated. In this section I will treat these well-known topics once more; but my aim is not to resolve or smooth away the contradictions inherent in Calderón's text, but rather to explore them as cultural phenomena with reference to the notions of trace and inscription introduced earlier. The prescriptive dichotomy of pernicious excess and benevolent essence will yield to the less coercive (and more productive) action of the 'supplement'. I take three main questions in turn (rhetoric, honour, and women) and relate each to a founding inscription already in place in Calderón's text (linguistic, social, and sexual). The problem of excess is essential to each of these areas of concern.

But let us begin with a theoretical passage written by the dramatist himself. In his treatise in defence of painting, Calderón offers a classically derived, mythical origin for representation itself. On emerging from the sea a group of naked youths notice how closely the shadows cast by the sun on the beach approximate to the form of their bodies. Playfully, they trace a pattern in the sand, following the edge of the shadows with their fingers, and, after repeated attempts, succeed in creating perfect likenesses of themselves. In such a way was the art of painting founded.[43] This myth of origin has at least three (unintended) implications that are relevant to our understanding

---

[42] *Calderón y su teatro* (Buenos Aires, 1946), 323.

[43] Cited by Evangelina Rodríguez and Antonio Tordera in their *La escritura como espejo de palacio: 'El toreador' de Calderón* (Kassel, 1985), 15–16.

of Calderón's drama. First, the male body is both subject and object of representation. The artistic process is essentially narcissistic, even homosexual, an imaging of self performed by the male hand (or phallus). Second, this representation is perfectible, and hence interminable. The youths trace sketches ('borrones') in the sand, only to erase them and begin once more in their pursuit of proper likeness. And third, if representation has no end, it also has no beginning: the youths make their 'hollowed out signs' on the sandy 'embryo' already offered them by the beach; and their 'insistent lines' strive only to displace the perfect and authentic image that is the shadow already cast by the sun. Thus the painterly depiction of nature is an essential function of nature itself. Art can only mimic this natural depiction, and is thus superfluous to its object. Yet it bases its claim to legitimacy on its identity with that object: Calderón concludes that, because of its association with nature, painting must be granted the status of numen, or divine inspiration. However, as in the case of Tirso's appeal to husbandry, the status of art is called into question by the exempla used to 'illustrate' it. For the distinction between nature and culture (already blurred in Lope and Tirso) is wholly subverted by Calderón's incorporation of the latter within the former.

The hidden complexities of Calderón's anecdote may be derived from a certain confusion between painting and writing: in painting the artist superimposes pigment on the empty canvas. Calderón's beach, on the other hand, is closer to a wax tablet, indented or incised by the (male) instrument. Calderón's image of representation is thus one of inscription, rather than of depiction: the finger hollows out a space in a medium which is not neutral, but at once yielding and resistant. And like Freud's magic writing-pad, Calderón's beach permits continuous and continuing erasure, as the hand moves time and again over its surface. In its implicit appeal to the intermittent presence and reiterated movement of the body, Calderón's allegory of representation is perhaps more appropriate for drama than it is for painting.

The overt 'artificiality' of much of Calderón's language, no doubt also the result of successive revisions, remains a cause of some anxiety for many modern critics. An early article by Wilson vindicates the unifying, functional nature of imagery relating to the four elements in Calderón.[44] And the latest full-length study of Calderón's imagery uses similar terms of reference: the worst work is marred by 'superfluous' ornament, his best distinguished by organically 'necessary' figures of speech.[45] Calderón's linguistic formality has lent itself to studies based on historical rhetoric, like that of John V. Bryans.[46] Bryans praises the vividness of Calderón's tropes, the symmetry of his figures, and the power of *ornatus* to both amplify a topic and produce an affective distancing in the audience. The sensuous pleasure of ornament is thus quite properly related to moral propriety or decorum and to the intellectual disengagement of the audience's emotions (pp. 181–6). There is thus no facile distinction between argument and ornament (essence and excess). The author does, however, distinguish between 'persuasive' and 'passionate' oration in Calderón, and takes care to subordinate an instrumental or functional model of language to the mastery of an omnipotent dramatist (pp. 186–7). The humanist and prescriptive bias of traditional scholars remains inherent in more recent rhetorical readings.

Yet it may be that Calderón's language is indeed excessive, if not quite in the way that early critics believed it to be; and that this linguistic excess is linked to specific kinds of cultural and sexual redundancy represented within the plays. The work I treat here is one of Calderón's most famous (even notorious) dramas, *El médico de su honra*, first performed in 1635.[47] This play may seem 'atypical' of Calderón in that it depicts an extreme case of the honour code: the murder of an innocent wife by her husband on the mere suspicion of infidelity. But it is just this extremity of position that will prove *a fortiori* my general thesis: that the significance of the Spanish honour code is not confined to the time and place in which it originated, but rather points, in typically heightened fashion, to structures of 'original redundancy' inherent in the operation of language, desire, and sexuality as general, cultural concerns.

Like *Peribáñez*, *El médico* begins with an unconscious man

[44] 'The Four Elements in the Imagery of Calderón', *MLR* 31 (1936), 34–47.

[45] William R. Blue, *The Development of Imagery in Calderón's 'Comedias'* (York, SC, 1983).

[46] *Calderón de la Barca: Imagery, Rhetoric, and Drama* (London, 1977).

[47] I have referred to the edn. by C. A. Jones (rev. Oxford, 1976).

being carried into the house of a married woman. In this case the man is the Infante Enrique (brother of King Pedro, known as the Cruel or the Just), and the woman is Mencía, wife of the noble Gutierre. And like *El burlador*, it presupposes a body of action anterior to the play itself: Mencía had once been courted by Enrique and Gutierre engaged to another woman (Leonor). Gutierre is convinced by circumstantial evidence that his wife is committing adultery with the passionate Enrique: first, he finds in his house a dagger left inadvertently by Enrique; later, he surprises Mencía in the act of writing to the infante. Finally, Gutierre has a surgeon bleed his wife to death. After this act, he is joined by the king in marriage to Leonor, his former fiancée. There is also a comic sub-plot involving the buffoon Coquín, which regularly interrupts the main action at apparently inappropriate moments.

The intensity of narrative violence in the play is matched by an unusual concentration of linguistic virtuosity. Perhaps the most prominent examples of formal patterning (and typical of Calderón) are *Summationsschema* and *rapportatio*. These schemes are prominent from the very beginning. Thus in Mencía's description of Enrique's arrival on horseback (1. 45–72) and her comparison of him to a phoenix (1. 174–84), a succession of transelemental images are summed up at the end of the speech; and a number of nouns are followed by a number of verbs which they govern. Previous critics have taken such passages in one of two ways: either they are ornamental and artificial (and hence excessive); or they are organic and thematically relevant (and hence essential). But the flagrant rhetoricity of such speeches offers a third possibility: that these most self-conscious devices make the spectator or reader aware of the twin status of spoken or theatrical language, as both movement and residue, duration and completion. *Rapportatio* wilfully disrupts the coherent progression of words on which meaning depends: we are offered not a single subject and a single verb, but a number of subjects followed by a number of verbs which we attempt to derive from those subjects. The intermittence of the syntagm is underlined by the final summing up: items plucked from a lengthy speech are reassembled in the last few lines. Like the elaborate staggering of the plot ('enredo') by which fragments of information are released at intermittent intervals, the rhetorical patterning of Calderón's language serves to interrupt the smooth procession of the dramatic trace by calling attention to the single moment as it both adds to and is subsumed by the general movement of the play as a whole. The linguistic and dramatic functions are thus (provisionally, at least) 'denaturalized', their artificiality made visible to a partially disengaged public.

One critic has noted the use of forensic language in this play: characters appeal quite openly to legal postures and terminology as they attempt to persuade their listeners.[48] Yet I would suggest that the rhetoricity of Calderón is significant in so far as it exceeds the purely instrumental or functional model of discourse we may associate with the law-courts. Indeed Lacan has proposed that human speech ('parole') may be defined by a linguistic surplus, claiming that what is redundant to communication is precisely what serves as resonance in speech ('Fonction et champ de la parole', p. 181). And the resonant excesses of Calderón's figures of speech are matched by the semantic superfluities of his figures of thought. For here the favourite technique is *significatio*, the infusion of multiple meanings into a single word or phrase. Thus in the first act Enrique claims that he will surely die (of love, understood), even as he recovers his (physical) health (I. 274–6); and in the second, Gutierre's speech on the (actual) candle blown out by the wind is overlaid by a secondary (figurative) allusion to Mencía's life as a light, soon to be extinguished with equal resolution (II. 973–80). Where everyday language is fluent and transparent, Calderón's is halting and opaque. And this very particular formal and conceptual overloading reveals the order of words to be arbitrary and their signifying value to be conventional. Moreover, there is in Calderón no neutral or non-figurative language from which the characters may be said to deviate, for it is the most passionate moments (those of greatest self-revelation) which provoke the most elaborate orations (those of greatest dissimulation). Linguistic surplus is characteristic of both human personality and cultural practice.

The appeal to extra-dramatic vocabularies fails to resolve this problem of authentic utterance, for there is no 'meta-

---

[48] The critic is A. K. G. Paterson in an untitled paper delivered to the Congreso anglo-germano sobre Calderón (Cambridge, 1984).

language' outside the play which can transcend the characters' predicaments within it. Thus they employ, as we have seen, a legal vocabulary, but one which is empty of value in the contexts of the play: the domestic, personal space of marriage and the uncertain, courtly space of an inadequate and fallible monarch. The language of alchemy which also occurs in the play also fails to 'explain' it.[49] For it seems to be linked to another linguistic trait frequent in Calderón, namely tautology. Thus Mencía claims, near the beginning once more, that like the precious metals distilled in crucibles made of themselves, so her honour has been purified within the vessel of her own body (I. 144–52). Calderón has his characters appeal to the phoenix, which is both father and son to itself, and to the diamond whose strength is matched only by itself. And he has them exclaim at climactic moments: 'I am who I am'. Yet this apparent assertion of absolute identity or perfect equivalence serves (no less than the more overtly 'artificial' figures) to call into question both language as statement and subjectivity as essence. For Mencía and Gutierre make this claim at precisely those moments when its value is compromised by their predicament: when the married woman is confronted by her former lover and when the loving husband feels obliged to kill his wife. All the characters could say with Coquín to the king: 'I am he who you would wish me to be' (I. 711–13), because (as in *Peribáñez*) the action of the play suggests that human identity is an arbitrary juxtaposition of incompatible discourses or subject-positions. Wife and lover; husband and killer: neither of these contradictions can be resolved in a single person. As Parker has suggested, Calderón's tragic world is one in which 'the human individual, *qua* individual, cannot exist'.[50] But this state is the result of socio-linguistic determination not ethico-religious abstraction.

The linguistic question, then, is also cultural or social, and is in particular related to honour. As in *Peribáñez*, cultural practice in *El médico* consists of a redundant circulation, in which the fact of exchange precedes the objects themselves. Once more, the role of Coquín is exemplary here. The fool makes a bargain

---

[49] See Alan K. G. Paterson, 'The Alchemical Marriage in Calderón's *El médico de su honra*', *RJ* 30 (1979), 263–82.

[50] 'Towards a Definition of Calderonian Tragedy', *BHS* 39 (1962), 222–37 (p. 237).

with the king that if he cannot make him laugh then he will consent to have his teeth pulled (1. 781–3). The principle of equivalence practised throughout the play (one thing in exchange for another) could hardly be more arbitrary than here. It is determined wholly by power relations: objects of use value to the powerless are reduced to objects of exchange value for the powerful (the teeth can have no purpose for the king as they do for the fool). Both people and commodities are subject to a constant displacement or circulation over which they have no control.

The main objects of this insistent, yet redundant, circulation are the dagger and the letter. In the course of the action Enrique's dagger moves from its owner to Gutierre to the king to Enrique and back to Gutierre again. It traces with its movement the dramatic action of the play. Yet it serves as an empty marker of social and cultural difference: the value attributed to it by the jealous husband (proof of his rival's potency and his wife's infidelity) is quite imaginary and is by no means inherent in the object itself. Likewise the letter written by Mencía to Enrique and discovered incomplete by Gutierre is both essential to the workings of the plot and arbitrary in its significance: if Mencía asks Enrique not to leave, it is not (as Gutierre believes) because she loves him. This interrupted circulation is reminiscent of Poe's 'The Purloined Letter', a text which is the object of a famous reading by Lacan.[51] For Lacan the moral of Poe's tale is that a letter, even when mislaid ('en souffrance') always reaches its destination. This is because if the subject receives a message, it is one already sent by him or herself, which returns in an inverted form. Thus, at the specific level of the play's action, Gutierre receives not Mencía's true message in her letter, but his own hysterical projection: Mencía's supposed guilt is the mirror image of his own obsessive fear of betrayal. And at the more general level of the play as a whole, the male audience or readership receive a message they have also emitted themselves and which reconfirms their own preconceptions as to the status of women: if Mencía is both powerless and innocent it is because women must be both excluded from cultural practice and elevated to the position of Truth or

---

[51] 'Le Séminaire sur "La Lettre volée"', in *Écrits*, i. 19–75.

Platonic essence.[52] Thus Mencía's physical extinction and metaphysical assumption both re-enact and reinforce the conventional values of patriarchy.

I return to the problem of gender in a moment. But first I will suggest that in its overt redundancy and excess the Spanish honour code reproduces in the cultural sphere the structure of desire as described in Lacanian psychoanalysis. Lacan distinguishes between biological need ('besoin') which is particular and psychic demand ('demande') which is absolute. Desire is the gap which opens up between these two. It is thus superfluous to the mere satisfaction of need. The purest desire, the most absolute demand (because the most impossible to gratify), is the desire for nothing, as in the case of the anorexic who asks precisely nothing of those who love her.[53] Each of these points may be related to honour. Honour is superfluous or gratuitous, because it goes beyond the biological needs of the male and the cultural needs of society. Indeed it threatens the very existence of psychic and social equilibrium. The space of the husband's desire lies in the gap between particular need (the wife's actual conformity to the conditions imposed on her) and absolute demand (the husband's insistence that the whole world recognize that conformity). What the husband requires of his wife (and what she cannot of course give him) is nothing: a lack of action and a lack of speech which will preserve a social reputation over which she has very little control. This desire, by definition, cannot be gratified. For the wife's demonstrations of innocence in particular circumstances can never displace or refute the husband's constant suspicion of guilt as moral and social absolute. Hence the comedia's obsession with adultery, real or imagined; for adultery may be defined as an excess of sexual practice which goes beyond that required for the reproduction of the species and of society.

Women, then, serve as objects of exchange, both excluded from and essential to the male circulation whose operation they precede. Under the aegis of the king, the dead Mencía is replaced by the living Leonor. Each is precisely equal to the other as object of exchange. Order is restored and social practice con-

---

[52] See Derrida's reading of Lacan on Poe: 'Le Facteur de la vérité', in *La Carte postale de Socrate à Freud et au-delà* (Paris, 1980), 441–524.

[53] For the distinction between 'need' and 'demand', see 'Fonction et champ', p. 177.

tinues. Like the playful youths on Calderón's sunlit beach, the brooding husbands of his darkened houses re-enact the movement of the signifying trace. A male hand, steeped in Mencía's blood, leaves its print on Gutierre's doorpost. The king orders it to be effaced, but the husband will have it reproduced in paint as a permanent sign of his newly cleansed honour. Thus the male hand (identified by at least one critic of the play with the phallus[54]) reveals itself in the intermittent play of inscription and erasure. Its prestige seems unshakeable.

Yet, as in the cases of *Peribáñez* and *El burlador*, this legitimizing male 'presence' is highly compromised by its origin. As Robert ter Horst has suggested, both men and women in the play are deprived of speech at critical points. In particular, the status of the king is highly ambivalent. Previous critics have debated whether he is 'cruel' or 'just'.[55] Ter Horst speaks rather of his 'feminine wiles' and the 'mismanaged logos' which will turn against him as surely as against Mencía: historically, the monarch will later be killed by his brother Enrique.[56] The unexpected moral of *El médico*, for the modern reader at least, is perhaps the fallibility of the father, or the inability of the patriarch to bound or control an exorbitant cultural practice. As with the magic writing-pad, any permanence of sign or value gives way to the indeterminacy of graphic inscription. And the allegory of this inscription is already suggested by Calderón himself: it is medicine, the science which can both kill and cure. This coincides with Derrida, for whom writing in general is like Plato's 'pharmakon', at once poison and elixir.[57] Thus it could be argued that *El médico de su honra* subverts the privilege of male writing, as it demonstrates its mortal potency; and that Calderón inadvertently undermines the social order of his day as he vindicates its 'naturalness'. This is not to claim that Calderón was 'really' a liberal or progressive or to deny the cruelty of his representation of women. Rather it is to suggest that in the very extremity of his vision Calderón obliges us to

---

[54] See Don N. Cruikshank, '"Pongo mi mano en sangre bañada en la puerta": Adultery in *El médico de su honra*', in *Studies in Spanish Literature of the Golden Age presented to E. M. Wilson*, ed. R. O. Jones (London, 1973), 45–62 (p. 51).

[55] See A. I. Watson, 'Peter the Cruel or Peter the Just? A Reappraisal of the Role played by King Peter in Calderón's *El médico de su honra*', *RJ* 14 (1963), 322–46.

[56] *Calderón: The Secular Plays* (Lexington, Ky., 1982), 93.

[57] 'La Pharmacie de Platon', in *La Dissémination* (Paris, 1972), 71–197.

re-examine our unthinking bias towards that naturalistic diction and those humane values that he so resolutely refuses to give us.[58]

5. DRAMA AS TRACE

How might we define the comedia? By now my answer should be clear. Just as Spanish lyric calls attention to the supplement as intermittent play of presence and absence, and Spanish picaresque calls attention to the parergon as both inside and outside of representation, so the Spanish comedia calls attention to the trace as both movement and residue of dramatic inscription. Drama as trace is neither the embodiment of eternal values, nor the reflection of historical incident, but the evidence of material process. That is, its character is neither ideal nor empirical, but theoretical (not abstract, but turning back on itself). The comedia is inscriptional, not pictorial: the dramatist does not 'paint' on a blank surface, but incises his mark on an active medium (wax or sand) already saturated with earlier writing. It is no accident that the major dramatists so often borrow plots and titles from each other. The dramatic process is communal and interminable, lacking in both origin and end. The magic writing-pad of the comedia is thus at once the author's imagination and the audience's memory, the cumulative residue of a continuing theatrical process which permits an ever-increasing stylization of language and economy of means, as the 'performance' of the dramatist and the 'competence' of the public feed reciprocally off one another.

The comedia is theoretical because it turns back on itself; it is material because it makes us aware of real social relations (but as founding inscription, not surface phenomenon). Thus *Peribáñez* reveals an 'authentic' oral nature to be shot through with

---

[58] In his *The Limits of Illusion: A Critical Study of Calderón* (Cambridge, 1984), Anthony J. Cascardi also suggests that the dramatist has a distancing or alienating effect on the spectator. In his treatment of *El médico*, however, he retreats from the physicality of the final scene into a Platonic vision of ineffable essence: 'As the images are displayed before us, they shimmer as pure presences, more phenomenological than representational.' (p. 79). Critics are fond of attributing to Calderón a Brechtian alienation effect which fails none the less to unsettle their own faith in humanism and patriarchy. See also José M. Ruano de la Haza, 'Hacia una nueva definición de la tragedia calderoniana', *BCom.* 35 (1983), 165–80.

alienating, cultural process; *El burlador* reveals 'instinctive' sexual passion to be underscored by socio-linguistic and psychic determinants; and *El médico* reveals the 'eternal' values of the Spanish male to be wholly compromised by social and cultural convention. Nature, desire, and honour can no longer be taken for granted: they are made strange, or defamiliarized. But, contrary to the opinion of many critics, this is not a once-and-for-all 'alienation effect', cleverly contrived by the author and greedily consumed by the spectator. The particularities of any genre are always renaturalized by a willing audience, however non-naturalistic those generic conventions may be. Any disengagement of the spectator must be wilful and persistent, a dogged unravelling of the 'symbolic' skeins of the text, not a facile submission to its 'imaginary' coherence (for which 'alienation' is just another, if more sophisticated, piece of evidence).

That the comedia is not the direct reflection of historical circumstance is self-evident. It is more difficult to suggest the ways in which writing and history might coincide. Thus Melveena McKendrick has recently suggested that the marital honour represented so obsessively on the stage (and in all probability absent in 'real' life) is a neurotic transference of a genuine, historical anxiety (conspicuously absent on the stage): the racist concern for 'purity of blood'.[59] On the surface this is a persuasive argument. However, there is no theoretical or empirical link between the supposedly discrete areas of art and life. The process is ineffable, and guaranteed only by the critic's authority. If we go beyond the terms of debate set by the critic, the use of the word 'transference' implies a Freudian subtext of libidinal or affective displacement, which is not developed in the article. But, as we have seen, later developments in psychoanalysis warn us against this hydraulic or homeostatic view of desire as a pressure which must find release in whatever channel is open to it.

There is however a term which can mediate between history and drama. It is the Marxian one of ideology. If we take the form of the comedia as ideological, then its particularities bear specific but indirect witness to the social and economic relations

[59] 'Honour–Vengeance in the Spanish Comedia: A Case of Mimetic Transference?', *MLR* 79 (1984), 313–35.

in Spain in the period. Thus the absence of 'three-dimensional' characters in the comedia was seen by Parker as the result of a moral concern for the demonstration of Catholic prescription at the expense of 'individuality'. But as George Mariscal hypothesizes, its ultimate origin could be socio-political: 'the successful "elimination" of bourgeois ideologies in Calderón's Spain precluded the notion of an autonomous subject, a notion which underlies the creation of any "great" fictional individual such as Hamlet, Macbeth or Lear'.[60] Ideology as mediation thus anticipates and disables both the naïve question: 'Were people in the Golden Age really like Peribáñez or Mencía?' and its more sophisticated variant: 'In what ways did they really differ from the fictional characters?' For ideology may be defined as a cultural inscription always in place within which individuals both live their lives and see those lives represented. Like the concept of decorum so dear to characters and authors of the comedia, ideology combines ultimate prestige with indefinite flexibility: its very adaptation to particular circumstance guarantees its appearance of universality.

What is more, ideology, like the comedia, has no verifiable origin, either 'inside' or 'outside' social practice. Like the trace, it is both the process and the product of history. And this reciprocal or dialectical relation also defines the enabling conditions of the comedia, written by an individual, but elicited by and performed for an active and vigorous public. Spanish popular drama confirms Marx's theory in the *Grundrisse* that production and consumption reproduce one another: '[Consumption] creates the objects of production in still subjective form. No production without a need. But consumption reproduces the need.'[61] The role of the trace, then, is not to reinstate a new hierarchy, a simple inversion of the old: audience before author; inscription before depiction; ideology before history. Rather it is to suggest a web of dialectical relations in which each is (in Marx's word once more) *immediately* the other.

These questions may seem abstract. But if we observe their implications, then they affect both a general critical approach

---

[60] George Mariscal, 'Re-reading Calderón', *BCom.* 36 (1984), 131–3. This is a response to Walter Cohen's 'Calderón in England' of the previous year.

[61] *Grundrisse: Foundations of the Critique of Political Economy*, trans. Martin Nicolaus (London, 1973), 91.

and specific cases of textual analysis. Thus two formal characteristics of the comedia are its stress on song and polymetry. We
saw in the introduction to this chapter that song has an ambivalent position in Aristotelian poetics, and it is perhaps significant that in each of the plays we have studied the singing of
songs bears a particular emphasis: thus the reapers sing of the
threat to Peribáñez's honour, the chorus sing of Don Juan's
complacent wager and impending punishment, and the king's
musicians sing of Enrique's departure, which will lead in-
directly to Mencía's death. In each case the song is both inside
and outside the represented action; indeed, in *Peribáñez* a
popular song precedes and provides the motive for that action.
Likewise, polymetry problematizes the dramatic medium itself:
as prose or single, consistent verse form, language may safely be
taken for granted. At any moment of the comedia, however, the
form of the language (like the actions of the characters) has a
proper yet variable status. The literary choice of polymetry is
comparable to the ethical choice of decorum. Thus, as ideological and formal components, song and polymetry enforce
illusionism as they undermine it, and promote both rhetorical
persuasion and critical disengagement at one and the same
time. Reichenberger claimed long ago that 'the Spanish play-
wright is the voice that artistically moulds and expresses the
ideals, convictions, aspirations and beliefs of his people'.[62] And
it is in the contradiction (unnoticed by the critic himself)
between the active 'moulding' and the passive 'expression' that
the theoretical and historical complexities of the comedia lie.

To put it more simply, the 'uniqueness of the comedia' lies in
formality without continuity. Spanish theatre is formal like the
French, in its appeal to verse and stock situations; but it undermines that formality by the use of polymetry (the calling into
question of verse form) and tragicomedy (the calling into question of genre). And it is discontinuous like the English, in its
lack of respect for Aristotelian unities; but it fails to develop
that loose illusionism by offering its audience 'autonomous'
characters. Historically, the comedia transgresses the law of
Aristotelian precept. But this transgression of law is preceded

---

[62] Cited by Richard A. Young in *La figura del rey y la institución real en la comedia lopesca*
(Madrid, 1979), 115.

by a law of transgression: Lope, the founding father, institutes and legitimizes a sense of Spanish drama as eternal deviance from alien, classical practice. Thus, if we can trace an increasing formality or artificiality from Lope to Tirso to Calderón, then that formality is already implicit in Lope's highly self-conscious position, both inside and outside Aristotelian and Horatian poetics, yielding to both the (natural) demands of a traditional craft and the (cultural) requirements of a specific audience.

The formality of oration in the comedia at all periods (and the evident potency of effect it held for the audience) suggests that in Spanish drama there can be no distinction between figure and ground, ornament and essence. But once more, this is hardly a new idea. For Scaliger had claimed in his Latin grammar *De causis* (xii. 176) that all discourse was figurative: 'Omnis oratio figurata est'.[63] Like the tendons of the body ('lineamenta') the so-called figures of speech are the very substance ('materia ipsa') of the oration. The stress on the body is telling. For what Spanish drama tells us is that if all discourse is figurative, then all figuration is discursive: the textual body expands to fill the representational space; no area is uninscribed, no object uncompromised by cultural construction. To use a metaphor common in the period (and employed by Lope himself with reference to relics of the saints),[64] the actor on the Spanish stage is a 'written body' ('cuerpo escrito'). And if this body is a male one, then it carries within itself, none the less, its possible displacement by the female. At a vital moment of the action each of the three lovers in the plays we have studied (Don Lope, Don Juan, and Don Enrique) is deprived of consciousness. The unconscious male body cradled in the arms of a woman re-enacts the helplessness of the child (the trauma of castration), that founding lack which the postures of the adult seek in vain to conceal.

Formality without continuity is, thus, the defining characteristic of the comedia; and ornament without essence is the force of its language. The rise of an 'excessive' diction in the lyric,

---

[63] Heidelberg, 1584. I owe this reference to Professor Pierre Lardet.

[64] See Lope de Vega, *Obras poéticas*, ed. José Manuel Blecua (Barcelona, 1969), p. 508 l. 133.

picaresque, and drama of seventeenth-century Spain may be related to a general epistemological shift in the same period. And, according to some critics, that shift or semiotic crisis is best illustrated in the work of Cervantes.

5

THE ERASURE OF RHETORIC
IN CERVANTES

I. SIMPLICITY, AUTHORITY, LANGUAGE

It seems impossible to write on Spanish literature of the Golden Age without referring to Cervantes. Yet this 'inevitability' is by no means self-evident or natural. Rather, it is the result of the particular limits of critical debate set in our time, and of the historical conditions in which Golden Age texts have been received in the centuries since they were produced. In many ways I have placed Cervantes outside the parameters of this study from the very beginning. For I started from the twin presuppositions that Spanish culture has been marginalized, banished to the fringes of a received European tradition; and that the overt cause of this marginalization was a perceived excess of language and sentiment, which was held to be intrinsic to Spaniards and radically alien to outsiders. Cervantes, however, is generally considered to be exceptional on both accounts. He is the sole writer in Castilian who is granted the status of 'universal genius', and who is known (if not read) throughout the world. And he is the purveyor of a simple 'clarity' of style, supposedly distinct from the baroque excesses of his younger contemporaries. My aim in this chapter is not to propose a new 'interpretation' of Cervantes's work (such a project lies beyond the scope of this study), but to examine recent criticism of Cervantes in the light of issues I have already raised in previous chapters. The readings already provoked by Cervantes's works are extraordinarily varied and frequently incompatible. Their multiplicity confirms my previous suggestion that a text is not a Platonic essence, whose changeless qualities are somehow preserved intact by the zealous author who has created them, but is rather a material product, whose variable value is the result of a constant dialectic between the writer and a historically determinate reader.

The questions to be answered here, then, are whether Cervantes can truly be exempted from the rhetorics of excess characteristic of his time; and, if not, whether any intuition of this excess or superfluity essential to all literary discourse is revealed (overtly or otherwise) in the latest criticism of his works. I treat these questions with reference to two major and rather complex areas of critical concern: literary genre and textual authority; and linguistic practice and psychological process. The problems raised here (which Cervantes shares with the lyric, picaresque, and drama of his time) are fundamentally those of the 'presence' of the author, the limits of representation, and the constitution of the human subject. That Cervantes's work has certain preoccupations in common with that of his contemporaries need not make his texts (or our reading of them) less significant.

We may begin with the question of genre: Cervantes's continuing (albeit qualified) reputation as the 'inventor of the modern novel'. Recent critical debate on this topic has been typically inconclusive. Thus Ruth El Saffar has argued that Cervantes's career as a whole moves from *Novel to Romance* (Baltimore, 1974), a shift exemplified in the particular by the passage from the 'early' *Novelas* (such as *Rinconete y Cortadillo*) to the 'later' (such as *La señora Cornelia*); and in the general by the passage from the 'realistic' *Don Quijote* I to the 'idealistic' *Persiles y Sigismunda*. El Saffar thus removes Cervantes from the facile, historical teleology of previous critics, for whom the artificiality of some works was held to be superseded by the 'natural' maturity of others. But she risks setting up a reverse hierarchy in which the positive term is displaced by the negative. Such is the case in a recent reading by Riley, in which Cervantes is said to 'prefer' romance to novel.[1] Edwin Williamson has argued that Cervantes favours neither of the two, at least as far as the interpolations to the *Quijote* are concerned. For if reality is often shown here to exceed the fixed patterns of romance, then this apparent 'realism' of Cervantes is purely negative, the result not of direct reproduction of life, but of ironic infringement of

---

[1] Edward C. Riley, '"Romance" y novela en Cervantes', in *Cervantes: Su obra y su mundo, Actas del I Congreso internacional sobre Cervantes*, ed. Manuel Criado de Val (Madrid, 1981), 5–13 (p. 13).

literary formula.[2] In a later study Williamson claims that the
Quijote is a 'half-way house' between novel and romance. But
this does not mean that it reconciles the two opposites: there is
no simple dichotomy between the two genres, since at least one
of them (the novel) can be defined only by its indeterminacy.[3]
The famous Cervantine irony thus promotes not coherence but
undecidability: it destabilizes the dualism of Quijote and
Sancho, while encouraging us to take that dualism as symbolic;
and it creates an opportunity for the naturalistic development
of character and plot, which it ultimately fails to develop
(p. 160, 202).

   Alban K. Forcione also argues the case for generic instability, this time with reference to the *Novelas ejemplares*. Cervantes's
refusal to conform to literary convention here denies the reader
'the comfort of a stock response'.[4] Yet Forcione identifies this
'non-linearity' with the humanist discourses of the sixteenth
century. Like Cervantes, writers such as Erasmus used paradox
and irony to provoke their readers' collaboration and to offer
them the opportunity to employ that creative 'freedom' which
they have exercised themselves (p. 29). Cervantes's habitual
lack of resolution, then, is by no means unique. It is preceded
by an authoritative tradition of sceptical libertarianism in
which, we might say, transgression is laid down as a general
Law. In a complementary study of *El casamiento engañoso* and *El
coloquio de los perros*, Forcione derives the formal discontinuity of
these texts from Cervantes's simultaneous impulse towards
both scepticism and dogmatic certainty; and he contrasts the
'unassertive voice' of Cervantes, so close to those of his humanist
ancestors, with the less tolerant tones of his ascetic Christian
contemporaries.[5] For Forcione, Cervantes leads us quite de-
liberately into a moral and epistemological 'darkness'. Once we
perceive the light of truth he offers us, however, 'we recognize
that it has been there all along' (p. 18). In such metaphors

   [2] 'Romance and Realism in the Interpolated Stories in the *Quijote*', *Cervantes*, 2
(1982), 43–67 (p. 67).
   [3] *The Half-way House of Fiction: Don Quijote and Arthurian Romance* (Oxford, 1984),
p. ix.
   [4] *Cervantes and the Humanist Vision: A Study of Four Exemplary Novels* (Princeton, 1982),
28.
   [5] *Cervantes and the Mystery of Lawlessness: A Study of 'El casamiento engañoso' and 'El
coloquio de los perros'* (Princeton, 1984), 17.

Forcione's approach, which is at once scholarly and imaginative, reveals none the less the inescapable limits of its own cognition. For if the light is always already implicit in the dark, is it not because the faith in such wilful illumination (like our belief in the presence of the author as speaking 'voice') is no quality inherent in the text itself but an 'imaginary' projection of the reader? And is the 'unassertive' voice which provokes this response *necessarily* more humane or liberating in its effect that its more overtly tyrannical alternatives? In previous chapters I suggested that Góngora, Quevedo, and Calderón call the reader's attention to the power invested in all authors and to the potentially oppressive nature of their works by means of a relatively opaque and excessive language. The modesty or reticence of a Cervantes (the refusal to direct the reader or give definite form to the work) elicits a more affectionate, but perhaps more self-deluding, response. The 'lawlessness' prized by Forcione in Cervantes may be a new and more subtle version of Law itself, all the more effective because of its very transparency.

In general, however, the discontinuities of Cervantes's texts, their manifest status as collages of literary fragments (novel and romance; realism and idealism), have not received the subtle attention of a Forcione. Thus Howard Mancing treats *The Chivalric World of Don Quijote* (Columbia and London, 1982), but still praises the 'timelessness' of the story (p. 5). For Mancing it seems that this fixity of value is not incompatible with the text's main function, which is to satirize a historically specific literary genre, well known in Cervantes's time and almost forgotten today. This ahistorical bias recurs in the conclusion, in which Mancing quotes Avalle Arce on the difference (supposedly exemplified in the work) between *ser* and *valer* ('existence' and 'value'). Alonso Quijano merely 'exists', while Don Quijote 'leads a worthwhile life' (p. 215). But it is precisely this essentialist understanding of value which is called into question by Cervantes's text. For the values of the chivalric world are not those of Cervantes's time, and those of the seventeenth century are no longer those of the twentieth. Each age considers it own values to be eternal, and each is deluded. The *Quijote* demonstrates at the surface level of the plot the historical specificity (and perhaps relativity) of value and meaning.

That even the most historical scholars tend to ignore this lesson is a sign of the continuing potency of its illusionist and rhetorical effect.

The problem of value and the related question of textual authority remain popular with critics. As in the case of picaresque, most seek to resolve formal contradictions by assigning them to a unified, omnipotent author. Thus for Juan Ignacio Ferreras the parodic structure of the *Quijote*, although halting and intermittent, merely reconfirms the 'harmony' and 'coherence' of the work, and the genius of its creator.[6] Another critic notes the discontinuities between different manuscript versions of the *Novelas*, and concludes from this evidence that Cervantes cannot be the author of the whole collection.[7] For most critics the essential 'unity' of the creative imagination must remain dominant, in spite of the fact that, as Anthony Close suggests, Cervantes's conception of the comic fable is typically Spanish in its variety and hybridism.[8] It is doubly curious, then, that those critics who praise Cervantes for his 'elusiveness' in the use of techniques such as the fictitious authorship device are those most anxious to reconfirm his status as founding father of the text and ultimate authority over it.[9] The more inconsistent the author's writing and the more elaborate the fictional devices which mediate between him and the reader, the more the critic seems compelled to invoke the author as absolute presence and single origin of value.

This sense of an insistent, if submerged, scepticism towards the very possibility of an authoritative interpretation of Cervantes may be related to shifts or contradictions in the discursive practice of his own time. Thus Juergen Hahn uses the solider's tale in *Don Quijote* I to suggest that any epistemological standard in the text must be based on a recognition of both the permanent truth of religion and the specific truth of history.[10] And Maureen Ihrie's study of *Skepticism in Cervantes* (London,

[6] *La estructura paródica del 'Quijote'* (Madrid, 1982), 131.

[7] E. T. Aylward, *Cervantes: Pioneer and Plagiarist* (London, 1982).

[8] 'Cervantes's *Arte nuevo de hazer fábulas cómicas en este tiempo*', *Cervantes*, 2 (1982), 3–22 (p. 22).

[9] See, for example, R. M. Flores, 'The Role of Cide Hamete in *Don Quijote*', *BHS* 59 (1982), 3–14.

[10] '*El capitán cautivo*: The Soldier's Truth and Literary Precept in *Don Quijote* Part I', *JHP* 3 (1979), 269–303.

1982) ends with an unresolved contradiction between an empirical (yet unknowable) truth and a legitimizing (yet unverifiable) faith (p. 116). Ihrie claims that there is a steady progression in Cervantes's œuvre from Truth to Faith. But we might add that, at any moment of his career, Cervantes's Pyrrhonism and his Fideism will be at once mutually exclusive and inextricable.

The ultimate question raised by these debates on truth, authority, and interpretation is whether meaning is intrinsic or extrinsic to the literary text. This question is not as simple as it may seem. For example, one leading exponent of a historical or contextualizing criticism also reveals an unfailing trust in the immanence of meaning and the universality of 'artistic sensibility': 'The poem (novel, play) points mutely at the rules for understanding it, if only we will look.'[11] Even E. C. Riley, who in *Cervantes's Theory of the Novel* (Oxford, 1962) seeks the author's meaning within the discursive context of his age, ends his study with a paean to *Don Quijote* as the 'illumination' of an (implicitly) unchanging 'human experience' (p. 225). In the previous pages Riley has treated the Copernican revolution of Cervantes's time, which led ultimately to the rise of rationalism and empiricism. But Riley dare not admit that such shifts in the framework of knowledge might affect the concept (even the experience) of humanity itself. In the final analysis, Cervantes's ability to perceive and represent that humanity remains immediate and unproblematic.

We shall return to the problem of 'Man' in a moment. But it is linked to the question of Cervantes's language as instrument or mediation. Cervantes is still praised for the moderation and 'clarity' of his style. Yet Elias L. Rivers compares him to Góngora, in that he is the culmination ('superación') of a process of literary elaboration and perfection.[12] Other critics have stressed the rhetoricity of Cervantes's language at the expense of its 'transparency', particularly with reference to oration and

[11] Anthony Close, *The Romantic Approach to 'Don Quijote': A Critical History of the Romantic Tradition in 'Quijote' Criticism* (Cambridge, 1977), 250–1.
[12] 'Cervantes and the Question of Language', in *Cervantes and the Renaissance: Papers of the Pomona College Cervantes Symposium*, ed. Michael D. McGaha (Easton, Pa., 1980), 23–33 (p. 33).

gesture;[13] or its overtly citational character, which invokes discourses such as the Petrarchan which we might not expect to appear.[14] Yet if, as I suggested in the first chapter, 'clarity' is taken in the twin senses of 'brilliance' and 'simplicity', then there need be no contradiction in using the word to describe Cervantes's remarkably fluid style. And if, as I suggested in the second chapter, we take the 'excessive' conclusions of Góngora to be already implicit in the 'moderate' beginnings of Garcilaso, then Cervantes can be seen (like Góngora) to be at once moderate and excessive, traditional and innovatory. For, as Riley says, Cervantes's fundamental problem is one which we have seen is shared by all his contemporaries: the relationship of art to nature (*Theory*, p. 222). This problem is discussed at length by Francisco Garrote Pérez, who cites the canon's comment on Don Quijote's description of the *locus amoenus* (that art by imitating nature comes to conquer it) and reproduces on the cover of his work an emblem bearing the motto: 'Ars naturam adiuuans'.[14] For Cervantes too, art is the essential supplement to a faltering nature. A 'supplementary' understanding of Cervantes's style (such as we have learned from Golden Age lyric) thus eliminates a compulsory choice between the prescriptive dichotomies of art and nature, Renaissance and baroque. Cervantes partakes of both terms simultaneously.

The possibility remains, moreover, that, as in the case of the comedia, our sense of the 'real' in Cervantes's texts and of the psychological constitution of the subject in his fiction are themselves determined by language. This is suggested by Elias L. Rivers in his *Quixotic Scriptures* (Bloomington, 1983). Rivers cites Don Quijote's use of 'a three-level system of conversational, second-person address' ('tu', 'vos', and 'vuestra merced') to produce or reproduce a social hierarchy that is material and not merely verbal in character (p. 117). And Ramón Saldívar, in his subtle and complex article 'Don Quijote's Metaphors and the Grammar of Proper Language',[16] makes a similar point by citing the Knight's own

---

[13] Antonio Roldán, 'Cervantes y la retórica clásica', in *Cervantes: Su obra y su mundo* (Madrid, 1981), 47–57.

[14] Alicia de Colombí-Monguió, 'Los "ojos de perlas" de Dulcinea (*Quijote* II, 10 y 11): El antipetrarquismo de Sancho (y de otros)', *NRFH* 32 (1983) 389–402.

[15] *La naturaleza en el pensamiento de Cervantes* (Salamanca, 1979), 49.

[16] *MLN* 95 (1980), 252–78.

speech on the Golden Age, in which he associates the fall from earthly paradise with the use of the linguistic modifiers 'yours' and 'mine'. For Saldívar this expresses 'a longing for a mythic world in which there was no gap between the expression and the understanding of meaning, in which there was, in short, no need for the mediation of language' (p. 263). As I have argued throughout this book, such a desire (which is shared by many critics of Golden Age literature) is as seductive as it is illusory. Saldívar follows Foucault in claiming that authority is a construct, or textual effect, not a transcendent essence or presence (p. 257). And he sees Don Quijote's madness as a predominantly linguistic error based on a Derridean phonocentricism (the erroneous equation of 'voice' and meaning), a Foucaldian reduction of difference to similarities (typical of the pre-Classical 'epistemè'), and an implicitly Lacanian infinity of displacement (the Knight's proliferating metaphors are curtailed only by death). Saldívar concludes by attributing to Cervantes a knowledge we have already discovered in Scaliger, namely that all discourse is figurative: 'Don Quijote shows ... that human speech as a whole, and in its various modes of discourse, is not immediate. It is rather constitutively figurative, and hence burdened with ambiguity, confusion and undecidability.' (pp. 277–8.) This is not to say that it is any the less 'real': speech and writing are necessary human activities. Indeed they form the very texture of our lives and ourselves.

Many North American critics, however, have inclined to a prescriptive psychologism reminiscent of their treatment of the comedia. Thus Carroll B. Johnson both posits a fictional space 'outside' the text (the character's psychic 'prehistory') and reads this space within a resolutely ahistorical framework (the Knight's adventures as 'mid-life crisis').[17] John G. Weiger's earlier study begins by claiming to offer an analysis based not on individualism (a twentieth-century preoccupation), but on individuation or 'the process of becoming an individual' (under particular circumstances).[18] However, Weiger's faith in the existence of a 'true self' and in the capacity of the individual to discover that self (p. 149) remains unshaken by his initial pre-

[17] *Madness and Lust: A Psychoanalytical Approach to 'Don Quijote'* (Berkeley, 1983), ch. II, and p. 197.

[18] *The Individuated Self: Cervantes and the Emergence of the Individual* (Ohio, 1979), 3.

miss that subjectivity is, to some extent at least, historically determinate. Louis Combet offers a more sophisticated psycho-analytical reading of Cervantes's entire œuvre.[19] Combet is remarkably broad in his terms of reference, presenting psychic event as a discursive figure not a neurological phenomenon, and refusing to reduce the main concerns of his study (erotics and masochism) to overtly sexual behaviour (pp. 15, 39, 165). Nor is he concerned (until the final chapter at least) with 'ana-lysing' the fictional characters or the historical author as if the first were real people and the second an immediately accessible presence. His stress on the inversion of gender stereotypes in Cervantes and on the typically passive stance of his male char-acters and narrators is also a strategic (and necessary) attack on the prestige of Cervantes as active or masterful author. Yet in his constant reference to a paradigm of 'échec' or disfunction, Combet tends none the less to smuggle back the prescriptive view of characters 'failing' to achieve sexual maturity, and of Cervantes himself as being 'unable' to resolve Oedipal con-flict.[20] I would suggest, then, that any alternative reading of language and psychology in Cervantes will involve redefini-tions of both the place of women in the œuvre and the historical conditions of representation itself.

One theorist often cited in this last context, and who touched in his own work on Cervantes's fiction, is Michel Foucault. Foucault's trace has been both explicit and implicit in recent criticism. Salvador Jiménez Fajardo cites Foucault's descrip-tion of the Knight as a 'graphisme' or inscriptional mark: Quijote is composed of language itself, of texts and stories already written or printed before his own (discursive) body has initiated its movement.[21] For Foucault, Quijote is the 'hero of the same', the man who continues to see in terms of resemb-lances in an age when the structure of knowledge was begin-ning to shift to the discrimination of difference and the perception of unique identity. Riley had compared Don Quijote to Velázquez's *Meninas* as an example of 'an act of

---

[19] *Cervantès, ou les incertitudes du désir: Une approche psychostructurale de l'œuvre de Cervantès* (Lyons, 1980).

[20] See Ruth El Saffar's review essay on Combet in *MLN* 97 (1982), 422–7.

[21] 'The Sierra Morena as Labyrinth in *Don Quijote* I', *MLN* 99 (1984), 214–34 (p. 217).

mental detachment which is a distinguishing mark of European thought around 1600' (*Theory*, p. 223). Yet Foucault's reading of the same painting (which Riley could not have known) stresses precisely the absence of this external or distanced mastery. Velázquez does indeed depict the material tools of representation (painter, brush, canvas). But what he cannot depict in the same picture is the gaze of the painter as he addresses the real painting and that of the monarch as he addresses the represented painter. The painting may serve as an allegory of representation in what Foucault dubs the 'Classical' period, but only in so far as it functions as an absence or void. For only in the modern period will Man emerge as both subject and object of representation at one and the same time, creator of the world and of his own imaging within it. Velázquez and, I would argue, Cervantes fail to offer that affective individualism for which they are prized today, because Man itself as discursive construct had not yet come into existence.

The formal condition of Classical representation, then, is that work and author cannot appear in the same artistic space. Ruth El Saffar seems to hint at this point (without explicit reference to Foucault) in an early study of *Don Quijote*.[22] She claims that for Cervantes 'in the perfect work of art in which the present can be viewed both in process and past at one time, either the work or the artist must be absent'. This is rather similar to the question of the 'trace' as both duration and termination which we have seen in relation to the comedia: the story of a man's life is both movement and residue. El Saffar's example is Ginés de Pasamonte's projected autobiography in *Don Quijote* I, which is contrasted with the same character's puppet show (under the name of Maese Pedro) in Part II: 'In Part I Ginés presents the theory, but not the work; in Part II he presents the work, but not himself.' The author can take up no position either 'inside' or 'outside' the work, and is manifest only as a highly contingent and intermittent authority.

This is not quite the same as the 'Perspectivist' model by which Cervantes is thought to be blurring the boundaries between an art and a life which have changed little from his time to our own. For this epistemic crisis, unlike that of the

---

[22] *Distance and Control in 'Don Quijote': A Study in Narrative Technique* (Chapel Hill, 1975), 139.

Perspectivists, is historically specific in character and can have no unchanging effect on a variable audience. In a later article El Saffar appeals openly to Foucault in seeing in the *Quijote* 'the intuition of a threatened severance of world and word that would ... plunge us into chaos'.[23] El Saffar distinguishes between *Don Quijote* and the *Persiles* in this regard: '*Don Quijote* shows us that fiction and illusion are products of our material experience in time and space ... What *Persiles y Sigismunda* shows us ... is that fiction and illusion need not wrest the traveler from his/her consciousness of origin and destiny.' It does not follow, however, as El Saffar claims, that the subject is thus 'free to manipulate the material world'. Indeed it is precisely the mastery of subject over circumstance which is called into question by the unresolved appeal to both material contingency and ideal essence made by Cervantes throughout his œuvre. Perhaps, as El Saffar suggests elsewhere, the key to these asymmetries rests in the 'recovery' of the woman in Cervantes's texts, in the feminine as 'fourth term' that transcends difference and contradiction at the same time as it destabilizes the prison-house of patriarchal narrative.[24]

I would suggest myself that Cervantes's work permits neither the facile resolution of difference nor the simple opposition of dichotomies. Novel versus romance; truth versus faith; empiricism versus Aristotelianism: these terms are not simply contraries. Rather they are incommensurate: that is, they do not belong to the same epistemological categories or classes and can therefore be neither compared nor contrasted with one another. For example, romance may be assimilated to epic as neo-Aristotelian genus; and novel may be assimilated to confessional lyric as post-Romantic ideological construct. But there exists, in Foucault's terms, no table of resemblances or mutual co-ordinates on which novel and romance may be mutually defined, for they share no historically specific determinants. Likewise, empirical truth and authoritative faith are incommensurate, for each has its meaning only within an epistemè or discursive configuration wholly discontinuous from

[23] 'Cervantes and the Games of Illusion', in *Cervantes and the Renaissance* (Easton, Pa., 1980), 141–56 (p. 143).

[24] *Beyond Fiction: The Recovery of the Feminine in the Novels of Cervantes* (Berkeley, 1984), pp. xii, 10–12, 170.

that of the other. Hence if the generic, linguistic, and psychic contradictions in Cervantes's work are determined, in the final instance, by the historical period in which he lived, this does not mean that they can be explained or resolved by cultural or ideological 'context'. It does mean, however, that they are shared, to a varying extent, by Cervantes's contemporaries, in whose lyric, picaresque, and drama difference and incommensurability are equally apparent. And if the works have much in common, then so does the criticism. Readings of Cervantes share with those of other authors the longing for a 'presence' absent in the text, the repression of a narrative frame too emphatic within the text and the erasure of an original literary inscription previous to the text, without which it could not have come into existence.

We are left however, with the historical problem of Cervantes's unique reception abroad. English translators of the eighteenth century stress the universality of Don Quijote:

Every Man has something of *Don Quixote*, in his Humour, some darling *Dulcinea* of his Thoughts, that sets him very often upon mad Adventures. What *Quixotes* does not every Age produce in Politicks and Religion, who fancying themselves to be in the Right of something, which all the World tells them is wrong, make very good sport to the Publick, and shew that they themselves need the Chiefest Amendment![25]

They also praise the copiousness of the *Persiles*, a characteristic less popular today: 'The Fecundity of Invention [is] marvellous; insomuch that he is even *wasteful* of his Wit, and excessive in the Multitude of his Episodes.'[26] But, as time passes, there is increasing reference to the specificity of the humour: 'the genius of knight-errantry having been so long expired all over *Europe*, excepting in *Spain*, yet this book has been translated into most languages, and every where read with universal applause; though the humour was long ago spent, and the satire affected none but the *Spaniards*.'[27] What is more, the artificiality of the

[25] *The History of the Renowned Don Quixote de la Mancha*, trans. by several hands (London, 1706), fo. A5^r.

[26] *Persiles and Sigismunda: A Celebrated Novel* (London, 1741), intro. 'Extract from Mr Bayle's General Historical Dictionary' (unnumbered).

[27] *The Life and Exploits of the Ingenious Gentleman Don Quixote de la Mancha*, trans. Charles Jarvis (London, 1742), 'Translator's Preface' (unnumbered).

language (already noted in 1706) is also offered as a peculiarly Spanish characteristic: 'He [the translator] has endeavoured to retain the spirit and ideas, without servilely adhering to the literal expression of the original; from which, however, he had not so far deviated, as to destroy that formality of idiom, so peculiar to the Spaniards, and so essential to the character of the work.'[28] By 1788 a French translator of the *Novelas* claims that their interest is mainly documentary, and of concern more to the Spaniards than to anyone else in Europe.[29]

The *Quijote* is prized, then, because it appears to be at once universal and particular. It seems to testify to both the ideal generality of an eternal 'human nature' and the material specificities of a particular time and place. The reception of the *Quijote* by foreigners thus confirms that curious coexistence of the ideal and the empirical which we have noted in Cervantes's œuvre as a whole. Far from praising his language as moderate or clear, however, the translators are struck by its formality and artificiality, which is held to be typical of Spain. I would suggest, then, that the success of the *Quijote* abroad (and, inversely, the relative failure of Cervantes's other works and those of his fellow Spaniards in the centuries which followed) may be explained by a transference of the principle of excess from the means to the object of representation. Cervantes's and Don Quijote's language is frequently rhetorical or artificial, but the reader may safely assign this quality to the madness of the Knight or the extravagance of the fictitious author. *Don Quijote* thus permits the foreign reader the flattering 'recognition' of a linguistic excess considered typical of Spain and the distancing of that excess by its attribution to figures represented within the fiction. When such an operation is performed by the reader Cervantes appears not to engage with those problems of linguistic materiality or 'dominance' so awkwardly posed by other authors of his time. The supposed transparency of his style confirms an intimate intuition of his 'presence' in the text, which is thought to register as a moderate and prudent irony. It remains the case, however, that the problems we have found in Cervantes (of genre, authority, and subjective constitution)

---

[28] *The History and Adventures of the Renowned Don Quixote* (London, 1755), i, fo. Cʳ.

[29] *Nouvelles espagnoles de Michel de Cervantes*, trans. Lefebvre de Villebrune (Paris, 1788), notes to *L'Illustre Frégone* and *Les Filoux* (p. 3).

recur more overtly perhaps, but with no less complexity, throughout the literature of the Spanish Golden Age. The text of the *Quijote* thus facilitates an erasure of the habitual rhetorics of excess and marginality, an erasure with which the modern reader is only too willing to collude.

2. KNOWLEDGE AND IGNORANCE: *EL LICENCIADO VIDRIERA*

The questions raised by the *Quijote* recur on a more manageable scale in the *Novelas ejemplares*. As in the *Quijote*, literary genre and textual authority are both, to some extent, called into question. Cervantes claimed to be the first to write *novelas* in Spanish. But the innovatory role in which he casts himself does not make the creative process any simpler. In the introduction to his *Cervantes and the Humanist Vision*, Alban K. Forcione cites Cervantes's further claim (made in the *Viaje del Parnaso*) to have opened a way or path in the *Novelas* through which the Castilian language can 'display an absurdity with propriety' (p. 3). Forcione takes this phrase as exemplary of a contradiction latent in the *Novelas*: on the one hand, Cervantes acknowledges the low status of prose fiction ('desatino'); on the other, he seeks to defend his own essays in the genre by appeal to the principle of decorum ('propiedad') (pp. 7–8). For Forcione Cervantes's ambivalence towards the genre is shown by his rejection of the narrative frame or *cornice* traditional in such collections. Cervantes introduces no external fictional speakers to tell his tales for him. Hence he rejects the 'closed, determining structure which reduces the contained fictions to a univocal exemplarity' (p. 6). In their concern for allegorical or latent truth (the 'mystery' to which Cervantes alludes in his introduction) the stories may be compared to a favourite motif of Erasmian hermeneutic, the 'Silenus Alcibiadis' or treasure chest in the form of a grotesque monster: the rough exterior conceals a precious mystery inside, which readers must seek out for themselves (p. 9).

And, as in the *Quijote* once more, the question of language and subjectivity is also problematic. Freed from both narrative framework and direct authorial intervention, the collection is disturbingly intermittent and discontinuous. Some stories are couched in relatively plain language and present us with psychologically 'rounded' characters; others are written in relatively ornate language and offer artificially 'flat' characters. The apparently random order of the collection, which resists definitive explanation, heightens this sense of heterogeneity, as the *Novelas* oscillate between Spanish realism, Italianate romance, and intermediate hybrids of the two. Hence many critics of the *Novelas* agree with critics of the *Quijote* in thinking that Cervantes's ultimate skill is in the leaving of formal or evaluative 'blanks' for the active reader to fill.

Even within a collection that is so disparate, my choice of *El licenciado vidriera* may seem perverse. The early date of its composition and the consequent inferiority of its structure (opinions which most critics seem to share) make its position appear marginal, relatively unimportant. Yet its theme, that of madness, must be central to any approach to Cervantes. And Cervantes's treatment of madness as a kind of privileged (yet deranged) insight takes up a general question raised in the first half of this chapter: the order of knowledge and its relation to discourse. I shall argue that *El licenciado* offers a critique of knowledge and of perspicacity; and that this critique occurs at precisely those points where the story is held by many critics to be imperfect. Not surprisingly, other critics, eager to 'improve' on earlier, more negative evaluations, have sought (as in the case of picaresque) to erase or smooth out these supposed faults or contradictions. One main area of dispute is the disjointedness of the story: in particular, the lengthy description of the protagonist Tomás's travels in Italy has no obvious connection with the string of apothegms to which he later gives vent in Spain. But for critics who seek to prove the 'structural unity' of the story this randomness and disjointedness are merely apparent. Rather they are a 'device employed to simulate the learning process' which points implicitly to the story's underlying theme: the 'discreción' or prudence which the character fails to achieve and which the reader must strive to attain.[30] The somewhat cursory conclusion (Tomás dies in battle) is hailed as exemplary. It reveals that Tomás has not managed to acquire the harmony that comes from proper self-knowledge. Again, as

---

[30] Frank P. Casa, 'Structural Unity in *El licenciado vidriera*', *BHS* 41 (1964), 242–6 (p. 245).

in the case of the picaresque novel, the critic who resolves formal contradictions also attempts to erase other troubling inconsistencies. These include the frequent and scantly motivated changes in Tomás's character; the alternate copiousness and austerity of Cervantes's language; the fluctuations in narrative voice or perspective. Such critics salvage psychic, stylistic, and narrative coherence in the name of the author. And one recent reader appeals to 'specular oppositions' to produce the necessary unity. Thus he claims that the opening scene in Spain is a mirror image of the closing scene abroad. Likewise, repeated changes in the character's name and clothing also point to a reflexive or specular symmetry.[31] The most recent critic claims that the failure of Tomás to achieve his ambition is a transcendent moral which saves the story from semantic vacuity and formal discontinuity: 'it is necessary [for Cervantes] to create absurdities that seem to lack integrity, that reflect an apparently episodic plot structure'.[32]

It is perhaps ironic that this last scholar appeals to Ruth El Saffar in this context. For she herself does not share his own faith in the authenticating 'substance' of the author. El Saffar argues persuasively that the story reveals Cervantes's 'unreconciled ambivalence' to literature which is at once necessary and futile; and that there is a clear 'disjunction' between story and apothegms, highlighted by the 'frailty of the link' between the two (*Novel to Romance*, pp. 50–1). She also stresses the story's narrative incoherence and its consequent lack of psychological realism (pp. 55, 61). El Saffar implies that to acknowledge these contradictions need not be to suggest a negative evaluation of the story. And I myself shall argue that it is not so much the inconsistencies but the sameness of *El licenciado* that produces the most unsettling effects: by failing to draw a clear distinction between the voice of the character and that of the narrator, by failing to keep a consistent distance from his creation, Cervantes reveals, unwittingly, the necessary role of difference in the production of narrative illusion.

Forcione's reading of the story, perhaps the most complex of

[31] Jacques Joset, 'Bipolarizaciones textuales y estructura especular en *El licenciado vidriera*', in *Cervantes, su obra y su mundo: Actas del I Congreso internacional sobre Cervantes* (Madrid, 1981), 357–63.

[32] John G. Weiger, *The Substance of Cervantes* (Cambridge, 1985), 36.

all, bears the title 'the mystery of knowledge'. He begins with the structural problem noted by previous critics: the relation between what he takes to be the 'frame' of the story (Tomás's adventures) and the substance (his satirical fragments) (p. 227). For Forcione the story achieves integration at an epistemological level, which can be perceived only in the context of Renaissance humanism. Like Erasmus's *Ciceronianus*, *El licenciado* is the story of an improper and excessive love of knowledge: Tomás's early travels and later madness reveal the same tendency towards indiscriminate superficiality. Tomás, when mad, is like a Cynic philosopher, prone to the particular vice of that school, a destructive misanthropy untempered by Christian *humanitas* (pp. 241–60). The 'mystery of knowledge' is in part that it is reflexive or recursive, always turning back on itself. It is significant that Tomás the satirist is stung by a wasp, for the wasp is a conventional symbol of satire itself (p. 281). Likewise knowledge can heal the sick, but in excessive doses its effect is poisonous, even deadly (pp. 302, 307). The only problem with Forcione's immensely detailed reading is a general, theoretical one: the relative status of the discourses invoked. At times the story itself seems to disappear under the weight of the critic's erudition. The very exhaustiveness of the reading, the very breadth of the parallels cited (from the immense corpus of Erasmus himself, to classical myth and Renaissance theology) confront the reader with the central problem of humanism itself: the unlimited proliferation of commentary. Of course, Forcione does not seek, naïvely, to prove the 'influence' of Erasmus on Cervantes, and there can be no simple distinction between relevant and irrelevant collation. But the problem of intertextuality is insoluble, because it is endless. For example, Forcione discerns a biblical subtext in the story: the tree under which Tomás is surprised sleeping at the beginning is the tree of knowledge in the Garden of Eden; the fruit offered Tomás which precipitates his madness is the apple of the same tree, cause of man's Fall (pp. 239–40). However (as Forcione knows very well) this kind of subtext does not resolve the story or curtail its play of meaning. Indeed, its effect is quite the reverse: it opens up the *novela* to a potentially infinite number of intertextual readings. Hence in his very subtlety, erudition, and copiousness Forcione reproduces, perhaps unwittingly, the motive and structure of Tomás's madness: the endless displacement of desire in the insatiable quest for knowledge.

I do not claim myself to resolve the mystery of *El licenciado vidriera*. But I would suggest that the story displays a rhetorical surplus which is characteristically Spanish, and which underlies the discontinuities of its form, characterization, style, and narrative voice. We need neither lament these contradictions like some critics, nor seek to erase them like others, but attempt like Forcione to place them within the epistemè or discursive configuration of Cervantes's time (and to confront it with that of our own). The form of the story is nomadic. It begins with Tomás asleep and alone, lacking both consciousness and company until he is woken by the gentlemen scholars. Even then he suffers from a selective amnesia, claiming to have forgotten his family and place of birth, but remembering his name.[33] Thus the point at which the story begins is indeterminate, nonspecific. Tomás is sleeping on the banks of the river Tormes, but the name functions more as the sign of the picaresque genre than as an index of a geographical location. More symptomatic of the story is that it is a wilderness ('soledad'). And this opening moment, already indistinct, is further qualified in that it refers the reader back to an absent origin: the character's family of whom no further mention is made throughout the rest of the story. Tomás is thus presented from the very beginning as a kind of self-erasing trace always already in motion, with no fixed or ascertainable source either inside or outside the text. His passage is like that of knowledge itself: it has always begun and is never ended. And the events which ensure the persistence of this ceaseless displacement are strangely, even scandalously, unmotivated. Thus the meeting with the captain is as fortuitous as the meeting with the students. We are told that Tomás now loves learning, but he is easily tempted abroad by Diego de Valdivia. The reasons offered by the narrator are hardly pressing. For example, Tomás reasons that he can always go back to university after a few years (p. 17). By placing the principle of chance at the very heart of his narrative, with these random encounters and half-hearted preferences, Cervantes comes close to destroying all sense of necessary con-

---

[33] *Novelas ejemplares*, ii, ed. Francisco Rodríguez Marín (Madrid, 1975), 9–10.

nection between the episodes he recounts. The result is that the death of the character at the end seems to be by no means inevitable. If Tomás is indifferent to military life at the start of the story it seems improbable (though not impossible) that he consider it his only refuge at the end. Cervantes's own concern for the arms and letters controversy is well known. But by displacing it on to his character (and by describing the causes and consequences of this choice in such a brief and cursory manner) Cervantes makes the Licenciado's death more bathetic than heroic, lacking as it does both adequate motivation and discernible effect.

This brings us to the disproportionate length allotted the various elements of the story. The travel scenes are replete with arbitrary lists: of wines, of Roman streets and hills, of offerings to Our Lady of Loreto (pp. 22, 27, 29). Critics have displaced the unease they feel at such aimless prolixity by assigning the catalogues to the character rather than to the narrator who offers them: they are often held to be a symptom of Tomás's improper curiosity, not of Cervantes's lack of concern for narrative relevance. The question posed by the lists, however, is more radical than this. It is, quite simply, whether such a thing as a 'proper' relationship between narrative and description (or between narrator and character) can be said to exist. By exceeding the limits of narrative relevance and coherence Cervantes reveals such limits to be arbitrary and conventional. His own reminiscences seem to force their way into the text as direct source of the travel scenes. Thus our sense of the aimless proliferation of knowledge cannot be restricted to the character. By improperly intruding into the fictional space the author becomes just another contributor to the boundless expansion or inflation to which the economy of knowledge is subject.

Cervantes's contempt for structural causality and psychic motivation appears most openly in the episode of the poisoning. The *femme fatale* is scarcely described at all. Indeed, the meaning of the one phrase by which she is defined ('dama de todo rumbo y manejo' (p. 32)) has proved obscure to the commentators. Her love of Tomás and rejection by him are allotted just a few lines, and once her deed is done, she simply disappears. The woman is thus invoked as a general example of infamy, rather than a specific case of psychological process. The effect of the potion is contrary to that expected: far from gaining in amorous strength, Tomás is so weakened he almost dies. And the narrator himself undermines any faith the reader may have in the efficacy of magic by stating that free will is more than a match for any potions or spells (p. 34). Here Cervantes sabotages the pivotal point of the narrative: the supposed cause of Tomás's madness is presented as both improbable and illogical. Cervantes devotes even less attention and provides even less motivation for Tomás's next metamorphosis, the cure of his insanity effected by a friar (p. 79). In his lack of attention to the necessary links between fictional episodes, Cervantes seems to go against a basic principle of story-telling. In a well-known essay on the structural approach to narrative, Barthes suggests that the dynamics of all plots rest on a slippage between consecution and consequence. Thus in narrative (but not in life) the event which follows another is generally thought to do so because of it. Barthes cites a scholastic dictum in this context: 'post hoc, ergo propter hoc'. The writer relies on (and the reader colludes in) this formal sleight of hand.[34] In *El licenciado vidriera*, on the other hand, the absence of probable or even possible connection between successive events prevents readers from performing the conventional collapse of consequence and consecution, of the chronological and the logical. There is a conflict between the sequence of actions and the relation we seek to draw between them. The story does not satisfy the demands of a coherent, seamless narration. But through this failure it makes us question those demands and our unthinking submission to them. The incoherence of *El licenciado* thus needs no interpretation. Its value is not hermeneutic but heuristic.

If the changes in Tomás's character seem arbitrary, then the other figures in the story barely merit the name 'characters' at all. The captain is the only one to be dignified with a name. And the Licenciado's own names suggest not a stable personality but a radical indeterminacy: he is a doubting Thomas, uncertain of the status of what he sees; and a wheel or pulley ('rueda', 'rodaja'), spinning uncontrollably over Europe before coming to rest at an arbitrary point. When asked who is the

[34] 'Introduction to the Structural Analysis of Narratives', in *Image Music Text*, ed. and trans. Stephen Heath (London, 1982), 79–124 (p. 94).

happiest man in the world, Tomás replies, 'Nemo' ('Nobody'): because 'Nobody knows his father; Nobody goes to heaven; Nobody is happy with his lot.' According to the modern editors, the idea is an old one, stretching back at least to Seneca (pp. 65–6). But the saying is almost emblematic of a work which strips all individualizing characteristics from the human beings it claims to represent. And the motives of this depersonalization are magic and madness. Magic is, of its essence, irrational, beyond human understanding. As we have seen, its effect is inexplicable, outside the control of individuals. Likewise, madness is the discourse of the unmotivated and the inconsequential, the irreducibly different. Cervantes presents us with two moods or moments of madness: Tomás's curious delusions concerning his glass body and his lucid comments on the vices of contemporary society. These moments are quite inconsistent: how can Tomás be so deluded and so perspicacious at the same time? But they suggest that madness is incoherent even in its alterity, that it is different even from itself. Like Cervantes's contradictory and depersonalized characters, madness offers no consistent or unified 'face' to the reader, not even that of an unspeakable Other, which remains eternally foreign to our own good sense. Of course, the wise fool is a common figure in the period. What is more important is that Cervantes refuses us the interpretative strategy it normally requires: a simple, consistent reversal in which folly becomes wisdom and wisdom folly. Cervantes both praises folly as the antidote to an immoral 'sanity', and decries it as a delusion incompatible with social order. He thus refuses to reduce the difference between sanity and madness to one of simple opposition.

The final problem raised by *El licenciado* is that of authority and language. At various points in the story we must ask ourselves, 'Who is speaking?' The narrator sometimes serves up the dullest of clichés with the straightest of faces: Salamanca is 'bewitching'; Venice, the wonder of the Old World, is rivalled only by Mexico, the wonder of the New (pp. 12, 30). In spite of the opinions of the more confident critics it is by no means clear that these observations are to be attributed to the naïve and undiscriminating Tomás. Likewise, as the satirist who seeks to reform society, Tomás sometimes seems to speak with the voice of Cervantes. But his anti-Semitic gibes to the washerwoman

and to the two men entering church (pp. 40, 42) are uncharac-
teristic of the author's general good humour and relative toler-
ance. Forcione would say that Cervantes shares Tomás's
scepticism, but not his lack of discrimination. But in the absence of any stable narrative framework, the distinction is very
difficult to draw. It is ironic, then, that Tomás speaks in senten-
tiae or aphorisms; for his words are deprived of the moral authority generally associated with such a form. His relentless copia
suggests an alternative, however; that madness is a function of
language itself. Thus, on the one hand, madness is a kind of
metonymic contagion: Tomás displaces the clarity of vision
from his intellect to his body. And his humour often derives
from the unexpected swerve or diversion of meaning also
known as displacement.[35] Thus in the example of the washerwoman Tomás cites a verse from the Gospels, and thus displaces the scriptural address to the Jews on to the woman in
front of him, hinting cruelly at her *conversa* origin. Or again, in
the case of the two men entering church, he displaces the order
of the days of the week into the area of names and holy days:
the Christian Domingo (Sunday) must wait for the Jewish
Sabbath to pass. Elsewhere madness and humour are based on
condensation. Thus Tomás condenses the various qualities of
glass (brilliance, clarity, fragility) into the single space of his
mutated body. And he makes frequent use of puns (the condensation of multiple meanings in a single word) in his witty
apothegms. For example, he tells a mother, out promenading
her ugly daughter who is decked with gems, that she does right
to 'stone' her in order to 'walk' her (where 'to stone' is both 'to
apply jewels' to a person and 'to lay flagstones' on a road)
(p. 63). This is one of the simpler examples of concentrated
word-play. The importance of displacement and condensation
is not (or not merely) that they permit us to analyse Tomás's
madness and his humour; it is that they suggest that neither can
be extricated from the endless play of language itself. Tomás's
statements cannot be attributed wholly to the character, to the
author, or to supposed 'sources' outside the text. And this is
because humour and madness are precisely those marginal dis-

---

[35] In the discussion which follows I use the terms 'displacement' and 'condensation'
in the senses proposed by Freud in his *Jokes and their Relation to the Unconscious*
(Harmondsworth, 1983), 50–66, 86–93.

courses which resist subjective closure, which demand intersubjective space.

But to argue simply that it is madness (or language) that
'speaks' in Tomás's mouth is to offer a generalization as indiscriminate as those of the madman himself. *El licenciado vidriera* is
not entirely unfocused. It also seems to offer an implicit critique
of knowledge and of representation. Thus there are hints that
suggest the nostalgia for an original basis for authority. When
Tomás visits Rome he describes the ruins of the ancient city as
the 'lion's claw', the only surviving trace of its former glory
(p. 26). This is an allusion to the proverb 'ex ungue leonem':
the witness to contemporary decadence must work back from
the current fragment to the original whole. Yet elsewhere the
text suggests that Ancient Rome cannot be taken as the image
of an original and authoritative presence. When asked his
opinion of poets, Tomás cites Ovid's *Ars amatoria*: once upon a
time ('olim') poets were properly concerned for the welfare of
their state, and their ancient choruses received great rewards
(p. 46). This quote (the longest and first of several) fails to
prove Tomás's point. For his own lament for a lost, cultural integrity, his own nostalgia for authoritative utterance, are also
to be found in the supposed source of that integrity and utterance. Rome is invoked as the guarantor of an authentic tradition. But, according to Tomás's own quote, it already betrays
within itself a decline from that tradition. The quest for a fixed
cultural or epistemological standard (for the mighty beast from
which the artistic trace derives) stands revealed as an infinite
return to a mythical origin always already lost. The decadence
for which the Licenciado berates his own time is a permanent
state of affairs.

Elsewhere, Tomás suggests (again, in spite of himself) that
there is a lack of 'fit' or correlation between the means and the
object of representation. The images and arguments he uses are
very similar to those we saw used by López Pinciano in the first
chapter. Thus in his discussion of poets, once more, Tomás
claims that poetry is universal in scope: it encompasses all other
sciences (p. 46). But if art is infinite in scale, representation is no
easy matter. On seeing some ill-painted statues outside a
church, Tomás says that good painters imitate nature
('imitar'), bad painters spew it up ('vomitar') (p. 49). Tomás

offers other examples of improper imitation: the chemists whose medicines have the opposite effect to that required, and the tailors and cobblers whose garments must be forced unnaturally to fit the parts of the body for which they are intended (pp. 55, 60). These images turn back on the story itself, whose language and structure seem alternatively inadequate for or excessive to its chosen subject matter. Cervantes fails to 'digest' his disparate matter (narrative and apothegms) and thus vomits it up in all its variety and incongruity. The labour of many orthodox critics is analogous to that of the unfortunate shoppers in the text: they must stretch or bend the literary garment until it assumes the appearance of their own body of preconception. When Tomás goes off on his travels he takes with him an edition of Garcilaso 'without a commentary' (p. 20). The reference implies a bias towards the self-sufficiency or plainness of text we might be tempted to attribute to Cervantes himself. However, this self-sufficiency is achieved neither by the character nor by the author: both Tomás and Cervantes embroider their stories with increasingly redundant decoration. And this is because the ideal of an object untouched by representation (of a text innocent of commentary) is a seductive but impossible delusion. The inconsistent fabric of the story and the contradictory readings of its critics disprove the notion of an original object outside the text or an objective, uncompromised reading of it.

In the first half of this chapter I cited Foucault's definition of Don Quijote as the 'hero of the same'. In this reading of *El licenciado* I have stressed the role of difference in the text: of difference within the form and characterization of the story, within its style and narrative voice. These differences approach incommensurability. That is, they juxtapose terms which have no common frame of reference. Yet it could be argued that in this story Cervantes himself is the 'hero of the same'. By lending the mad protagonist his own scepticism and irony and by abolishing (intermittently at least) the habitual difference between character and narrator, Cervantes disrupts the fictional illusion and disorientates the reader. Ironically, then, the intervention of the author tends to undermine any faith in his transcendent authority as source of knowledge. For in such passages as the travelogue and the praise of poetry it is as an arbitrary collection of prejudices and preferences that he makes his presence felt. By failing to carry through his customary pose of neutrality or non-intervention, by participating himself in his character's encyclopaedic ambitions, Cervantes destabilizes the order of knowledge at the same time as he asserts its universality. There can be no escape from the discursive configuration of the age; but that configuration is by no means immutable.

El licenciado vidriera thus raises a number of questions associated with the work of the best-known theorist of knowledge, Michel Foucault. It suggests first that madness is not an essential or unchanging state but a marginal discourse, through which society enforces the boundaries of its power. Secondly, it confirms (as in the case of the *Quijote*) that the subject who embraces the same as a cognitive principle and refuses to experience the world in terms of difference and identity will find himself excluded from the increasingly empiricist world-view of the early seventeenth century. Thirdly, it implies that the order of knowledge is bound up inextricably with the omnipresence of power and the tyrannical privilege of sight.[36] Indeed, the story can be read as a burlesque of the principle of clarity or perspicacity, which (as we have seen throughout this book) is fundamental to all writing in the period. The critical gaze of the madman defines and subjects others in a kind of parody of the scientific or encyclopaedic method. All human life is classified and dissected by the penetrating action of Tomás's eye and tongue. But this gaze is reflected or deflected back on to his own body, a perfectly lucid and perfectly absent space. The look of light erases the subject from whom it issues: the madman is deprived of both the flesh that would make him human and the authority which would legitimate his speech. In the Introduction to this book I cited Lacan's dictum 'You never look at me from the place from which I see you.' The moral of *El licenciado vidriera* is slightly different, but more radical: 'I can never look at myself from the place from which I see you.' There can be no

[36] These three points are explored, at great length and with great subtlety, in the following three works: *Histoire de la folie à l'âge classique* (Paris, 1972); *Les Mots et les choses*; *Surveiller et punir*. For an excellent guide to these works see Alan Sheridan, *Michel Foucault: The Will to Truth* (London and New York, 1982), part I, chs. 1 and 2; part II, ch. 2. For the tyranny of sight see Martin Jay, 'In the Empire of the Gaze: Foucault and the Denigration of Vision in Twentieth-century French Thought', in *ICA Documents 4: Postmodernism* (London, 1986), 19–25.

pure or innocent subject position, no place from which one can scrutinize one's own specificity. The place of pure transparency, of perfect freedom from individual determination, is that of madness.

The character's blind spot, then, is that knowledge is unlimited. Even if we achieved absolute knowledge of the world, we could never have access to the space occupied by our own body, to those unknowable forces that shaped the way we see. The critics' blind spot is that absence is irremediable. Struggling to gain access to the creative processes of Cervantes the immortal genius, they fail to note the return of the author in a relativized, non-transcendental guise. Where Tomás denies or erases the particularities of his body, Cervantes projects his likes and dislikes, wholly undigested, into the fictional space of the story. Cervantes thus hints at the meaning of Barthes's apparently senseless statement: 'Writing passes through the body.'[37] For if (as the story reveals) the erasure of the body is impossible, then the only alternative is to acknowledge the specificity of its determination. In his fragmentary autobiography Barthes offers lists of favourite things such as food and drink (pp. 120–1), which seem almost as random as the rather similar lists in Cervantes's story. But in neither case does this signify the return of the author as an integrated, if idiosyncratic, individual. Rather it suggests the material constitution of the subject, who is neither authoritative nor transcendent.

A Foucaldian reading of *El licenciado* foregrounds the marginality of madness, the deviance of the same, and the tyranny of vision. But it also calls attention to another effect of the will to knowledge: the compulsion to 'speak the truth' in sexuality.[38] For sex is the displaced or repressed term in the story. As many critics have noted, Tomás recoils from the only offer of love made to him, that of the unnamed *femme fatale*. But, at a deeper level, it is the gift of love that is the vehicle for the return of the repressed. It is a poisoned quince ('membrillo'), thought to be an aphrodisiac, and speaking in its supposed etymology the forbidden knowledge of the female genitals the fruit is thought to resemble ('membrum'). A superficial 'Freudian'

---

[37] *Roland Barthes par Roland Barthes* (Paris, 1980), 83.
[38] This is a central theme of the first volume of Foucault's history of sexuality, *La Volonté de savoir*.

reading might claim that Tomás goes mad because of sexual frustration. But, as we saw in the last chapter, the sexual economy is not one of simple homeostasis or hydraulics. What is suggested by the 'membrum–membrillo' is that sexuality is indeed central to subjectivity, but that it is always bound up with linguistic structure. The false etymology implied but unstated by Cervantes's text involves both the displacement of logical reasoning and the condensation of multiple meaning. The quince is at once and alternatively fruit and organ, food and sex. And Cervantes, like Foucault again, does not take it for granted that sex forms the essence of a person's being. Rather he questions that assumption, through his lack of attention to amorous intrigue and the cursory way in which he depicts it. Thus there is no simple opposition between sexuality and repression, any more than there is between madness and sanity. Likewise the distinctions between knowledge and ignorance or light and dark are more complex than they first appear. They are not contraries, but privatives: the second term is defined by the absence of the first. If the story seems fragmented and hollow it is because it is based in part on a general economy of knowledge which is prone to structural asymmetry.

The story ends in death. But, yet again, death is not the opposite of desire. Indeed, it is in death that Tomás achieves his desire for glory ('fama'). The nature of such glory is one concern of a work which treats the problem of absolute knowledge, Derrida's most intimidating text, *Glas* (Paris, 1981). Derrida's title is appropriate for the end of our story: 'glas' (from the vulgar Latin 'classus') once meant a military fanfare, and now means a death knell. In the opening pages Derrida's text (which purports to be a commentary on Hegel and Genet) weaves together a number of dislocated, apparently random motifs, drawn from a variety of sources. Thus the catafalque is at once a dais for the elevation of the body and a scaffold for its execution (i. 2^r; 3^r); the masterpiece is an erection which swells in its author's signature, but fills it like a sarcophagus (fo. 15^r); the flowers of rhetoric, neither natural nor artificial, rot like wreaths on the walls of a cemetery (fo. 17^r). It would be easy to offer interpretations or paraphrases of these fragments: glory is predicated on the death of the hero, writing on the absence of the author, and figuration on the difference between trope and referent. The problem is that to adopt such univocal readings is to reintroduce those delusions of absolute knowledge and objective commentary that *Glas* works so hard to unsettle. It is perhaps better to dwell on the most persistent motif in *Glas*: the monolith or colossus. The monolith is at once the raised phallus and the site of death, a pointer to the continuing presence and definitive absence of its originator. The literary monument, like its military equivalent, is a vain construction or a phantom erection because it must always testify to the absence of the author it claims none the less to embody. As character, Tomás achieves his goal, but is banished at once from the story; as author, Cervantes constructs his monument, but is reduced to the status of a cultural institution. Like the anamorphic skull in Holbein's *Ambassadors*, literary glory is a distorting lure, a trap for the gaze, a swollen phallus which cannot conceal the necessary pre-eminence of death.[39]

We may now return to the image cited by Forcione in connection with Cervantes's humanist 'vision', the 'Silenus Alcibiadis'. As I said at the beginning of this section, the Silenus is generally taken as the symbol of a binary process of interpretation: the grotesque monsters on the outside of the treasure chest open to reveal the precious objects within. In just this way, Forcione implies, the sometimes inconsistent surface of the *Novelas* reveals to the active reader the mystery hidden inside. Yet I have suggested that the action of *El licenciado vidriera* tends to subvert our belief in internal essence or transcendent meaning. And if we look at Renaissance and classical treatments of the Silenus its moral becomes less self-evident. Thus Covarrubias offers a picture of two 'coarse and fearsome' monsters perched on a chest, which itself resembles a catafalque or coffin. The motto reads: 'Meliora latent' (iii. 25ʳ). But what exactly are these 'better things' hidden inside? It is perhaps significant that Covarrubias gives no source for his motto. The verse below the picture says the Silenus contains 'jewels and precious things' ('joyas y preseas'); but the prose text on the verso calls the chest an 'escritorio', a case for storing papers and writing implements. A later emblem book, Picinellus's *Mundus*

---

[39] For Holbein's skull as phallus see Lacan's *Four Fundamental Concepts* (pp. 86–90). For anamorphosis as the death of representation see Jean-François Lyotard, *Discours, figure* (Paris, 1971), 376–9.

symbolicus (Cologne, 1681), states that the Sileni contain 'gods and jewels' ('deos et gemmas') (lib. 3, numer. 133).

If we look back to Forcione's favourite authority, Erasmus, the hidden object becomes even less certain. Editions of the *Adagia* state that what is revealed when the statues open is a 'numen'. Deriving originally from a root meaning 'to nod with the head', 'numen' comes to mean, variably, a human command or authority, or divine will and majesty. One edition of the *Adagia* places the Silenus in a section titled 'Simulatio et dissimulatio'.[40] Erasmus seems to quicken this play of concealment and revelation already implicit in the image by placing an abstract noun (not a concrete object) at the centre of his metaphorical treasure chest. The *Adagia* themselves, rather like the lists of objects and apothegms in Cervantes's story, seem to exemplify the proliferating manner of the humanist vision. But Erasmus's treatment of the Silenus calls into question the existence of the authority it is his intention to affirm. As Forcione notes (p. 9), for Erasmus the greatest example of the Silenus is Christ, his homely exterior concealing the numinous presence within. However, the slippage between literal and figurative in the Silenus must undermine the ability of allegory to serve as a vehicle for ultimate truth.

The main authority cited by both Erasmus and Covarrubias is Plato's *Symposium*. In his speech in praise of Socrates, Alcibiades likens his tutor (apparently ugly, foolish, and lustful) to the brutish, lascivious demigods, the Sileni (216 E). This much is clear enough. But the word he uses to describe the treasure within the chest is even more problematic than 'numen'. It is 'agalma', a noun denoting variously delight, glory, or honour; a pleasing gift, especially for the gods; a statue in honour of a god; a statue, a portrait, or a picture; or an image, expressed by painting or words. The lexicon which gives all these meanings claims that the last is appropriate for its use in the *Symposium*.[41] Yet there could hardly be a linguistic image inside the chest. And if it is a painted image (or a statue, of whatever kind) then the inner treasure must be itself a representation; not an original source of knowledge or power, but a

---

[40] Published in Frankfurt, 1629 (pp. 653–7).

[41] Henry George Liddell and Robert Scott, *A Greek–English Lexicon* (Oxford, 1968), s.v. ἄγαλμα.

signifier improperly occupying the place of privilege, referring elsewhere to its absent origin. Hence, the Silenus is a *mise-en-abyme*. Reflecting back only on to itself, it sends the observer's eye hurrying ever inwards or backwards in search of the ultimate truth it claims to conceal within. But as Tomás Rodaja discovered to his cost, the quest for knowledge it initiates is interminable, the desire for meaning it stimulates is insatiable. If the Silenus is an image of the *Novelas*, it is because it undermines the search for absolute meaning while appearing to underwrite it. And if it is an image of Cervantes's œuvre as a whole, it is because it gives an illusion of presence or authority which it must ultimately fail to deliver. But this does not make the search any less valuable, nor the illusion any less necessary.´

CONCLUSION
THE MARGINALITY OF SPANISH CULTURE

THERE can be little doubt that Spanish literature is considered to be marginal today, outside the Hispanic world at least. That this was also the case in the years of Spanish political and military hegemony in Europe is far from certain. Madame de Sévigné and Samuel Pepys were just two of those familiar with the Castilian language and versed in its writings. While I have not attempted in this study to explore the very complex historical problem of the relationship between Spanish writers and a European public, it seems undeniable that, even at the height of their power, Spaniards often felt themselves to be different (and frequently inferior) from others. As I have tried to show, this difference reveals itself within the texture of the writing as a persistent attempt to attain an impossible goal: that of fixing once and for all the boundaries between inside and outside, defining the limits between essence and excess. A number of motifs which have occurred in the course of this study seem emblematic of this literate self-consciousness. Garcilaso's curiously prominent 'tongue', still singing in the mouth of the poet's severed head, suggests to us the virtuosity and ingenuity of Spanish lyric; Mateo Alemán's inverted painting, whose position the reader is invited to correct, suggests the concern of picaresque narrative for the act of perception and the limits of representation; Calderón's sunlit beach, criss-crossed with shadows and traces, suggests the ceaseless play of inscription and erasure typical of the comedia. These images of qualified abundance or copia are complemented by the work of Cervantes, which is equally concerned with language, perception, and convention, but more easily assimilated by readers outside Spain.

Perhaps now the time has come for a wider and more sympathetic knowledge of these texts. Gracián complained that, before the *Agudeza*, Spanish 'conceptos' had been orphaned at birth, thrust into an alien world which failed to recognize their unique quality. The reception of Golden Age writing by humanist critics is not so different, whether they praise or blame the objects they have chosen to study. Confronted by texts which exhibit diversity and discontinuity, they react by praising the moderate prudence of 'Renaissance' authors and reducing even the 'baroque' works to formal unity and moral orthodoxy. The complex linguistic pleasure offered by all Golden Age writing, the persistence with which it exceeds the arbitrary limits of plain speech and organic structure (and thus calls into question the very possibility of such criteria), is simply repressed or ignored. Thus Góngora is vindicated in the name of an active, virile intelligence, a 'wit' which brings unity to á fragmented world and thus renders verbal complexity 'essential' to the poem. Or again, Quevedo, the most rhetorical of poets, is praised for the 'modernity' of his style and his supposed expression of personal feeling. The text is thus both floated free from its historical conditions and weighted down by anachronistic conceptions of the 'individual' and 'humanity'. As I read the great body of Golden Age criticism produced by modern scholars I feel a curious sense of enclosure or confinement. For the majority of readings are caught in a web of arbitrary and self-generating dichotomies: conceptismo and culteranismo, Renaissance and baroque, natural and artificial. Even those works which promise a new perspective or new approach seem confined within the limits of conventional debate. Indeed, any intervention from 'outside' those limits risks either absorption into the critical canon or petrification into a mannered posture of revolt.

The newer theories of writing may seem Byzantine to many. Their adherents share with Renaissance rhetoricians a mistrust of unadorned language and a love of technical vocabularies. But what can be seen only now is that the humanist's belief that it was possible, even necessary, to discuss literature in language readily accessible to the 'common reader' is itself a historically specific tenet, and one whose life-span was relatively short. Derrida is surely closely to Scaliger (or Quintilian) than is F. R. Leavis (or A. A. Parker). It may be literary criticism in the late twentieth century is returning to the philosophy from which it emerged in the sixteenth. Thus when Herrera or Barthes use such terms as metalepsis or anacoluthon they are not merely drawing attention to their own status as practitioners of an élite discipline. They are also acknowledging implicitly that the literary object they treat is a complex linguistic phenomenon, not a simple organic growth. What is more, it could be argued that such traditional terms as 'symbol', 'tension', or 'experience' (all of which were unknown to the Renaissance) are as much 'jargon' as their gaudier rhetorical equivalents. For, like all abstractions, they find their meaning only within a particular discursive context and can have no claim to universal prescription. The true difference between the critical schools is the traditionalists' claim to be theoretically neutral or disengaged, a status denied all writing by the modern theorists.

Hence, if I call in this study for an end to the resistance to theory in Hispanism, I use theory in the sense of reflexivity, not abstraction: a turning back on our own activity, not a dissolution of material ties. This attention to theory would require a shift in the horizon of analysis, backwards or outwards to the most basic concerns of criticism. Language, representation, and subjectivity would no longer be 'given' or taken for granted, but would themselves be objects of analysis. This theoretical perspective would also require an awareness that there can be no definitive reading of a text: each is partial, deficient, and wholly compromised by the reader's strategic or conceptual bias. Thus I am not proposing a 'New' or an 'Anti-' Hispanism. Such a movement (if one were to appear) would inevitably reinscribe itself as opposite and equal to the Academy. As Jean-François Lyotard has claimed, deconstruction is itself a construction.[1] It can no longer claim to be innocent of the oppressive mastery it sought to displace or decentre.

However, if there can be no escape from the structures of power and of institutions (and what space can there be 'outside' the Academy for those who write and teach within it?), then the particular significance of Spain and its Renaissance writers might be as an example of persistent and irreducible marginality. For Spain is the 'woman' of European culture. She is excluded from the main currents of political and cultural power, scorned for her supposed emotionalism and sensualism, and pitied for her lack of that serene classicism or rationalism which once presented itself as the ideal. But, at a time when

---

[1] *Économie libidinale* (Paris, 1974), 305.

both the Utopian projects of the Enlightenment and the objective authority of empirical science are increasingly called into
question, then the advantages of a marginal position, less compromised by a dominant intellectual tradition, are self-evident.
Like the concept of 'woman' under patriarchy, Spain embodies
that lack on which Law is predicated, serves as the term which
can neither be excluded from the system, nor allowed to participate in it. As supplement, trace, or parergon, Golden Age
writing defines by its very marginality the arbitrary parameters
of the European culture which cannot absorb it and dare not
admit it. And in doing so it suggests a final characteristic of
literary discourse in general, namely the coexistence of specificity and indeterminacy. Thus one of the leading thinkers of
the period, Juan Caramuel, claims in his *Rationalis et realis philosophia* that the infinite, created object can neither exist nor be
conceived: 'Ens infinitum creatum nec esse nec concipi potest.'[2]
Caramuel classes this unthinkable object, with customary
rigour, under 'aperantologia', the science of the boundless. Yet
we may identify this object with the literary idiom itself. For the
latter is both produced by human beings under particular circumstances ('creatum') and caught up in the endless displace-
ments of desire and language ('infinitum'). The necessary
superfluities of Golden Age writing thus point mutely towards
this paradox: the literary text as both finished product and endless process. And the unique position of Spanish culture
(neither equal nor opposite to its more confident rivals) offers
the attentive reader both the pleasures of difference and the
access of excess.

[2] Published in Louvain, 1642 (table at end, fo. Nnnʳ).

BIBLIOGRAPHY

Alemán, Mateo, *Guzmán de Alfarache*, ed. Francisco Rico (Barcelona, 1983).
Almeida, José, *La crítica literaria de Fernando de Herrera* (Madrid, 1976).
Alonso, Dámaso, *La lengua poética de Góngora* (Madrid, 1935).
—— *Góngora y el 'Polifemo'* (Madrid, 1961).
—— *Cuatro poetas españoles* (Madrid, 1962).
—— Intro. to *Antología de la poesía española: Lírica de tipo tradicional* (Madrid, 1969).
—— 'Garcilaso y los límites de la estilística', in *La poesía de Garcilaso*, ed. Elias L. Rivers (Barcelona, 1974), 269–84.
Althusser, Louis, *Lenin and Philosophy*, trans. Ben Brewster (London, 1971).
Archer, Robert, 'The Fictional Context of *Lazarillo de Tormes*', *MLR* 80 (1985), 340–50.
Arias, Joan, *'Guzmán de Alfarache': The Unrepentant Narrator* (London, 1977).
Aubrun, Charles V., 'Le Don Juan de Tirso de Molina: Essai d'interprétation', *BHisp.* 59 (1957), 26–61.
Aylward, E. T., *Cervantes: Pioneer and Plagiarist* (London, 1982).
'Azorín' [José Martínez Ruiz], 'Garcilaso', in *La poesía de Garcilaso*, ed. Elias L. Rivers (Barcelona, 1974), 35–9.
Barthes, Roland, *Mythologies* (Paris, 1957).
—— *Le Plaisir du texte* (Paris, 1973).
—— *Roland Barthes par Roland Barthes* (Paris, 1980).
—— 'Introduction to the Structural Analysis of Narratives', in *Image Music Text*, ed. and trans. Stephen Heath (London, 1982), 79–124.
Bataillon, Marcel, *Défense et illustration du sens littéral* (Leeds, 1967).
—— *Pícaros y picaresca: La pícara Justina* (Madrid, 1969).
Beverley, John, 'Hispanism Today: A View from the Left', paper read at the Midwest MLA Conference (Iowa, 1982).
Bjornson, Richard, 'Moral Blindness in Quevedo's *El buscón*', *RR* 67 (1976), 50–9.
—— *The Picaresque Hero in European Fiction* (Madison, 1977).
Blue, William R., *The Development of Imagery in Calderón's 'Comedias'* (York, SC, 1983).
Bowie, Malcolm, 'Lacan and Literature', *RS* 5 (1984–5), 1–26.
Bruck, Jan, 'From Aristotelian Mimesis to Bourgeois Realism', *Poetics*, 11 (1982), 189–202.
Bryans, John V., *Calderón de la Barca: Imagery, Rhetoric, and Drama* (London, 1977).
Calderón de la Barca, Pedro, *El médico de su honra*, ed. C. A. Jones (Oxford, 1976).
Caramuel, Juan, *Rationalis et realis philosophia* (Louvain, 1642).
—— *Mathesis audax* (Louvain, 1644).
Carballo, Luis Alfonso de, *Cisne de Apolo*, ed. Alberto Porqueras Mayo (Madrid, 1958).

Carrillo y Sotomayor, Luis, *Libro de la erudición poética*, ed. Manuel Cardenal Iracheta (Madrid, 1946).

Casa, Frank P., 'Structural Unity in *El licenciado vidriera*', *BHS* 41 (1964), 242–6.

Casalduero, Joaquín, Intro. to Tirso de Molina, *El burlador de Sevilla* (Madrid, 1982).

Cascardi, Anthony J., *The Limits of Illusion: A Critical Study of Calderón* (Cambridge, 1984).

Castro, Américo, 'El *Lazarillo de Tormes*', in *Hacia Cervantes* (Madrid, 1967), 143–9.

Cave, Terence, '*Enargeia*: Erasmus and the Rhetoric of Presence in the Sixteenth Century', *L'Esprit créateur*, 16. 4 (Winter 1976), 5–19.

—— *The Cornucopian Text: Problems of Writing in the French Renaissance* (Oxford, 1979).

Cavillac, Michel and Cécile, 'A propos du *Buscón* et de *Guzmán de Alfarache*', *BHisp.* 75 (1973), 114–31.

Cervantes Saavedra, Miguel de, *The History of the Renowned Don Quixote de la Mancha*, trans. various (London, 1706).

—— *Persiles and Sigismunda: A Celebrated Novel* (London, 1741).

—— *The Life and Exploits of the Ingenious Gentleman Don Quixote de la Mancha*, trans. Charles Jarvis (London, 1742).

—— *The History and Adventures of the Renowned Don Quixote* (London, 1755).

—— *Nouvelles espagnoles*, trans. Lefebvre de Villebrune (Paris, 1788).

—— *Novelas ejemplares*, ii, ed. Francisco Rodríguez Marín (Madrid, 1975).

Cicero, Marcus Tullius, *De oratore*, ed. E. W. Sutton and H. Rackham (London and Cambridge, Mass., 1967).

Close, Anthony, *The Romantic Approach to 'Don Quijote'* (Cambridge, 1977).

—— 'Cervantes's *Arte nuevo de hazer fábulas cómicas en este tiempo*', *Cervantes*, 2 (1982), 3–22.

Cohen, Walter, 'Calderón in England: A Social Theory of Production and Consumption', *BCom.* 35 (1983), 69–77.

Collard, Andrée, *Nueva poesía: Conceptismo, culteranismo en la crítica española* (Madrid, 1967).

Colombí-Monguió, Alicia de, 'Los "ojos de perlas" de Dulcinea (*Quijote* II, 10 y 11): El antipetrarquismo de Sancho (y de otros)', *NRFH* 32 (1983), 389–402.

Combet, Louis, *Cervantès, ou les incertitudes du désir: Une approche psychostructurale de l'œuvre de Cervantès* (Lyons, 1980).

Covarrubias Orozco, Sebastián de, *Emblemas morales* (Madrid, 1610).

Cros, Edmond, *Protée et le gueux: Recherches sur les origines et la nature du récit picaresque dans 'Guzmán de Alfarache'* (Paris, 1967).

—— *Mateo Alemán: Introducción a su vida y a su obra* (Madrid, 1971).

—— *L'Aristocrate et le carnaval des gueux: Étude sur le 'Buscón' de Quevedo* (Montpellier, 1975).

Cruikshank, Don N., '"Pongo mi mano en sangre bañada en la puerta": Adultery in *El médico de su honra*', in *Studies in Spanish Literature of the Golden Age presented to E. M. Wilson*, ed. R. O. Jones (London, 1973), 45–62.

Culler, Jonathan, 'Poetics of the Lyric', in *Structuralist Poetics* (London, 1983), 161–88.

Curtius, Ernst Robert, *European Literature and the Latin Middle Ages*, trans. Willard R. Trask (London, 1953).

Darst, David H., *The Comic Art of Tirso de Molina* (Chapel Hill, 1974).

Davies, Gareth Alban, '*Pintura*: Background and Sketch of a Spanish Seventeenth-century Court Genre', *JWCI* 38 (1975), 288–313.

Derrida, Jacques, *De la grammatologie* (Paris, 1967).

—— *L'Écriture et la différence* (Paris, 1967).

—— *La Dissémination* (Paris, 1972).

—— *Marges, de la philosophie* (Paris, 1972).

—— *La Vérité en peinture* (Paris, 1978).

—— *La Carte postale de Socrate à Freud et au-delà* (Paris, 1980).

—— *Glas* (Paris, 1981).

Deyermond, A. D., *Lazarillo de Tormes* (London, 1975).

Díaz-Migoyo, Gonzalo, *Estructura de la novela: Anatomía de 'El buscón'* (Madrid, 1978).

Dunn, Peter N., *The Spanish Picaresque Novel* (Boston, 1979).

—— 'Problems for a Model of the Picaresque and the Case of Quevedo's *Buscón*', *BHS* 59 (1982), 95–105.

Eagleton, Terry, *Criticism and Ideology* (London, 1978).

—— *Literary Theory: An Introduction* (Oxford, 1983).

Easthope, Anthony, *Poetry as Discourse* (London, 1983).

El Saffar, Ruth, *Novel to Romance* (Baltimore, 1974).

—— *Distance and Control in 'Don Quijote': A Study in Narrative Technique* (Chapel Hill, 1975).

—— 'Cervantes and the Games of Illusion', in *Cervantes and the Renaissance*, ed. Michael D. McGaha (Easton, Pa., 1980), 141–56.

—— Review of Louis Combet, *Cervantès*, *MLN* 97 (1982), 422–7.

—— *Beyond Fiction: The Recovery of the Feminine in the Novels of Cervantes* (Berkeley, 1984).

Erasmus, Desiderius, *Adagia* (Frankfurt, 1629).

Evans, Peter W., '*Peribáñez* and Ways of Looking at Golden Age Dramatic Characters', *RR* 74 (1983), 136–51.

Fernández, Xavier A., '¿Cómo se llamaba el padre de don Juan?', *REH* 3 (1969), 145–59.

Fernández Morera, Dario, *The Lyre and the Oaten Flute: Garcilaso and the Pastoral* (London, 1982).

Ferreras, Juan Ignacio, *La estructura paródica del 'Quijote'* (Madrid, 1982).

Flores, R. M., 'The Role of Cide Hamete in *Don Quijote*', *BHS* 59 (1982), 3–14.

Forcione, Alban K., *Cervantes and the Humanist Vision: A Study of Four Exemplary Novels* (Princeton, 1982).

—— *Cervantes and the Mystery of Lawlessness: A Study of 'El casamiento engañoso' and 'El coloquio de los perros'* (Princeton, 1984).

Fothergill-Payne, Louise, '*El caballero de Olmedo* y la razón de diferencia', *BCom.* 36 (1984), 111–24.

Foucault, Michel, *Les Mots et les choses* (Paris, 1966).

Foucault, Michel, *L'Ordre du discours* (Paris, 1971).

—— *Histoire de la folie à l'âge classique* (Paris, 1972).

—— *Surveiller et punir: Naissance de la prison* (Paris, 1975).

—— *La Volonté de savoir* (Paris, 1976).

Freud, Sigmund, *Jokes and their Relation to the Unconscious* (Harmondsworth, 1983).

Fumaroli, Marc, 'L'Apologétique de la langue française classique', *Rhetorica* 2.2 (1984), 139–61.

Gallego Morell, Antonio (ed.), *Garcilaso de la Vega y sus comentaristas* (Madrid, 1972).

Garcilaso de la Vega, *Obras completas con comentario*, ed. Elias L. Rivers (Madrid, 1974).

Garrote Pérez, Francisco, *La naturaleza en el pensamiento de Cervantes* (Salamanca, 1979).

Gates, Eunice Joiner, *Documentos gongorinos* (Mexico City, 1960).

Gaylord Randel, Mary, 'Proper Language and Language as Property: The Personal Poetics of Lope's *Rimas*', *MLN* 101 (1986), 220–46.

Gilman, Stephen, 'The Death of Lazarillo de Tormes', *PMLA* 81 (1966), 149–66.

Góngora, Luis de, *Sonetos completos*, ed. Biruté Ciplijauskaité (Madrid, 1969).

Gracián, Baltasar, *Agudeza y arte de ingenio*, ed. Evaristo Correa Calderón (Madrid, 1969).

Grimaldi, William M. A., *Studies in the Philosophy of Aristotle's Rhetoric* (Wiesbaden, 1972).

Guillén, Claudio, 'La disposición temporal del *Lazarillo de Tormes*', *HR* 25 (1957), 264–79.

Hahn, Juergen, '*El capitán cautivo*: The Soldier's Truth and Literary Precept in *Don Quijote* Part I', *JHP* 3 (1979), 269–303.

Herrera, Fernando de, *Obra poética*, ed. José Manuel Blecua (Madrid, 1975).

Hesse, Everett W., *New Perspectives on Comedia Criticism* (Potomac, 1980).

—— *Theology, Sex, and the Comedia* (Potomac, 1982).

Ife, B. W., *Reading and Fiction in Golden Age Spain* (Cambridge, 1985).

Iffland, James, *Quevedo and the Grotesque*, i. (London, 1978).

Ihrie, Maureen, *Skepticism in Cervantes* (London, 1982).

Irigaray, Luce, *Speculum, de l'autre femme* (Paris, 1974).

—— *Ce sexe qui n'en est pas un* (Paris, 1977).

Jay, Martin, 'In the Empire of the Gaze: Foucault and the Denigration of Vision in Twentieth-century French Thought', in *ICA Documents, 4: Postmodernism* (London, 1986), 19–25.

Jiménez Fajardo, Salvador, 'The Sierra Morena as Labyrinth in *Don Quijote* I', *MLN* 99 (1984), 214–34.

Johnson, Barbara, Intro. to Derrida, *Dissemination* (London, 1981).

Johnson, Carroll, B., *Inside 'Guzmán de Alfarache'* (Berkeley, 1978).

—— *Madness and Lust: A Psychoanalytical Approach to 'Don Quijote'* (Berkeley, 1983).

Jones, R. O., *A Literary History of Spain: The Golden Age: Prose and Poetry* (London and New York, 1971).

Jones, R. O., 'Garcilaso, poeta del humanismo', in *La poesía de Garcilaso*, ed. Elias L. Rivers (Barcelona, 1974), 53–70.

Jordan, Barry, 'Between Discipline and Transgression: Re-tracing the Boundaries of British Hispanism', *RS* 5 (Winter 1984–5), 55–74.

Joset, Jacques, 'Bipolarizaciones textuales y estructura especular en *El licenciado vidriera*', in *Cervantes, su obra y su mundo: Actas del I Congreso internacional sobre Cervantes* (Madrid, 1981), 357–63.

Kahn, Victoria, *Rhetoric, Prudence, and Skepticism in the Renaissance* (Ithaca, 1985).

Kallendorf, Craig, 'The Rhetorical Criticism of Literature in Early Italian Humanism from Boccaccio to Landino', *Rhetorica*, 1. 2 (1983), 33–59.

Kennedy, George, 'Authorial Intent in the Aristotelian Tradition of Rhetoric and Poetics', paper read at the Fifth Biennial Conference of the International Society for the History of Rhetoric (Oxford, 1985).

Kennedy, Ruth Lee, *Studies in Tirso*, i: *The Dramatist and His Competitors, 1620–6* (Chapel Hill, 1974).

Lacan, Jacques, *Écrits*, i (Paris, 1966).

—— *The Four Fundamental Concepts of Psychoanalysis*, trans. Alan Sheridan (Harmondsworth, 1977).

Lapesa, Rafael, *La trayectoria poética de Garcilaso* (Madrid, 1968).

Lausberg, Heinrich, *Manual de retórica literaria*, trans. José Pérez Riesco (Madrid, 1966–8).

Lázaro, Fernando, *Estilo barroco y personalidad creadora* (Salamanca, 1966).

Lida de Malkiel, María Rosa, 'Sobre la prioridad de ¿*Tan largo me lo fiáis?* Notas al *Isidro* y a *El burlador de Sevilla*', *HR* 30 (1962), 275–95.

Liddell, Henry George, and Robert Scott, *A Greek–English Lexicon* (Oxford, 1968).

López de Ubeda, Francisco, *La pícara Justina* (Barcelona, 1968).

López Pinciano, Alonso, *Philosophía antigua poética*, ed. Alfredo Carballo Picazo (Madrid, 1953).

López Quintás, Alfonso, 'Confrontación de la figura del hombre "burlador" (Tirso), el "estético" (Kierkegaard), el "absurdo" (Camus)', in *Homenaje a Tirso* (Madrid, 1981), 337–80.

Lyotard, Jean-François, *Discours, figure* (Paris, 1971).

—— *Économie libidinale* (Paris, 1974).

McKendrick, Melveena, *Woman and Society in the Spanish Drama of the Golden Age* (Cambridge, 1974).

—— 'Honour–Vengeance in the Spanish Comedia: A Case of Mimetic Transference?', *MLR* 79 (1984), 313–35.

Macrí, Oreste, *Fernando de Herrera* (Madrid, 1959).

Mancing, Howard, 'The Deceptiveness of *Lazarillo de Tormes*', *PMLA* 90 (1975), 426–32.

—— *The Chivalric World of Don Quijote* (Columbia and London, 1982).

Mariscal, George, 'Re-reading Calderón', *BCom.* 36 (1984), 131–3.

Martí, Antonio, *La preceptiva retórica española en el siglo de oro* (Madrid, 1972).

Marx, Karl, *Grundrisse: Foundations of the Critique of Political Economy*, trans. Martin Nicolaus (London, 1973).

Menéndez y Pelayo, Marcelino, *Calderón y su teatro* (Buenos Aires, 1946).

Menéndez y Pelayo, Marcelino, *Historia de las ideas estéticas en España* (Santander, 1947).

Moi, Toril, *Sexual/Texual Politics: Feminist Literary Theory* (London and New York, 1985).

Molho, Maurice, *Introducción al pensamiento picaresco* (Salamanca, 1972).

Montori de Gutiérrez, Violeta, *Ideas estéticas y poesía de Fernando de Herrera* (Miami, 1977).

Morris, C. B., 'Metaphor in *El burlador de Sevilla*', *RR* 55 (1964), 248–55.

Norris, Christopher, *Deconstruction: Theory and Practice* (London and New York, 1982).

Olivares, Julián, *The Love-poetry of Francisco de Quevedo: An Existential and Aesthetic Study* (Cambridge, 1983).

Ong, Walter, J., 'The Writer's Audience is always a Fiction', *PMLA* 90 (1975), 9–21.

—— *Orality and Literacy: The Technologizing of the Word* (London, 1982).

Orozco Díaz, Emilio, *En torno a las 'Soledades' de Góngora* (Granada, 1969).

Pallares, Berta, Intro. to Tirso de Molina, *La huerta de Juan Fernández* (Madrid, 1982).

Parker, Alexander A., *The Approach to Spanish Drama of the Golden Age* (London, 1957).

—— 'Towards a Definition of Calderonian Tragedy', *BHS* 39 (1962), 222–37.

—— *Literature and the Delinquent: The Picaresque Novel in Spain and Europe 1599–1753* (Edinburgh, 1967).

Paterson, Alan K. G., Intro. to Tirso de Molina, *La venganza de Tamar* (Cambridge, 1969).

—— '*Ecphrasis* in Garcilaso's "Egloga tercera"', *MLR* 72 (1977), 73–92.

—— 'The Alchemical Marriage in Calderón's *El médico de su honra*', *RJ* 30 (1979), 263–82.

Peale, George, '*Guzmán de Alfarache* como discurso oral', *JHP* 4 (1979), 25–57.

Picinellus, Philippus, *Mundus symbolicus* (Cologne, 1681).

Prieto, Antonio, Intro. to Tirso de Molina, *El vergonzoso en palacio* and *El condenado por desconfiado* (Barcelona, 1982).

Pring-Mill, R. D. F., 'Spanish Golden Age Prose and the Depiction of Reality', *ASSQJ* 32–3 (1959), 20–31.

—— 'Escalígero y Herrera: Citas y plagios de los *Poetices libri septem* en *Las anotaciones*', in *Actas del segundo congreso internacional de hispanistas* (Nimega, 1967), 489–98.

—— 'Some Techniques of Representation in the *Sueños* and the *Criticón*', *BHS* 45 (1968), 270–84.

Quevedo, Francisco de, *Obras completas: Prosa*, ed. Luis Astrana Marín (Madrid, 1932).

—— *Poesía original*, ed. José Manuel Blecua (Barcelona, 1974).

—— *La vida del buscón llamado Don Pablos*, ed. B. W. Ife (Oxford, 1977).

Quintilian [Marcus Fabius Quintilianus], *Institutio oratoria*, ed. H. E. Butler (London and Cambridge, Mass., 1968).

Raimondi, Ezio, 'Poesia della retorica', in *Retorica e critica letteraria* (Bologna, 1978), 123–50.

Rey Hazas, Antonio (ed.), *Lazarillo de Tormes* (Madrid, 1984).

Rico, Francisco, *The Spanish Picaresque Novel and the Point of View*, trans. Charles Davis with Harry Sieber (Cambridge, 1984).

Rico Verdú, José, *La retórica española de los siglos xvi y xvii* (Madrid, 1973).

Riley, Edward C., *Cervantes's Theory of the Novel* (Oxford, 1962).

—— '"Romance" y novela en Cervantes', in *Cervantes: Su obra y su mundo, Actas del i Congreso internacional sobre Cervantes* (Madrid, 1981), 5–13.

Rivers, Elias L., 'The Pastoral Paradox of Natural Art', *MLN* 77 (1962), 130–44.

—— (ed.), *La poesía de Garcilaso: ensayos críticos* (Barcelona, 1974).

—— 'Cervantes and the Question of Language', in *Cervantes and the Renaissance* (Easton, Pa., 1980), 23–33.

—— *Quixotic Scriptures: Essays on the Textuality of Hispanic Literature* (Bloomington, 1983).

Rodríguez, Evangelina, and Antonio Tordera, *La escritura como espejo de palacio: 'El toreador' de Calderón* (Kassel, 1985).

Rogers, Daniel, 'Fearful Symmetry: The Ending of *El burlador de Sevilla*', *BHS* 41 (1964), 141–59.

Roldán, Antonio, 'Cervantes y la retórica clásica', in *Cervantes: Su obra y su mundo* (Madrid, 1981), 47–57.

Rose, Constance Hubbard, 'Pablos' *Damnosa Heritas*', *RF* 82 (1970), 94–101.

Ruano de la Haza, José M., 'An Early Rehash of Lope's *Peribáñez*', *BCom*. 35 (1983), 5–29.

—— 'Hacia una nueva definición de la tragedia calderoniana', *BCom*. 35 (1983), 165–80.

—— 'Malicia campesina y la ambigüedad esencial de *Peribáñez y el comendador de Ocaña* de Lope', *Hispanófila*, 84 (1985), 21–30.

Salcedo Coronel, García de (ed.), *Soledades ... comentadas* (Madrid, 1636).

—— *Obras ... comentadas*, ii (Madrid, 1649).

Saldívar, Ramón, 'Don Quijote's Metaphors and the Grammar of Proper Language', *MLN* 95 (1980), 252–78.

Sánchez de Lima, Miguel, *Arte poética en romance castellano*, ed. Rafael de Balbín Lucas (Madrid, 1944).

Sánchez Escribano, Federico and Alberto Porqueras Mayo, *Preceptiva dramática española del renacimiento y del barroco* (Madrid, 1965).

Scaliger, Julius Caesar, *Poetices libri septem* (Lyons, 1561).

—— *De causis linguae latinae* (Heidelberg, 1584).

Shepard, Sanford, *El Pinciano y las teorías literarias del siglo de oro* (Madrid, 1962).

Shergold, N. D., *A History of the Spanish Stage from Medieval Times until the End of the Seventeenth Century* (Oxford, 1967).

Sheridan, Alan, *Michel Foucault: The Will to Truth* (London and New York, 1982).

Sieber, Harry, *The Picaresque* (London, 1977).

—— *Language and Society in 'La vida de Lazarillo de Tormes'* (Baltimore, 1978).

Smith, C. C., 'On the Use of Spanish Theoretical Works in the Debate on Góngora', *BHS* 39 (1962), 165–76.

Smith, Paul Julian, 'Barthes, Góngora, and Non-sense', *PMLA* 101 (1986), 82–94.

Smith, Paul Julian, 'Affect and Effect in the Lyric of Quevedo', *FMLS* 22 (1986), 62–76.

—— *Quevedo on Parnassus: Allusion and Theory in the Love-lyric* (London, 1987).

Spitzer, Leo, 'Sobre el arte de Quevedo en el *Buscón*', in *Francisco de Quevedo: El escritor y la crítica*, ed. Gonzalo Sobejano (Madrid, 1978), 123–84.

Stern, Charlotte, 'Lope de Vega, Propagandist?', *BCom.* 34 (1982), 1–36.

Sullivan, Henry W., *Tirso de Molina and the Drama of the Counter Reformation* (Amsterdam, 1976).

—— 'La razón de los altibajos en la reputación póstuma de Calderón', paper read at the Congreso anglo-germano sobre Calderón (Cambridge, 1984).

Tarr, F. Courtney, 'Literary and Artistic Unity in the *Lazarillo de Tormes*', *PMLA* 42 (1927), 404–21.

ter Horst, Robert, *Calderón: The Secular Plays* (Lexington, Ky., 1982).

Terry, Arthur, 'The Continuity of Renaissance Criticism: Poetic Theory in Spain between 1535 and 1650', *BHS* 31 (1954), 27–36.

—— *An Anthology of Spanish Poetry 1500–1700 Part 1: 1500–1580* (Oxford, 1965).

—— 'Thought and Feeling in Three Golden Age Sonnets', *BHS* 59 (1982), 237–46.

Tesauro, Emanuele, *Il cannocchiale aristotelico* (Bad Homburg, 1968).

Tirso de Molina [Gabriel Téllez], *El burlador de Sevilla*, ed. Américo Castro (Madrid, 1980).

Valdés, Juan de, *El diálogo de la lengua*, ed. Cristina Barbolani (Madrid, 1982).

Vega, Lope Félix de, *Obras poéticas*, ed. José Manuel Blecua (Barcelona, 1969).

—— *Peribáñez y el comendador de Ocaña*, ed. J. M. Ruano and J. E. Varey (London, 1980).

Walters, D. Gareth, *Francisco de Quevedo, Love Poet* (Cardiff, 1985).

Wardropper, Bruce W., 'El trastorno de la moral en el *Lazarillo*', *NRFH* 15 (1961), 441–7.

Watson, A. I., 'Peter the Cruel or Peter the Just? A Reappraisal of the Role played by King Peter in Calderón's *El médico de su honra*', *RJ* 14 (1963), 322–46.

Weiger, John G., *The Individuated Self: Cervantes and the Emergence of the Individual* (Ohio, 1979).

—— *The Substance of Cervantes* (Cambridge, 1985).

Weinberg, Bernard, *A History of Literary Criticism in the Italian Renaissance* (Chicago, 1961).

Welles, Marcia L., 'The *pícara*: Towards Female Autonomy, or the Vanity of Virtue', *RQ* 33 (1986), 63–70.

Williamson, Edwin, 'The Conflict between Author and Protagonist in Quevedo's *Buscón*', *JHP* 2 (1977), 45–60.

—— 'Romance and Realism in the Interpolated Stories in the *Quijote*', *Cervantes*, 2 (1982), 43–67.

—— *The Half-way House of Fiction: Don Quijote and Arthurian Romance* (Oxford, 1984).

Willis, Raymond S., 'Lazarillo and the Pardoner: The Artistic Necessity of the Fifth *Tractado*', *HR* 27 (1959), 267–79.

Wilson, Edward M., 'The Four Elements in the Imagery of Calderón', *MLR* 31 (1936), 34–47.

Wilson, Edward M., 'Images et structure dans *Peribáñez*', *BHisp.* 51 (1949), 125–59.

—— 'Images et structure dans *Peribáñez*', *BHisp.* 51 (1949), 125–59.

—— and Duncan Moir, *A Literary History of Spain: The Golden Age: Drama 1492–1700* (London, 1971).

Wilson, Margaret, *Tirso de Molina* (Boston, 1977).

Woods, M. J., 'Gracián, Peregrini, and the Theory of Topics', *MLR* 63 (1968), 854–63.

—— 'Rhetoric in Garcilaso's First Eclogue', *MLN* 84 (1969), 143–56.

—— *The Poet and the Natural World in the Age of Góngora* (Oxford, 1978).

—— 'Pitfalls for the Moralizer in *Lazarillo de Tormes*', *MLR* 74 (1979), 580–98.

—— 'Herrera's Voices', in *Medieval and Renaissance Studies on Spanish and Portuguese in Honour of P. E. Russell* (Oxford, 1981), 121–32.

Wright, Elizabeth, *Psychoanalytic Criticism: Theory in Practice* (London and New York, 1984).

Young, Richard A., *La figura del rey y la institución real en la comedia lopesca* (Madrid, 1979).

Zahareas, Anthony N., 'The Historical Function of Art and Morality in Quevedo's *Buscón*', *BHS* 61 (1984), 432–43.

INDEX